MARITIME ANIMALS

Nigel Rothfels, General Editor

Books in the Animalibus series share a fascination with the status and the role of animals in human life. Crossing the humanities and the social sciences to include work in history, anthropology, social and cultural geography, environmental studies, and literary and art criticism, these books ask what thinking about nonhuman animals can teach us about human cultures, about what it means to be human, and about how that meaning might shift across times and places.

OTHER TITLES IN THE SERIES:

Rachel Poliquin, *The Breathless Zoo: Taxidermy and the Cultures of Longing*

Joan B. Landes, Paula Young Lee, and Paul Youngquist, eds., *Gorgeous Beasts: Animal Bodies in Historical Perspective*

Liv Emma Thorsen, Karen A. Rader, and Adam Dodd, eds., *Animals on Display: The Creaturely in Museums, Zoos, and Natural History*

Ann-Janine Morey, *Picturing Dogs, Seeing Ourselves: Vintage American Photographs*

Mary Sanders Pollock, *Storytelling Apes: Primatology Narratives Past and Future*

Ingrid H. Tague, *Animal Companions: Pets and Social Change in Eighteenth-Century Britain*

Dick Blau and Nigel Rothfels, *Elephant House*

Marcus Baynes-Rock, *Among the Bone Eaters: Encounters with Hyenas in Harar*

Monica Mattfeld, *Becoming Centaur: Eighteenth-Century Masculinity and English Horsemanship*

Heather Swan, *Where Honeybees Thrive: Stories from the Field*

Karen Raber and Monica Mattfeld, eds., *Performing Animals: History, Agency, Theater*

J. Keri Cronin, *Art for Animals: Visual Culture and Animal Advocacy, 1870–1914*

Elizabeth Marshall Thomas, *The Hidden Life of Life: A Walk Through the Reaches of Time*

Elizabeth Young, *Pet Projects: Animal Fiction and Taxidermy in the Nineteenth-Century Archive*

Marcus Baynes-Rock, *Crocodile Undone: The Domestication of Australia's Fauna*

Deborah Nadal, *Rabies in the Streets: Interspecies Camaraderie in Urban India*

Mustafa Haikal, translated by Thomas Dunlap, *Master Pongo: A Gorilla Conquers Europe*

Austin McQuinn, *Becoming Audible: Sounding Animality in Performance*

Karalyn Kendall-Morwick, *Canis Modernis: Human/Dog Coevolution in Modernist Literature*

Keith Botelho and Joseph Campana, eds., *Lesser Living Creatures of the Renaissance: Volume 1, Insects*

Keith Botelho and Joseph Campana, eds., *Lesser Living Creatures of the Renaissance: Volume 2, Concepts*

MARITIME ANIMALS

Ships, Species, Stories

EDITED BY KAORI NAGAI

THE PENNSYLVANIA STATE UNIVERSITY PRESS
UNIVERSITY PARK, PENNSYLVANIA

Library of Congress Cataloging-in-Publication Data

Names: Nagai, Kaori, editor.
Title: Maritime animals : ships, species, stories / edited by Kaori Nagai.
Other titles: Animalibus.
Description: University Park, Pennsylvania : The Pennsylvania State University Press, [2023] | Series: Animalibus : of animals and cultures | Includes bibliographical references and index.
Summary: "Explores nonhuman animals' involvement with human maritime activities in the age of sail, presenting the ship as a place where the ocean and animal species interact in often surprising ways"—Provided by publisher.
Identifiers: LCCN 2023002112 | ISBN 9780271095370 (hardback)
Subjects: LCSH: Animals—Transportation—History. | Human-animal relationships—History. | Ocean travel—History. | LCGFT: Essays.
Classification: LCC SF89 .M37 2023 | DDC 636.08/3—dc23/eng/20230215
LC record available at https://lccn.loc.gov/2023002112

Printed in the United States of America
Published by The Pennsylvania State University Press,
University Park, PA 16802–1003

The Pennsylvania State University Press is a member of the Association of University Presses.

It is the policy of The Pennsylvania State University Press to use acid-free paper. Publications on uncoated stock satisfy the minimum requirements of American National Standard for Information Sciences—Permanence of Paper for Printed Library Material, ANSI Z39.48–1992.

CONTENTS

ILLUSTRATIONS

ACKNOWLEDGMENTS

The idea of this volume originated in a conference titled "Maritime Animals: Telling Stories of Animals at Sea," held at the National Maritime Museum, Greenwich, London, on April 25–27, 2019, and seven of the chapters had their beginnings as papers presented at that event. I would like to thank the National Maritime Museum for hosting the conference and for their generous support for this project, which is based on the research I conducted in the museum as a Caird Short-term Research Fellow. I am particularly grateful to Robert Blyth, Lizelle de Jager, Nigel Rigby, Aaron Jaffer, Andrew Choong, Susan Gentle, and Liza Verity for their invaluable support and input, and to Sally Archer and Beatrice Okoro of the National Maritime Museum, Greenwich, for kindly granting permission to use two images from the museum in this book. My special thanks also go to Thom van Dooren, one of the conference's keynote speakers, for suggesting that all the contributors to this volume take on the challenge of telling maritime stories from the perspective of one particular species of animal. Several other papers from the "Maritime Animals" conference have been collected in the *Journal for Maritime Research*, the journal of the National Maritime Museum, as a special issue on "Animals at Sea," edited by myself (22, nos. 1–2 [2020]). Unlike the present volume, which takes a species focus, the essays collected there focus on particular ships and maritime operations to tell stories of animals at sea, and this issue will be of strong interest to readers of the present volume, as it sheds a complementary light on the topic.

The editing of this collection fell during the period of the COVID-19 crisis, which had affected all of us in many different ways, and I know some of the contributors were hit harder than others. I am very grateful to all of them for their support and understanding, without which this volume would never have been possible. I would also like to thank the two reviewers, Jakobina Arch and Andrew Kincaid, for their insightful comments and suggestions, which allowed us to improve the manuscript, and also to Ben Grant, Charlotte Sleigh, William Gervase Clarence-Smith, and John McAleer for their valuable input into this project. Last but not least, I am hugely grateful to Kendra Boileau and Nigel Rothfels at the Pennsylvania State University Press for their kindness and guidance throughout the process, and to Josie DiNovo, the Press's editorial assistant, for overseeing the final manuscript preparation. It was a real pleasure and privilege to work with them.

INTRODUCTION

Kaori Nagai

The HMS *Challenger* expedition of 1872–76 was a groundbreaking scientific mission, tasked to "investigate the physical and biological conditions of the great Ocean-basins."[1] To this end, it made a 68,890-nautical-mile trip around the globe, visiting every ocean and continent, including Antarctica, and gathering data at 362 observing stations.[2] Henry Nottidge Moseley (1844–1891), a young Oxford scholar, joined the expedition as one of its scientific staff. *Notes by a Naturalist on the "Challenger"* (1879) is Moseley's account of the expedition, which provides a detailed description of the fauna, flora, and peoples of the places the ship visited. Significantly, the book ends with a short section called "Zoology and botany of the ship," in which Moseley describes the nonhuman species who accompanied the *Challenger*. According to him, the ship "seemed nearly free of animals, other than men, dogs, and live stock required for food" when it sailed from Portsmouth to start its journey.[3] However, all kinds of creatures came on board the ship during its three-and-a-half-year journey. Moseley provides vivid accounts of these animals, which makes him an important chronicler of animals at sea in the nineteenth century.

The "navifauna" of the *Challenger*, as recorded by Moseley, included a wide variety of insects, such as red ants, clothes moths, mosquitoes, and house crickets, the latter of which established themselves in a staff cabin and were "as noisy as at home" (515). The most prominent insects of all were undoubtedly the cockroaches, which "became plentiful on board, and showed themselves whenever the ship was in a warm climate" (514). Moseley recalls "one huge winged Cockroach" that visited his cabin nightly and watched him closely from his bookshelf; once the light went out, it would come to "sip the moisture from [his] face and lips," which he found "decidedly unpleasant." This cockroach dodged Moseley's many attempts to get rid of it, but was eventually killed when he confronted it with an air gun; this incident "created some excitement on the upper deck, where the sound was plainly heard" (514).

The *Challenger* also had many exotic animals that the crew brought on board at various times as their companions. Chief among these was Robert, a young grey parrot bought at Madeira at an early stage of the journey, who "survived all the extremes of the heat and cold of the voyage and perils of all kinds, from heavy tumbles during gales of wind, and the falling about of books and furniture" (515–16). At Montevideo, the ship was joined by very young South American ostriches, the adults of which species had been observed by Darwin to use their wings as sails on the plains of Patagonia (516). Moseley likewise notes the way in which these young ostriches chased flies on the upper deck, "instinctively spreading their little wings as sails to catch tiny draughts reflected from the bulwarks" (516); away from home, they were like ships within a ship, riding the same wind as that which propelled the three-masted *Challenger.* Some animals spent only a short period on the ship, such as a young Aru Islands cassowary, which "roamed about the decks for some time, but was soon killed as a nuisance" (516), or a young fur seal that, "crying like a child," followed the crew around to be fed and petted, but soon died (517). Notably, the *Challenger* did not carry live monkeys. They were "strictly forbidden, by a special Admiralty regulation, on surveying ships" such as the *Challenger*, because "one once destroyed a valuable chart which had just been completed with great labour" (517).

To travel as a naturalist had been Moseley's dream since his childhood: "the study of *Robinson Crusoe* certainly first gave [him] a desire to go to sea," and this was further consolidated when he came across *The Voyage of the Beagle* (1839), Charles Darwin's account of his voyage around the world as the *Beagle*'s naturalist (466). His *Notes by a*

Naturalist, dedicated to Darwin, was written to emulate Darwin's travelogue and makes references to other "naturalists at sea" who accompanied scientific or survey expeditions.[4] Moseley was aware of the rich tradition of European travel and discovery and was proud to be part of it. In this sense, it is important that Moseley's book features a section on the shipborne animals; he recognizes them as an integral part of the maritime tradition and indeed as fellow travelers whose global paths crossed with his own. Among the navifauna of the *Challenger* was a kid taken on board at Juan Fernández Islands, famous for being the island on which Alexander Selkirk, the life model of Robinson Crusoe, was stranded for four years. The goat was supposedly "one of the direct descendants of Alexander Selkirk's Goats," who fed Selkirk and thereby Daniel Defoe's story, without which Moseley might not have gone to sea.[5] The stories of human travelers and those of nonhumans converge to share the same journey. The young goat, duly christened "Robinson Crusoe," became something of a ship's mascot, whose "gambols often roused the merry laughter of the ship's company."[6]

Maritime Animals: Ships, Species, Stories is a collection of essays that explore nonhuman animals' involvement with human maritime activities. Its central image is animals traveling on board ship, and it styles itself as an oceangoing ship, which carries all sorts of animals and their stories. Moseley's account of the animals on HMS *Challenger* seemed to me to be a fitting place to start, first as an example of how ships were once packed with nonhuman passengers, but more importantly because the *Challenger*'s global trajectory, touching every part of the world—land, sea, and even ocean floor—was their own: this voyage therefore demonstrates just how far and wide nonhuman animals traveled to be entangled with human maritime networks.

In recent years, the "oceanic turn" within environmental studies has drawn our attention to the historical, cultural, and ecological importance of the sea. It has led to powerful critiques of our human, land-based perspectives, which have facilitated the destruction of the ocean and its habitats, as well as to the emergence of what Elizabeth DeLoughrey calls "a new oceanic imaginary," exploring "ontologies of the sea and its multispecies engagements."[7] The ocean as a body of water has come to be seen as, to quote Astrida Neimanis, "a more-than-human hydrocommons," which "[presents] a challenge to anthropocentrism, and the privileging of the human as the sole or primary site of embodiment."[8] Drawing inspiration from these new oceanic insights, *Maritime Animals* seeks to uncover untold stories of animals at sea to challenge a standard and anthropocentric definition of "maritime history" as "humankind's relationship with the sea."[9] Despite the long history of maritime animal companionship, nonhuman animals have often been ignored or marginalized in the stories of ships and the sea. *Maritime Animals*, by contrast, takes seriously nonhumans as seafarers. There are ten chapters in total, each of which focuses on the oceanic journeys of a particular species. Eight of them deal with a nonhuman animal which came on board ship: these consist of animals transported as on-board food (the Galápagos tortoise), animal specimens for scientific study (the tuatara), animal cargoes (the sheep and the horse), vermin (the ship rat); and working animals (the sled dog), together with two marine species known to make the ship their "home": the shipworm and the sponge. The other two chapters follow a different type of oceanic traveler, with the ship as a reference point: the whale who accompanied the ship for centuries, and Hawai'i's terrestrial snails, who crossed the sea to scatter around the Hawaiian Islands. By weaving together these chapters, *Maritime Animals* characterizes the ship as a space in which countless animal stories coexist and intersect with each other. The book includes stories of the human-animal relationships formed on board and around the ship, as well as those of multispecies connections formed across different geographical locations, knitted together by the long history of global ship movements. It thereby explores the history of the ship as that of a contingent, multispecies assemblage, traveling through space and time, and, in the process, profoundly affecting the lives of innumerable individuals and species across the globe.

As a phrase, "maritime animals" overlaps with, yet differs from, "marine (or oceanic) animals," which refers to the denizens of the sea. The word *maritime* etymologically comes from the Latin word *maritimus*, meaning "of the sea, near the sea," derived from *mare* ("sea") and a superlative suffix *-timus*, denoting "close association with."[10] As Sidney I. Dobrin puts it, the word "conveys oceanic correlation such as living adjacent to the sea or a close relationship to the sea," rather than "of the sea itself."[11] A good example of this is *Ursus maritimus* (maritime bear), the Latin name for the polar bear, a land animal whose existence is bound up with the Arctic Ocean. Indeed, "maritime animals" can and should evoke animals that have a close relationship and engagement with the sea, regardless of whether they are terrestrial, coastal, or oceanic animals. However, the word *maritime* is now predominantly used "to describe human activity in relation to ocean," such as "military service, shipping, or navigation."[12] The ship has played a central role in this definition of *maritime*, as the main stage of human mastery over the sea, as well as the main vehicle of European colonization and global operations. Through its focus on the relationships of a variety of animals to ships and their role in European colonial expansion, *Maritime Animals* examines how human activities at sea have affected the lives of nonhuman animals. In so doing, it seeks to unravel the anthropocentric narratives of the ship as the seat of maritime history. Drawing on the etymological definition of *maritime* as oceanic correlation, this collection characterizes the ship as a place where the ocean and species interact with each other in multiple and often surprising ways. It is also where nonhuman animals, in their adjacency to the ocean, tell stories and make histories.

In our exploration into animal-centric ways of telling shipborne stories, we are conscious of the roles that the ship's pets and mascots played in maritime history. Dogs and cats were the most popular animal companions, but sailors also adopted a wide variety of unusual or exotic animals, as can be seen from the *Challenger*'s examples. The Royal Navy had animal mascots till the practice was eventually banned in the 1970s for health and safety reasons.[13] This maritime tradition gave rise to many animal celebrities, such as Trim the ship cat who accompanied Matthew Flinders in his historic circumnavigation of Australia in 1801–3, and Tirpitz the pig, rescued from a sinking German ship by the British, who adopted her as a ship's mascot during World War I.[14] Their stories, richly documented in the form of archival photographs and other materials, demonstrate that humans did not make maritime history alone; they were helped by many nonhuman shipmates, who "have demonstrated considerable courage and loyalty and have given much consolation to their sailor companions."[15] As common objects of sailors' affection, they also played a significant role in bringing together the human (and predominantly male) shipborne community.[16] However, it is also important to bear in mind that ships' pets and mascots, represented as loyal companions to their human masters, were an integral part of the maritime romance, told to celebrate the heroism and resourcefulness of human sailors.[17] As such, they helped shape the narratives of the sea as anthropocentric and androcentric adventures, which are inseparable from the European history of colonization and imperialism.

Maritime Animals does not feature chapters dedicated to the roles of ships' pets and mascots, in order to do justice to the full diversity of maritime animals, and to take a critical distance from the human-centered maritime animal storytelling that these animals came to embody. This, however, does not mean that the ship's pets and mascots are totally absent from this volume. Each chapter's species focus allows us to witness how the same species was entangled in different kinds of human-animal and interspecies relationships, of which the human-pet relationship was just one. Moreover, the borders between different animal categories—food, specimens, companions, and the like—were extremely thin in the enclosed space of the ship, with a limited number of live human and nonhuman animals on board.[18] For instance, rats, loathed as vermin, became valuable food/water sources when the ship ran out of these (see chapter 6), and the Galápagos tortoise, loaded on board as food or scientific specimens, could be adopted as a ship's pet (chapter 1). Terrestrial conventions and preconceptions about species were often tested and had to be remade on the waves, in the sailors' close proximity and constant companionship with other animals.

Steven Mentz, drawing on Donna Haraway, declares that "sailors are cyborgs," created through the coupling between organism and machine.[19] This provides another definition of "maritime animals": a cyborg entity comprised of animals (both human and nonhuman) and the ship as technology. Several of the chapters in *Maritime Animals* consider how the ship's physical construction and technology shaped the species' experience on board, and how it was conversely shaped by a range of nonhuman forces. As such, the maritime animal is both a part and an embodiment of what many theorists, building on Deleuze and Guattari's concept, have theorized as an "assemblage," to capture the inter-action and coming together of heterogeneous forces, which inform more-than-human entanglements.[20] Importantly, this biotechnological assemblage—animals traveling on the ship—was a driving force and embodiment of European colonization and mass migration, which has powerfully changed the dynamics of global ecology, with lasting consequences. It is then no wonder that maritime animal stories are often told to address the issues of extinction. Many of the chapters in this collection feature animals whose conservation status is (or was) critical (Hawaiian snails, the Galápagos tortoise, the tuatara, the blue whale), or animals whose global migrations have contributed to the decimation of ecosystems (e.g., the sheep and the rat).

Maritime animal stories were powered by the ship's movement as well as the ocean currents. In introducing the book's ten chapters, I draw on Moseley's descriptions of the HMS *Challenger* expedition again as a reference point. This is not only to bring these ten species' travel stories into conversation, but also to demonstrate the extent to which the ship was a nexus of many animal stories and interspecies connections.

While at the Hawaiian Islands, the *Challenger* received on board two living Galápagos tortoises from HMS *Peterel*, which had visited the Galápagos archipelago on a special mission to collect specimens of this species, which was known to be "nearly extinct as the whale ships kill them for food."[21] On the *Challenger*, the tortoises were "fed a good deal on pine-apples," which were stored in the paymaster's office. Moseley recalls how they "used to glare and sniff longingly at the fruit" as they "[propped] themselves up against a board put across the door of the office to keep out dogs."[22] The *Challenger*'s crew apparently took good care of the tortoises because they were such valuable specimens. The devastating impact of the whaling industries on the once abundant population of the Galápagos tortoise is the central focus of David Haworth and Lynette Russell's chapter, "Islands, Oceans, Whaling Ships, and the Mutable Ontologies of the Galápagos Tortoise" (chapter 1). Whaling ships frequented the Galápagos Islands to harvest the tortoises by hundreds, and once aboard ship they were "kept alive during the voyage, traversing the oceans in the darkness of the hold, as a convenient source of fresh meat for hungry whalers." In giving an account of the cruel destruction of tortoise lives, Haworth and Russell are critical of, and resist repeating, the straightforward, anthropocentric narrative of human exploitation and nonhuman extinction. Instead, they place the tortoise's extinction story within the shifting relationships among islands, oceans, and whaling ships to demonstrate how confluences of "cultural and biological, human and nonhuman, and living and nonliving forces and agencies" have shaped the tortoise's history.

Being a "modern" ship with metal sheathing on the hull, the *Challenger* was unlikely to have suffered from damage caused by the shipworm, a marine mollusk that feeds on wood submerged in saltwater. In chapter 2, "Shipworms and Maritime Ecology in the Age of Sail," Derek Lee Nelson and Adam Sundberg take us back to an earlier time, when these creatures were the bane of shipborne life. Endemic in warmer and tropical waters, the shipworm spread worldwide via oceangoing European ships, which they bored into and destroyed. The chapter discusses a variety of strategies and preventative measures taken to protect the ship, and in doing so, characterizes the ship as a maritime ecology shaped by human-shipworm interactions. The shipworm emerges as a key contributor to maritime technological advancements, as it precipitated the ship's transition to iron and steel.

When HMS *Challenger* arrived in Melbourne in March 1874, the first thing Moseley noted was the flocks of English house sparrows, making themselves "quite at home" on the beach and about the city.[23] He was clearly aware of the fact that the steady flow of migrants, both human and nonhuman, was having a considerable impact on the Australian landscape. In particular, sheep played a defining role in the making of Australia as a settler colony. In chapter 3, "Sheep from Cowes: Using a Shipboard Diary to Explore Animal Mobilities," Nancy Cushing follows a flock of sheep's voyage from England to Sydney in 1826, and in the process, she draws attention to the challenge of recovering the stories of animal cargoes, who "disappear from sight during the voyage, rendering their experiences of mobility unrecorded and unknowable." Cushing's examination of a shipboard diary kept during the voyage by the sheep's caretaker sheds valuable light on their living conditions, their mobility within the limited space of the ship, and their relationship with their caretaker, who regarded them only as commodities.

Understanding a nonhuman species' shipboard experience is also the focus of Donna Landry's chapter, "Weapons, Commodities, Subjects: Stories of Horses at Sea" (chapter 4). She tells maritime stories of different types of equine travelers, such as military horses and Arabian horses transported as exotic cargoes, with close attention to their entanglements in the web of human (class, material, political, etc.) relations. The chapter asks what it was like for a horse to travel on a ship by inviting us to imagine the equine *Umwelt*, or the horse's species-specific environmental world. In many ways, the ship, without sufficient space, air, and water, is at variance with what normally constitutes an equine world. The horses need the vigilance and constant care of their keepers to survive and feel safe, which makes the ship a unique space through which to think about the nature of human-animal companionship and responsibility of care.

On arrival in the United Kingdom, the *Challenger*'s two Galápagos tortoises were sent to the Gardens of the Zoological Society of London, where they were soon reunited with two other tortoises that had remained aboard HMS *Peterel*.[24] Enthusiastically received as the first living Galápagos tortoises to reach Britain, they were just one species among many that the *Challenger* collected during its journey. Indeed, it is frightening to think that Moseley's description of the zoology of the ship omits thousands of dead animal specimens stored in the holds of the ship. As a scientific survey ship, the *Challenger* embodied natural history's practice of collecting exotic and rare specimens, dead or alive; ships played a vital role in transporting these specimens. In chapter 5, "Repatriating Castaways: Travel Tales of the Tuatara," Anna Boswell considers the stories of the tuatara, a reptile endemic to Aotearoa / New Zealand, which was shipped to Europe and North America to be part of museum collections and displays. Focusing on the work of Andreas Reischek (1845–1902), an Australian naturalist who trafficked tuatara specimens, Boswell highlights the violence of the way in which Western scientific practices uprooted species from their localities and erased local knowledge practices of which they had been an integral part. She stresses the importance of "repatriating" these specimens stranded in European collections and maritime stories, and argues that this repatriation should include finding new ways of telling the tuatara's travel stories.

Moseley remembers that rats came on board when the *Challenger* was "moored at Bermuda, alongside the wharf in the dockyard," despite the fact that "boards were placed on all the mooring chains as a fence against rats."[25] The history of human navigation is never complete without that of seafaring rats, who chose a life at sea, unlike other animals who were taken aboard by humans. My chapter, "Rattus-Homo-Machine: Rats as Seafarers in the Nineteenth Century," considers the rats' global journey made in partnership with humans and their ships. During the period of colonial expansion, rats became the metaphor and embodiment of the force of European migration and settlement, due to the fact that they, as an invasive species, devastated local wildlife in European colonies and elsewhere. Alongside this representation of rats as a colonizing machine, the chapter discusses rats' resourcefulness in utilizing ships to make their own travel possible. The ship emerges as a site of homo-rattus multispecies flourishing, in which the sailors did not merely kill rats as vermin, but also had to take into account rats' need to eat, drink, and survive as part of the shipborne economy.

As already mentioned, dogs were a popular choice of maritime pets or mascots, and the *Challenger* had some dogs on board from the beginning of its journey. However, the human-canine relationship, which Lea Edgar discusses in chapter 7, is of a very different kind. Titled "Beloved Member of Our Team," the chapter uncovers the stories of the sled dogs of the *St. Roch*, a famous Royal Canadian Mounted Police vessel that patrolled the Canadian Arctic in the early twentieth century. These dogs, which included *qimmiq*, or the Inuit sled dog, were perceived as fierce and wild, and were hardly cuddly companions. They were working animals, whom the human crew relied on for their survival in the Arctic. Drawing on the archives of the Vancouver Maritime Museum, which now houses the *St. Roch* as a National Historic Site, Edgar documents the lives of these sled dogs and their human coworkers and shipmates, while bearing in mind the fact that the sled dogs, associated and identified with the Inuit, were part of the Canadian civilizing mission, which endangered the Inuit way of life by pushing them into settlements.

In the nineteenth century, the deep sea, hitherto unreachable, therefore unknown, became an object of scientific inquiry to which the *Challenger* expedition made a defining contribution. Robert the Parrot was a witness and chronicler of the ship's fathoming and dredging operations, as he learned to say, and repeated constantly: "What! two thousand fathoms and no bottom! Ah, Doctor Carpenter, F.R.S."[26] As Jimmy Packham and Laurence Publicover point out, such fathoming of the deep, conducted by European colonial powers, was driven by political and economic motives, and facilitated the exploitation of the ocean and its resources. Their chapter, "The Decontextualized Deep: Fathoming the Whale" (chapter 8), examines nineteenth-century human encounters with the whale, considered to embody the life and mysteries of the ocean. Drawing on the writings of three maritime travelers (Darwin, Beck, and Melville), it highlights the impossibility of *our* fully knowing the whale, as an animal inhabiting a space that is fundamentally alien to us. The ship, which horizontally glides across the ocean surface, marks the limit of our knowledge of the deep.

I have already evoked the picture of the *Challenger*'s safe return to Britain, carrying with it a wide array of animal cargoes and passengers. But let us now, instead of parting company with the *Challenger* at its final terrestrial destination, imagine an alternative journey that it might have taken with a bit of bad luck—one to the bottom of the sea. Indeed, the ocean floors are littered with the wrecks of innumerable ships, sunk for various reasons during the long history of human navigation, and these have become home to all sorts of maritime creatures. In chapter 9, "The Encrusting Ocean: Life-Forms of the Spongy Wreck," Killian Quigley explores the poetics and aesthetics of submerged shipwrecks as an integral part of deep-sea ontology. His focus is the sponge, one of the most accomplished colonizers of wreckage, which encrusts the surfaces of shipwrecks and thereby conserves them. Ornamented by, and merged with, the sponge, the shipwreck becomes a lively site of multispecies storytelling, which, to quote Quigley, "sustains maritime story at the same moment that it renders it richly, strangely, and irredeemably other-than-human."

Moseley was fascinated with the birds that visited the *Challenger* during its voyage. For instance, the pelagic petrels such as albatrosses were their "constant companions in the Southern Ocean, following the ship day after day, dropping behind at night to roost on the water and tracing the ship up again in the early morning by the trail of *débris* left in its wake."[27] Just like the whales, these avian visitors are a reminder of the fact that humans are hardly the sole ocean-going travelers, nor ships the only way to cross the ocean. In our final chapter, "Drifting with Snails: Stories from Hawai'i" (chapter 10), Thom van Dooren considers the oceanic journeys of Hawai'i's snails undertaken without the aid of human ships. Despite being terrestrial snails, they have dispersed themselves widely across the islands by means of, presumably, birds, waves, and other vectors. We can only speculate as to their journeys, which involve the processes of evolution and speciation, and are "an epic, deep-time story that has been slowly unfolding over millions of years," putting into perspective our shipborne maritime history in many ways. And if our recent maritime stories, in the form of rats and other introduced predators, or human activities, threaten the survival of these snails, it is not just their existence and their place in the ecological system that are at stake, but the memories of their deep-time oceanic journeys, which each snail embodies.

This concludes my tour of *Maritime Animals*; I am conscious that, even with the aid of the all-surveying HMS *Challenger*, the collection could cover only a selection of species, geographical ranges, and time frames. Nonetheless, I hope that our stories of ten species' journeys will provide a glimpse of the richness and complexity of maritime animal storytelling, and help us to imagine countless other stories that exist and are yet to be written. And the ship, by which we of the land have thrown ourselves into the middle of the oceans—an environment in which we need to be careful if we are to survive—is a good place through which to think about our relationship with more-than-human worlds, and the vulnerability and perishability that we share with other living creatures. Each of us is a maritime animal, and other animals are our fellow travelers. *Maritime Animals* point to the meeting of our various journeys, shaped according to the ways in which we have all been carried by, or have interacted with, ocean currents.

Notes

1. Thomson, *Atlantic*, 1:70.
2. Ibid., xvi.
3. Moseley, *Notes by a Naturalist*, 514.
4. See G. Williams, *Naturalists at Sea*. Moseley was also inspired by Joseph Dalton Hooker, the director of the Royal Botanic Gardens at Kew, who built his scientific career by participating in several voyages of discovery. During Moseley's journey on the *Challenger*, Hooker corresponded with him to give support and encouragement, as well as aiding him in collecting plants (Moseley, *Notes by a Naturalist*, vi). For a discussion of Hooker's observations of the animals on board *Erebus* and *Terror*, see Jones, "Animals."
5. Moseley, *Notes by a Naturalist*, 517.
6. "The Cruise of the 'Challenger,'" *Illustrated London News*.
7. DeLoughrey, "Submarine Futures of the Anthropocene," 32.
8. Neimanis, *Bodies of Water*, 2.
9. Williams, "Maritime History," 371.
10. *OED Online*, s.v. "maritime, adj. and n.," accessed October 27, 2022, www.oed.com/view/Entry/114163.
11. Dobrin, *Blue Ecocriticism*, 36.
12. Ibid.
13. Verity, *Animals at Sea*, 9.
14. See Flinders, Dooley, and Sandall, *Trim*; Mizelle, *Pig*, 104–5.
15. Verity, *Animals at Sea*, 11.
16. See Mäenpää, "Sailors and Their Pets."
17. Cohen, *The Novel and the Sea*, 3.
18. For a discussion of the interchangeability of animal categories on board ship, see Jones, "Animals," 35–36.
19. Mentz, *Ocean*, 55.
20. See, for instance, Bennett, *Vibrant Matter*, chap. 2; Bear, "Assembling Ocean Life."
21. Matkin, *At Sea*, 280.
22. Moseley, *Notes by a Naturalist*, 516.
23. Ibid., 222.
24. Cookson, "Letter," 526.

25. Moseley, *Notes by a Naturalist*, 515.
26. Ibid., 516.
27. Ibid., 494. For further insight into the marvel of maritime encounters with seabirds and fish, see McAleer, "As Pretty a Thing"; Mäenpää's article, "To Kill an Albatross," also gives an account of the fascinating maritime practice of catching albatrosses on Finnish windjammers in the 1930s.

Bibliography

Bear, Christopher. "Assembling Ocean Life: More-than-Human Entanglements in the Blue Economy." *Dialogues in Human Geography* 7, no. 1 (2017): 27–31.

Bennett, Jane. *Vibrant Matter: A Political Ecology of Things*. Durham: Duke University Press, 2010.

Cohen, Margaret. *The Novel and the Sea*. Princeton: Princeton University Press, 2010.

Cookson, Commander W. E. "Letter from, containing remarks on the Tortoises of the Galapagos." *Proceedings of the Zoological Society of London* (June 20, 1876): 520–26.

"The Cruise of the Challenger." *Illustrated London News*. 68, no. 1924 (June 10, 1876): 558.

Deleuze, Gilles, and Félix Guattari. *A Thousand Plateaus: Capitalism and Schizophrenia*. Translated by Brian Massumi. London: Continuum, 2003.

DeLoughrey, Elizabeth. "Submarine Futures of the Anthropocene." *Comparative Literature* 69, no. 1 (2017): 32–44.

Dobrin, Sidney I. *Blue Ecocriticism and the Oceanic Imperative*. London: Routledge, 2021.

Flinders, Matthew, Gillian Dooley, and Philippa Sandall. *Trim, the Cartographer's Cat: The Ship's Cat Who Helped Flinders Map Australia*. London: Adlard Coles, 2019.

Haraway, Donna. "A Cyborg Manifesto: Science, Technology, and Socialist-Feminism in the Late Twentieth Century." In *Manifestly Haraway*, 4–90. Minneapolis: University of Minnesota Press.

Jones, Cam Sharp. "Animals, Joseph Dalton Hooker and the Ross Expedition to Antarctica, 1839–1843." *Journal for Maritime Research* 22, nos. 1–2 (2020): 25–40.

Mäenpää, Sari. "Sailors and Their Pets: Men and Their Companion Animals Aboard Early Twentieth-Century Finnish Sailing Ships." *International Journal of Maritime History* 28, no. 3 (2016): 480–95.

———. "'To Kill an Albatross Is Unlucky': Maritime Animals as Symbols of Freedom on Finnish Windjammers in the 1930s." *Journal for Maritime Research* 22, nos. 1–2 (2020): 97–114.

Matkin, Joseph. *At Sea with the Scientifics: The* Challenger *Letters of Joseph Matkin*. Edited by Philip F. Rehbock. Honolulu: University of Hawai'i Press, 1992.

McAleer, John. "'As Pretty a Thing as I Have Ever Seen': Animal Encounters and Atlantic Voyages, 1750–1850." *Journal for Maritime Research* 22, nos. 1–2 (2020): 5–23.

Mentz, Steve. *Ocean*. New York: Bloomsbury Academic, 2020.

Mizelle, Brett. *Pig*. London: Reaktion, 2014.

Moseley, Henry Nottidge. *Notes by a Naturalist: An Account of Observations made during the Voyage of H.M.S. "Challenger" round the world in the years 1872–1876*. A New and Revised Edition. London: John Murray, 1892.

Neimanis, Astrida. *Bodies of Water: Posthuman Feminist Phenomenology*. London: Bloomsbury Academic, 2017.

Thomson, C. Wyville. *The Atlantic; a Preliminary Account of the General Results of the Exploring Voyage of*

H.M.S. "Challenger" during the Year 1873 and the Early Part of the Year 1876. 2 vols. London: Macmillan, 1877.

Verity, Liza. *Animals at Sea.* London: National Maritime Museum, 2004.

Williams, David M. "Maritime History: Contexts and Perspectives." *International Journal of Maritime History* 32, no. 2 (2020): 370–75.

Williams, Glyn. *Naturalists at Sea: Scientific Travellers from Dampier to Darwin.* New Haven: Yale University Press, 2013.

CHAPTER 1

ISLANDS, OCEANS, WHALING SHIPS, AND THE MUTABLE ONTOLOGIES OF THE GALÁPAGOS TORTOISE

David Haworth and Lynette Russell

In *Moby-Dick* (1851), Herman Melville's narrator Ishmael relates that certain individual whales can accrue such an "ocean-wide renown" among whalers and mariners that they are "admitted into all the rights, privileges, and distinctions of a name."[1] One of these renowned whales is known as Don Miguel, whom Ishmael addresses as "thou Chilian whale, marked like an old tortoise with mystic hieroglyphics upon the back!"[2] Melville returns to this image of a giant tortoise covered in writing in his novella "The Encantadas" (1856), based on his visit to the Galápagos Islands in 1841, while working on a whaleship. Melville writes:

> Such is the vividness of my memory, or the magic of my fancy, that I know not whether I am not the occasional victim of optical delusion concerning the Gallipagos [*sic*]. For, often in scenes of social merriment . . . I have drawn the attention of my comrades by my fixed gaze and sudden change of air, as I have seemed to see, slowly emerging from those imagined solitudes, and heavily crawling along the floor, the ghost of a gigantic tortoise, with "Memento * * * * *" burning in live letters upon his back.[3]

What meanings can be gleaned from this vivid, seemingly fantastical image of an ancient and giant tortoise with incandescent text emblazoned across its shell? On one level, it echoes the sacred tortoise of Chinese mythology, which emerges from a river carrying inscriptions of divination upon its back—additionally, some of the earliest examples of Chinese writing have been found inscribed on the shells and plastrons, or undershells, of tortoises. But since Melville invokes this inscribed tortoise within two works that reference his life at sea and his experiences as a whaler, on another level this depiction should be read in connection with the history of whaling in the Pacific Ocean, and the ways that Galápagos tortoises are embedded in that history. During the nineteenth century, ships en route to and from the Pacific whaling grounds would often stop at the Galápagos in order to harvest giant tortoises, sometimes by the hundreds. The tortoises were kept alive during the voyage, traversing the oceans in the darkness of the hold, as a convenient source of fresh meat for hungry whalers. There were tortoises on board the *Essex* when it was rammed and sunk by a sperm whale in 1820, inspiring Melville's *Moby-Dick*.[4] And a close look at the history of Galápagos tortoises in the whaling industry suggests that Melville's references to inscribed tortoises could have been inspired not only by the mythological Chinese tortoise but also by a real Galápagos tortoise. In 1925, the Director of the New York Aquarium, Charles Haskins Townsend, published a monograph titled *The Galápagos Tortoises in Their Relation to the Whaling Industry: A Study of Old Logbooks*, in which he recounts numerous stories of a "renowned tortoise that was supposed to weigh over a thousand pounds [with] names carved all over its back," and quotes from an interview with a Mr. George A. Grant, a whaler claiming to have seen on Albemarle (now Isabela) Island in 1881 "a tortoise of extraordinary size that was famous among the whalemen and was known as 'Port Royal Tom.' There were dates and names carved on his back, the oldest date being 1791."[5] Whether Melville actually encountered Port Royal Tom on Albemarle Island in 1841, or merely heard stories about this named, immense, and text-laden tortoise from other whalers, he certainly seems transfixed by the image of a giant and long-lived tortoise, overladen with meaningful symbols.

Curiously, a similar depiction of the Galápagos tortoise as inscribed with traces of the past appears in a vastly different context in the writing of evolutionary biologist Richard Dawkins, in his concept of the "genetic book of the dead." Dawkins writes that every animal's genome comprises a textual record of its evolutionary history,

> a kind of negative imprint of ancient worlds, a description of the ancestral environments of the species. . . . The genetic book of a giant tortoise most vividly portrays the Galápagos island habitat of its recent ancestors; before that the South American mainland where its . . . ancestors thrived. But we know that all modern land tortoises descend earlier from marine turtles, so our Galápagos tortoise's genetic book will describe somewhat older marine scenes. But those marine ancestral turtles were themselves descended from much older, Triassic, land tortoises. And, like all tetrapods, those Triassic tortoises themselves were descended from fish. So the genetic book of our Galápagos giant is a bewildering palimpsest of water, overlain by land, overlain by water, overlain by land.[6]

Dawkins depicts the evolutionary history of the Galápagos tortoise as leaving traces of its ancestral islands, oceans, and continents carved in multiple layers across its body. But Dawkins leaves out the maritime and anthropogenic forces that have left their own layered, indelible traces on the history of these animals. As indicated by the story of Port Royal Tom, upon whose shell was carved the record of a century of encounters with whalers and buccaneers, the story of the Galápagos tortoise is a thickly layered palimpsest not only of islands and oceans and distant continents, but also of ships and mariners and the desire for whales.

In this chapter we explore the different layers of this palimpsest, examining the ways that islands, oceans, whaling ships, and mariners have left their imprint upon the Galápagos tortoise. Forming an integral part of this palimpsest are the stories, often recorded in logbooks, of the lives and deaths of tortoises during their voyages aboard whaling ships. Like the mythical World Tortoise that carries the weight of the world on its back, the giant tortoise species of the Galápagos archipelago have become burdened, over time, with the weight of different meanings and value categories. We therefore also look at the shifting ontological status of the Galápagos tortoise: how, at various points in the history of whaling and its aftermath, individual tortoises have been framed in different ways, as antediluvian wonders, livestock, pets, mascots, scientific specimens, icons of evolution, or emblems of extinction and conservation. By thinking of the history and ontology of Galápagos tortoises within the whaling industry as a palimpsest of island, oceanic, and maritime forces, we are building on the multidisciplinary approach advocated by island studies scholars such as Jonathan Pugh. Pugh calls for a bringing together of island studies, critical ocean studies, and maritime history, writing that "islands, oceans and ships should not always be reductively conceptualized in isolation, because they are often inextricably interwoven into complex, multifaceted and shifting arrays of relations and assemblages."[7] Along these lines, stories of the shipborne voyages of Galápagos tortoises are inextricably interwoven with many other kinds of stories, and should not be considered in isolation from them. Thinking of islands, oceans, and ships as an interwoven assemblage is an especially significant intervention in studies of the Galápagos Islands and the giant tortoises that they are named for, because these islands and these animals have in many ways become icons of isolation, of being cut off from the rest of the world. We are therefore also building on the recent work of environmental history scholars who have called into question the imagining of the Galápagos and its wildlife as isolated, pristine, or untouched.[8] These scholars tend to focus only on the cultural and historical—that is, human—forces that have left their imprint on these islands and animals. We, however, are interested in how the Galápagos tortoises have been inscribed—almost "burning in live letters"—with cultural and biological, human and nonhuman, and living and nonliving forces and agencies: islands, oceans, and whaling ships.

Whaling and the Galápagos Islands

The maritime industry of whaling arose as a consequence of the industrial revolution of the eighteenth century, and the emergent need for oil to provide illumination and to grease the wheels of industry.[9] On a global scale, whale oil was important for creating export opportunities with Europe and Asia, most notably China, and after the Revolutionary War, large numbers of American vessels were fitted out to secure cargoes to carry to the Cantonese and European markets. From the 1770s onwards, the Southern Whale Fishery (SWF), dominated by British and

American ships, was perhaps the most successful and profitable. The SWF focused on the southern waters of the Pacific, Indian, and Atlantic oceans; American vessels also pursued whales in both Antarctic and Arctic waters. These oceans teemed with cetaceans, both the Mysticeti, or baleen whales, and the Odontoceti, or toothed whales, of which the Sperm whale (*Physeter macrocephalus*) was the largest. The vast majority of whales are migratory—baleen whales' diet is predominately krill, which is found in very cold (Arctic and Antarctic) waters, but warmer waters need to be sought for giving birth and while newborn whales lack the blubber needed to keep them warm.[10] Whaling fleets working the SWF followed these migratory patterns, particularly across the Pacific.

One of the first American vessels that arrived in the Pacific for the express purpose of whaling was the *Rebecca*, which traversed the region in 1791–93. By the 1840s, "[t]here were more than six hundred American vessels as well as smaller numbers of British and Australian vessels in the Pacific."[11] The Pacific, an idyllic location of great beauty and mild climate that was much desired by Europeans, quickly became the location for the slaughter of hundreds of thousands of whales. Records for this industry are notoriously inaccurate and many ships did not register the "take" at all, but the impact that these activities had on marine ecosystems is still evident today. Indeed, we may never really know what Pacific Ocean populations might have looked like prior to the resource raiders of the late eighteenth and nineteenth centuries.

Replenishing food and water was essential on long voyages that often lasted many years. Islands and archipelagos such as the Galápagos became refuges for whale ships, where they could secure the supplies they needed, and often replacement crew also.[12] The Galápagos Islands were first mapped by Europeans in the sixteenth century, but it was not until 1793 that the unique flora and fauna of the Galápagos were described, and James Colnett—British Royal Navy officer, explorer, and later a maritime fur trader—suggested that the region could be used as a base for whaling vessels. The Galápagos Islands were visited by whalers working the American whaling grounds out of New Bedford, and occasionally by British whalers working the colonial SWF out of London and Sydney.[13] As provisions frequently ran low, the Galápagos provided the opportunity to replenish fresh vegetables, fruit, and water. Meat was invariably highly sought after. Traditionally a whaling ship was kitted out with what was known as "salted horse"; this was rarely horse meat but rather salted dried beef. Access to Galápagos tortoises, a massive and highly desirable source of fresh meat, led to significant numbers of tortoises being harvested, bringing the population of these animals close to extinction by the later decades of the nineteenth century.

Darwin and the Galápagos Tortoises

Charles Darwin visited the Galápagos in 1835, on his five-year voyage aboard the *Beagle*. Famously, Darwin's curiosity for the idea of natural selection is thought to have arisen while he was looking at the beaks of what became known as "Darwin's finches." However, as Frank Sulloway and others have shown us, this is more myth than fact.[14] We do know that the various species of Galápagos Island tortoises, each uniquely adapted to its environment and food sources, fascinated Darwin. He writes:

> October 8th . . . I have not as yet noticed by far the most remarkable feature in the natural history of this archipelago; it is, that the different islands to a considerable extent are inhabited by a different set of beings. My attention was first called to this fact by the Vice-Governor, Mr. Lawson, declaring that the tortoises differed from the different islands, and that he could with certainty tell from which island any one was brought. I did not for some time pay sufficient attention to this statement, and I had already partially mingled together the collection from two of these islands. I never dreamed that islands, about fifty or sixty miles apart, and most of them in sight of each other, formed of precisely the same rocks, placed under a quite similar climate, rising to a nearly equal height, would have been differently tenanted; but we shall soon see that this is the case.[15]

Darwin goes on to explore the adaptation of species to different environments in his classic book *On the Origin of Species*; the finches feature, but, as he notes in the above journal entry, it was the differences between species of tortoise that were first brought to his attention.

The giant tortoises of the Galápagos also did more than energize and sustain Darwin's intellect and imagination: they energized and sustained his body. While camping in the highlands on James (now Santiago) Island, Darwin "lived entirely upon tortoise-meat: the breast-plate roasted (as the Gauchos do *carne con cuero*), with the flesh on it, is very good; and the young tortoises make excellent soup; but otherwise the meat to my taste is indifferent."[16] Evidently, the tortoise's status as a subject of scientific enquiry, one that helped to develop Darwin's thinking on evolution, did not preclude it also being accorded the status of meat. Darwin was quite aware that the Galápagos, rather than being cut off from outside forces, had "long been frequented, first by the Bucaniers, and latterly by whalers," and he was also aware of the extent to which the movement of large numbers of tortoises from islands to ships had caused their populations to be "greatly reduced. . . . It is said that formerly single vessels have taken away as many as seven hundred, and that the ship's company of a frigate some years since brought down in one day two hundred tortoises to the beach."[17] The *Beagle*, on its visit to the archipelago, did not take away quite so many: Captain Robert Fitz-Roy reported that forty-eight tortoises were brought aboard, and that while the majority were slaughtered and consumed during the voyage, "several were brought alive to England" as specimens, pets, and souvenirs.[18] For the remainder of the *Beagle*'s voyage, which included visits to Tahiti, New Zealand, and Australia, this ever-dwindling cohort of tortoises would probably have lived in the darkness of the hold, while also existing in a somewhat murky or multi-layered ontology: each individual tortoise was, at the same time, both a potential scientific specimen and a potential meal.

Islands and Oceans

It is no coincidence that both Darwin and Alfred Russel Wallace developed ideas about natural selection in light of their expeditions to island archipelagos. Islands are useful tools for learning or thinking about natural selection, not because they are evolutionary anomalies but because they are absolutely paradigmatic: they dramatize in stark relief the workings of natural selection. Famously, the isolation of island ecosystems creates conditions that encourage the evolution, speciation, and survival of seemingly fantastical creatures—marvels of nature like the Galápagos tortoises, the New Guinean birds of paradise, the Komodo dragon and the dodo of Mauritius—as well as making these island species intensely vulnerable to outside forces. Thinking about the isolation of islands in this way, as a producer of marvels, can encourage a rethinking of the entire notion of isolation, not as a neutral separation from external forces but as a powerful force in its own right, generating its own chains of cause and effect: a force that many people become keenly aware of during a long ocean voyage, or a global pandemic.

Isolation is never neutral because it is always maintained by some kind of physical or abstract barrier, a regime of distance. Rather than being thought of as an absence of relations, it is instead the channeling or coalescence of relations into one all-encompassing, immersive medium. Those able to shelter at home during a pandemic have relations with the outside world mediated through whichever resources and technologies are available within their immediate surroundings (their homes), and in a similar way, an island relates to the outside world via the immersive medium of the surrounding ocean. No island is an island "entire of itself": islands are constituted and defined by their oceans. Oceans help determine an island's size and its proximity to other land masses, which both have a profound influence on island ecosystems, as E. O. Wilson and Robert H. MacArthur demonstrate in their 1967 book *The Theory of Island Biogeography.*[19] Ocean currents and prevailing winds can bring new animal and plant species to islands, sometimes floating in on rafts of flotsam or on ships containing mariners, domesticated animals, and animals categorized as vermin. Crucially, oceans also shape an island's capacity to attract mariners, human settlers, and migratory animals: the presence or absence of desirable resources, safe harbors, or habitable landscapes, and the distance from human settlements, shipping routes, or migration patterns. Islands and the species found on them may be isolated from other land masses, but they are inextricably linked to and shaped by the oceans that surround them.

The lives of giant tortoises were shaped and defined by oceans, islands, and ships long before whaling ships ventured into the Pacific Ocean. In fact, the shifting relationship between oceans, islands, and ships enabled both the survival of giant tortoise species and their decimation. The extant giant tortoise species found on remote islands in the Pacific and the Indian Oceans had most likely already evolved to be giants by the time they reached these islands. Fossils of giant tortoises have been found on every continent except for Australia and Antarctica, and the fossil record suggests that their extinctions on these continents roughly coincided with the arrival of humans, which they were too large and slow-moving to escape or hide from.[20] In the 1970s, an 11,000-year-old giant tortoise fossil was found in a Florida sinkhole with a spear still lodged in its shell.[21] Giant tortoises arrived at the Galápagos between two and three million years ago, but because the archipelago has never been connected to a continent by a land bridge or a series of "stepping stone" islands, they most likely reached it by drifting across an immense expanse of open ocean, floating for six hundred miles along the Humboldt current from South America.[22] Giant tortoises are thought to have reached the Aldabra Atoll and the Mascarene Islands in the Indian Ocean by drifting in a similar way, although a recent study has hypothesized that they were introduced to Indian Ocean islands by early Austronesian sailors, to serve as provisioning stations on oceanic voyages.[23] Zoologist Peter Pritchard claims that while smaller tortoise species are able to reach and populate islands close to continents, only a giant tortoise could have survived the much longer ocean crossing to the Galápagos, its size allowing it to hold its head high above the waves, and its fat reserves allowing it to survive long periods without food or water.[24] Gigantism, in other words, is what enabled the presence of tortoises on the Galápagos Islands, rather than the reverse. In a quirk of fate, the very physiology that made these vast ocean crossings possible would, millions of years later, make Galápagos tortoises such a convenient source of fresh meat for whalers, since they could survive in the hold for months, sometimes years, without food or water.

The fossil record suggests that giant tortoises washed ashore and established themselves on many islands and archipelagos scattered across the Pacific and the Indian Oceans, but the only species to survive into modern times did so upon a handful of islands that somehow escaped being visited by extinction-level cataclysms such as eruptions or oceanic inundations: islands that, up until the arrival of European ships in the sixteenth century, were either not known or were not appealing destinations for the Indigenous maritime cultures of the Pacific and the Indian Oceans.[25] These islands were all remote volcanic islands or coral atolls, not part of any continental shelf, and were almost never visited due to a number of factors that kept ships away: their incredible distance from established settlements, prevailing ocean currents and winds, and a lack of fresh water, exploitable resources, and convenient harbors. Forces of the ocean, in other words, combined with volcanic and tectonic forces to produce islands that did not attract ships, and it was this particular relationship between islands, oceans, and ships that allowed giant tortoises to flourish and speciate, whereas their counterparts in more accessible locations did not. Giant tortoises became incredibly abundant in the Galápagos, numbering in their hundreds of thousands. As Townsend states, "All of the early navigators made mention of their abundance. Dampier who visited the Galápagos in 1684 says 'It is incredible to report how numerous they are.'"[26] This abundance was made possible by the absence of ships; giant tortoises flourished because the vicissitudes of oceanic forces and the quirks of human history granted them, for millions of years, relative safety, far from the eyes of humans. That safety in isolation was partly shattered by the arrival of buccaneers in the seventeenth century, and then was utterly obliterated by the arrival of far greater numbers of whaling ships in the centuries that followed.

Exploitation and Removal from Islands

The idea that the Galápagos tortoise might provide a steady food source appears to have intrigued British polymath Sir Joseph Banks, who in the nineteenth century was described as "founder" of Australia, with Captain James Cook as "discoverer." The British Library holds Sir Joseph's copy of the American sealer and whaler Amasa Delano's *A Narrative of Voyages and Travels in the Northern and Southern Hemispheres* (1818), and in this copy, each time Delano mentions Galápagos tortoises, Banks has noted in the book's margins "terrapin," meaning tortoise, and "food?" While it might seem improbable, it appears that Banks was keen for the tortoises to be considered a potential fresh meat supply for ships traveling across the Pacific to the new Antipodean colonies.

During the nineteenth century, thousands of Galápagos tortoises were captured, stored, and transported on ships. Many ships transported very large hauls, such as the *Isabella Hood*, which took 335 tortoises in just four days in 1831.[27] The New Bedford archive, a mecca for whaling historians (though it must be pointed out that most whaling journals probably did not find their way to the archive), lists seventy-nine whaling vessels that made 189 visits to the Galápagos between 1831 and 1868 for the purpose of securing tortoises. Their combined catch during this period was 13,013.[28] The study of a larger collection of logs would undoubtedly yield more information of statistical value, but the records already available afford a safe measure by which to gauge the effect produced by the fleet as a whole. In view of the fact that there were more than seven hundred vessels in the American whaling fleet at one time, and that the majority of these made repeated voyages to the Pacific during the above-mentioned period, called the golden age of whaling, it is evident that the recorded catch of 13,013 was a mere fraction of the number of tortoises actually carried away. On the logistics of tortoise collecting, Townsend writes:

> Tortoise hunters were sent ashore by the boatload. The log of the *Edward Carey* at Albemarle on November 9, 1862, in company with three other vessels, contains this record: "Each ship have sent one boat with nine men apiece after terrapin." Tortoises weighing from fifty to seventy-five pounds were the sizes most readily transported. A tortoise to a man was the usual load, the carrying of which was called "backing them down." Sometimes men were sent ashore with provisions for several days' work. The log of the ship *Pocahontas* at Chatham Island on August 30, 1861, says "sent two boats ashore with provisions and water for 3 days."[29]

David Porter, captain of the *Essex*, wrote in 1812 that he observed whaling ships taking two to three hundred tortoises at a time, each weighing between three and four hundred pounds, a sizable cargo on any ship.[30]

Giant Tortoises on Board Ships

The use of Galápagos tortoises on whaling ships is part of a broader history of tortoise exploitation, which includes the buccaneers of the seventeenth century as well as later colonists and collectors.[31] According to the Galápagos Conservancy, total tortoise numbers across the archipelago have declined from an estimated historical population of 200,000–300,000 to a low of roughly 3,000, and although numbers have now risen to roughly 20,000, this is still only 10 percent of their historical population: a literal decimation.[32] But the story of islands, oceans, whaling ships, and Galápagos tortoises does not end when tortoises are removed from their islands—an individual tortoise could live on board a whaling ship, piled up in the hold, for months on end, and sometimes longer than a year. Townsend writes:

> There are a few records respecting the length of time tortoises lived on board the whaleships. An entry in the log of the bark *Equator* of New Bedford, on September 8, 1846, reads: "killed our last Terpen which has lived on air for four months and made a good mess for all hands." This evidently was the last of the one hundred fifty tortoises taken by the *Equator* from Albemarle Island on April 22d of the same year—four and one-half months before.
>
> [American sea captain Benjamin] Morrell says "I have had these animals on board my own vessels from five to six months without their once taking food or water. . . . They have been known to live on board of some of our whaleships for fourteen months." Porter says, "No description of stock is so convenient for ships to take to sea as the tortoises of these islands. They require no provisions or water for a year. . . . They have been piled away among the casks in the hold of a ship, where they have been kept eighteen months."[33]

On a single ship, hundreds of living tortoises would be crammed into a dark, confined space, deprived of food, water, movement, and light, for months and sometimes years at a time. The fact that Porter refers to these conditions as a convenience suggests that tortoises on board whaling ships were not considered to be anything more than livestock, or perhaps even less than livestock, since they were not fed or watered: they were a living larder.

Human-animal relations often involve intense categorization, what Arnold Arluke and Clinton R. Sanders, in their book *Regarding Animals*, refer to as the sociozoologic scale.[34] Different cultures divide the animal kingdom into constructed categories that can include livestock, vermin, companion animals, working animals, mascots, celebrities, research specimens, zoological curiosities, and wild animals. These categories are often arbitrary and expedient, inconsistent and contradictory, and so maintaining them often requires a certain degree of moral blindness: a willingness to acknowledge the consciousness, personality, individuality, and, especially, the pain sensitivity of some animals, but to deny these qualities in others. Humans have a tendency to blind themselves to the suffering of certain animals, particularly those that are eaten. A rabbit acquired in a pet store is destined to be given a name, a personality, emotional attachments, and physical affection; a rabbit acquired from a butcher is destined to receive none of these things. In this way, animals bound for the dinner plate are never seen in their totality—there is a blindness towards some parts of them, such as their pain and discomfort.[35]

It is true that giant tortoises are physically capable of surviving extended periods without food or water by breaking down their fat reserves—as mentioned earlier, this capability enabled them to make impossibly long ocean crossings and populate incredibly remote islands. But when given the option, they will eat every day, up to eighty pounds of vegetation; juvenile Galápagos tortoises eat an average of 16.8 percent of their own body weight in dry matter per day.[36] While it might not kill giant tortoises to pile them up in the hold and deprive them of food and water, not to mention light and movement, it would certainly cause significant discomfort. Consequently, mariners had to be blind or indifferent to their pain and suffering in order to see them as a living larder, and a number of quotes from Townsend's study of whaling logbooks suggest that they were. He quotes from E. C. Cornell's book *Eighty Years Ashore and Afloat*: "Though they appear to enjoy eating as well as other animals, yet they will live and thrive on ship-board for months with nothing on which to subsist."[37] Note that Cornell acknowledges that tortoises prefer to and enjoy eating regularly, and yet are given nothing. Townsend also quotes from an interview with a Captain Smith, who said that "terrapin were seldom fed anything when kept on board whaleships. Sometimes, however, they were given a few bananas."[38] Finally, Townsend quotes a passage from Captain Thomas Crapo's book *Strange but True* showing that the tortoises could occasionally be used (in other words, categorized) as more than just a living larder: "We put them on deck and between decks, and let them crawl around as they chose. It was all of six months before they were all gone. I never knew one to eat or drink a drop while they were on board, and yet they looked as fat as a ball of butter when they were killed."[39]

When taken together, these references in logbooks to the lives of tortoises aboard whaling ships show a large degree of inconsistency and expediency in the ontological status that they could be accorded. While these brief morsels of sunlight, mobility, and food could be read as attempts to treat the tortoises with sympathy and compassion, it seems more likely that these were ways that whalers could break up the tedium of long days and nights at sea—given that the tortoises crawling on deck were all slaughtered and eaten in the space of six months. Accorded the status of a living larder, tortoises could occasionally and temporarily be re-designated as a source of entertainment and interspecies interaction. A few lucky tortoises were permanently re-designated, in the same way that, on a small farm, an individual cow, chicken, pig, or sheep can sometimes be adopted as a family pet, thereby escaping the slaughterhouse, Townsend writes that "whaleships frequently kept one or two [tortoises] throughout the voyage of two years or more, as pets, finally landing them alive at the home port."[40] While a very small number of tortoises were given the status of shipmates, mascots, specimens, or pets, and were brought back alive to the home port of whichever ship collected them, hundreds of thousands of tortoises were given the collective status of food, which meant that their individual consciousness and sensitivity were denied, their meat was consumed, and their carapaces and plastrons were thrown overboard to sink beneath the waves.

Giant Tortoises at Home Port

Townsend provides insight into the fate of some of the tortoises that made it alive to home port, writing that "Mr. Frank Wood, curator of the Whaling Museum at New Bedford, related his experience with two tortoises brought home in the early 'sixties by a whaleship owned by his uncle Mr. Edward W. Howland, who kept them in his garden. Mr. Wood spoke of riding on them, saying that a tortoise had first to be started, after which he got on its back."[41] Many tortoises, however, survived an ocean voyage with hungry whalers only to end up on the dinner plates of hungry miners. Recent work at the archaeological site of Thompson's Cove, San Francisco, which dates to the 1840s Gold Rush era, somewhat remarkably discovered evidence for both Galápagos tortoise and sea turtle remains. Colloquially known as terrapin, both giant tortoises and turtles were cooked and consumed on the goldfields, probably in commercial eateries.[42] Ships traveling across the eastern Pacific en route to the California goldfields called into the Galápagos archipelago, where they collected tortoises and sea turtles, as they were "easily caught . . . [and] could be stored alive for weeks (sometimes months or years at a time)."[43] Tortoise meat was highly desirable, and was by no means a mere starvation food, with one ship in 1855, the *WA Tarlton*, arriving in the port of San Francisco from the Galápagos Islands "with 500 terrapin onboard."[44] Such massive numbers of collected tortoises were far from rare, as Townsend documented in his catalogue of tortoises taken by whale ships.

The tortoises destined for the stomachs of whalers or gold miners died because they were not *seen* in their totality: the humans who collected them, slaughtered them, and consumed them did not see their consciousness and suffering. But in a twist of fate, one tortoise managed to survive its ocean voyage by not being seen at all. In Townsend's aforementioned interview with the whaler George A. Grant, Grant states: "Shortly after the ship *Niger* of New Bedford left the Galápagos, one tortoise disappeared. Two years later when the ship arrived at New Bedford, the tortoise was found alive among the casks in the lower hold."[45] While hundreds of thousands of tortoises were killed due to a pervasive moral blindness, this New Bedford tortoise survived by being invisible, by remaining undetected either through luck or pluck. And that lucky or plucky individual has a contemporary corollary, a kindred, in a female Fernandina tortoise (*Chelonoidis phantasticus*), long thought to be extinct, that was recently, in 2019, found living in its natural habitat.[46] Extinction, as an ontological status or category, is dependent upon recorded sightings, and no human had sighted this species for over a century. While the rest of its species encountered humans in an earlier, unluckier time, this particular tortoise (and most likely its immediate forebears) remained unseen for over a hundred years, long enough to survive into a time when being detected by humans is not, on the whole, a death sentence—at least not for charismatic megafauna such as giant tortoises.

This story of surviving by remaining invisible to humans is not only true of the New Bedford tortoise and of this recently discovered Fernandina tortoise—it is also true of giant tortoises in general. The giant tortoise species that survived into modern times all evolved on undiscovered or uninhabited islands, unseen by humans. So if there is one consistent trope throughout the entire story of the giant tortoises of the Galápagos, it is this trope of visibilities and invisibilities, of unfrequented islands, moral blind spots, the darkness of a ship's hold, and extinctions based on a lack of sightings.

Extinction, Endlings, Hybrids, and Survival

Extinction discourse, as Patrick Brantlinger and others have observed, has functioned across the natural and cultural worlds.[47] Since the eighteenth century, global expansion, European colonization, and the overexploitation of animal species—accompanied by forest clearing and air, soil, and water pollution—had led to what has been described as the sixth mass extinction.[48] In Australia, the last thylacine (Tasmanian tiger) died in the 1930s. The footage of this endling, pacing his too-small cage at the Hobart Zoo, is harrowing. The thylacine extinction followed the death of the Tasmanian Aboriginal woman named Truganini in 1876, which was heralded erroneously as the extinction of the Tasmanian people, also marked seven years prior by the death of the "last man" William Lanné.[49] In the American context, Ishi, the "last" California Yahi, functioned as a salutary tale of modernity and resource-hungry Europeans colliding with "primitivism" and nature.[50]

The inevitability of the "weak"—or those perceived to be inferior—perishing before the "strong"—or those assumed to be more advanced—inspired H. G. Wells, who writes in *War of the Worlds* (1898):

> We men, the creatures who inhabit this earth, must be to them [the Martians] at least as alien and lowly as are the monkeys and lemurs to us. [. . .] And before we judge of them too harshly we must remember what ruthless and utter destruction our own species has wrought, not only upon animals, such as the vanished bison and dodo, but upon its own inferior races. The Tasmanians, in spite of their human likeness, were entirely swept out of existence in a war of extermination waged by European immigrants, in the space of fifty years. Are we such apostles of mercy as to complain if the Martians warred in the same spirit?[51]

Endlings, as Dolly Jørgensen reminds us, are more than the mere "last of" a species, a lineage, or a family; they are stark and often painful reminders of new but diminished beginnings, where the endling might continue on "through dreams, memory and the subconscious."[52] In the animal world, the extinction of the iconic dodo and New Zealand moa, both classified as megafauna, are sobering examples of how being both large and slow might seal your fate.[53] By the late nineteenth century, it was apparent that many species were, like the dodo and moa, becoming extinct, or at least endangered. Whalers knew only too well that where whales had once been abundant, they were now significantly reduced, and many voyages led to losses; the industry was doomed. The earth and its produce were seen by many as rightfully belonging to "civilized man," who acted as resource raiders, plucking assets where they found them. Animals, plants, and even people deemed to be inferior were collateral damage.

For the Galápagos tortoises—whose shifting status saw them move from food source and living larder, to shipmates and even pets, before becoming scientific specimens and museum objects—perhaps the best known and most evocative individual of recent times was Lonesome George, the last Pinta Island tortoise.[54] George was shipped from his home island to the Darwin Research Station on Santa Cruz Island, where after nearly five decades of attempting to mate him with very closely related tortoises, George died and was taxidermied. As an endling, Lonesome George embodied the concept of extinction; however, as one of his keepers noted, while extinction usually takes place away from our eyes—an absence of sightings indicates the loss of a species—in George's case this loss was observed, marked, and memorialized.

In 2013, a group of genetic researchers, led by Harvard University, discovered that on Isabela Island there were at least seventeen first-generation genetic hybrids.[55] With links to the Pinta Island tortoises of which Lonesome George was assumed to be the last, these hybrids are thought to have been the result of whalers relocating tortoises. Indeed, in 1817, Delano described moving from James (now Santiago) Island "three hundred very good terrapins to the island of Massa Fuero," now known as Alejandro Selkirk Island after castaway Alexander Selkirk: a distance of nearly 4,000 kilometers.[56] Although Delano describes how many did not survive, there would seem to be at least the suggestion that some did. The relocation of animals, along with the seeding of plants, was part of a deliberate though ill-conceived strategy of resource-stocking potential stopping places across the oceans. Rabbits, goats, and pigs were experimented with, and carrots, garlic, onions, and cabbages were planted mosaic-like across the Pacific and the Indian Oceans. Facilitated primarily by the whaling industry, animals and plants were moved around these oceans, and perhaps no animal is more emblematic of this history than the Galápagos tortoise, nearly made extinct by overharvesting. Along with the recently "discovered" Fernandina tortoise, Lonesome George is a mascot for the trials and tribulations of these marvelous creatures.

Rewilding and Tortoise Agency

Over the course of this chapter we have explored the various forces that have left their traces upon the Galápagos tortoises—the ocean currents that first brought them to these islands, the island habitats far from the eyes of humans where they could flourish and evolve into different forms, and then the arrival of the whaling ships, the subsequent displacement of tortoises onto ships, and the application of an inconsistent and often expedient taxonomy, variously labeling giant tortoises as livestock, living larder, pet, entertainment, endling, emblem, or hybrid. But we do not want to suggest that the giant tortoises of the Galápagos archipelago are merely at the receiving end of all these oceanic, island, and maritime forces: they do in fact have their own agency. We therefore conclude by exploring some of the ways that giant tortoises exercise agency upon the ecosystems they are part of, and in which they were once tremendously abundant.

Recent research has examined how giant tortoises, as large-bodied herbivores, can have significant top-down effects on their ecosystems, acting as ecological engineers.[57] The use of GPS telemetry has shown that giant tortoises are surprisingly mobile within their habitats, moving between lower and higher ground in search of water and food, thereby dispersing seeds and crushing vegetation as they walk.[58] Researchers suggest that an abundance of giant tortoises moving across the surface of these islands has been a significant factor in regulating plant density and distribution, which in turn influences the populations of other herbivore species.[59] So while the Galápagos tortoises can be read as a palimpsest of island, ocean, and maritime stories, they have also told their own stories, carving their own palimpsest of legible and powerful traces into the landscape. Darwin hinted at this in 1835, when he noted that "broad and well-beaten paths branch off in every direction from the wells down to the sea-coast," forming a network of tortoise tracks that mariners learned to follow in order to find fresh water.[60] Current efforts to rewild the Galápagos involve harnessing the power of giant tortoises, either by restoring extant species to their former abundance, or by replacing extinct species with functional analogues.[61] But in yet another quirk of fate, this cultural—that is, human—shift towards encouraging, rather than obliterating, the agency of giant tortoises happens to coincide with the ocean's emerging response to anthropogenic climate change.[62] If these rewilding efforts can somehow withstand the myriad, proliferating consequences of rising seas, warmer seas, and more acidic seas, then we may look forward to a time when giant tortoises are restored to a position of abundance and agency.

Notes

1. Melville, *Moby-Dick*, 221.
2. Ibid., 222.
3. Melville, "The Encantadas," 186–87.
4. Conrad, "*Moby-Dick* and the Galápagos Tortoises."
5. Townsend, *Galápagos Tortoises*, 86.
6. Dawkins, "The Genetic Book of the Dead," 9.
7. Pugh, "The Relational Turn in Island Geographies," 1041.
8. Foote and Gunnels, "Exploring Early Human-Animal Encounters in the Galápagos Islands Using a Historical Zoology Approach"; Hennessy and McCleary, "Nature's Eden?"
9. Tønnessen and Johnsen, *History of Modern Whaling*.
10. Horton et al., "Straight as an Arrow."
11. Gray, "From Windfall to Copra," 38.
12. Russell, *Roving Mariners*.
13. McBride, "The Galapagos Islands"; Whitehead, Christal, and Dufault, "Past and Distant Whaling and the Rapid Decline of Sperm Whales off the Galápagos Islands"; Whitehead and Hope, "Sperm Whalers off the Galápagos Islands and in the Western North Pacific, 1830–1850."
14. Sulloway, "Darwin and His Finches."
15. Darwin, *Journal of Researches*, 419–20.
16. Ibid., 402.
17. Ibid., 400–401.
18. FitzRoy, *Narrative*, 504.
19. Wilson and MacArthur, *Theory of Island Biogeography*.
20. Pritchard, *Galápagos Tortoises*, 17.
21. Ibid., 17.
22. Ibid., 18.
23. Wilme, Waeber, and Ganzhorn, "Human Translocation as an Alternative Hypothesis to Explain the Presence of Giant Tortoises on Remote Islands in the South-Western Indian Ocean," 1.
24. Pritchard, *Galápagos Tortoises*, 19.
25. Ibid., 18.
26. Townsend, *Galápagos Tortoises*, 104.
27. Ibid., 66.
28. Ibid., 81.
29. Ibid., 59.
30. Porter, *Journal of a Cruise Made to the Pacific Ocean*, 137.
31. For a comprehensive account of this history of exploitation, see Conrad and Gibbs, "The Era of Exploitation."
32. Galápagos Conservancy, "Giant Tortoise Restoration in the Galápagos Islands."

33. Townsend, *Galápagos Tortoises*, 68.
34. Arluke and Sanders, *Regarding Animals*, 167.
35. Wicks, "Silence and Denial in Everyday Life."
36. Hatt et al., "Fiber Digestibility in Juvenile Galapagos Tortoises (*Geochelone nigra*) and Implications for the Development of Captive Animals," 188.
37. Townsend, *Galápagos Tortoises*, 95.
38. Ibid., 89.
39. Ibid., 98.
40. Ibid., 68.
41. Ibid., 69.
42. Conrad et al., "Hide, Tallow and Terrapin"; Conrad and Pastron, "Galapagos Tortoises and Sea Turtles in Gold Rush-Era California"; Chambers, *Sheltered Life*.
43. Conrad et al., "Hide, Tallow and Terrapin," 546.
44. Ibid., 546.
45. Townsend, *Galápagos Tortoises*, 68–69.
46. Galápagos Conservancy, "Breaking: Female Tortoise Found on Fernandina Island."
47. Brantlinger, *Dark Vanishings*.
48. Barnosky et al., "Has the Earth's Sixth Mass Extinction Already Arrived?"
49. Smith, *Spectre of Truganini*.
50. Kroeber, *Ishi in Two Worlds*.
51. Wells, *War of the Worlds*, 3.
52. Jørgensen, "Endling, the Power of the Last in an Extinction-Prone World."
53. Turvey and Cheke, "Dead as a Dodo"; Holdaway et al., "An Extremely Low-Density Human Population Exterminated New Zealand Moa."
54. Nicholls, *Lonesome George*.
55. Edwards et al., "The Genetic Legacy of Lonesome George Survives."
56. Delano, *Narrative of Voyages and Travels*, 377.
57. Gibbs, Sterling, and Zabala, "Giant Tortoises as Ecological Engineers."
58. Blake et al., "Seed Dispersal by Galapagos Tortoises."
59. Gibbs et al., "Giant Tortoises as Ecological Engineers," 213.
60. Darwin, *Journal of Researches*, 408.
61. Hansen et al., "Ecological History and Latent Conservation Potential."
62. Falcón and Hansen, "Island Rewilding with Giant Tortoises in an Era of Climate Change."

Bibliography

Arluke, Arnold, and Clinton R. Sanders. *Regarding Animals: Animals, Culture and Society*. Philadelphia: Temple University Press, 1996.

Barnosky, Anthony D., Nicholas Matzke, Susumu Tomiya, Guinevere O. U. Wogan, Brian Swartz, Tiago B. Quental, Charles Marshall, et al. "Has the Earth's Sixth Mass Extinction Already Arrived?" *Nature* 471, no. 7336 (2011): 51–57.

Blake, Stephen, Martin Wikelski, Fredy Cabrera, Anne Guezou, Miriam Silva, E. Sadeghayobi, Charles B. Yackulic, and Patricia Jaramillo. "Seed Dispersal by Galapagos Tortoises." *Journal of Biogeography* 39, no. 11 (2012): 1961–72.

Brantlinger, Patrick. *Dark Vanishings: Discourse on the Extinction of Primitive Races, 1800–1930*. New York: Cornell University Press, 2003.

Chambers, Paul. *A Sheltered Life: The Unexpected History of the Giant Tortoise*. St. Ives: John Murray, 2004.

Conrad, Cyler. "*Moby-Dick* and the Galápagos Tortoises." *Scientific American*, November 27, 2020. Accessed December 2, 2020. https://www.scientificamerican.com/article/moby-dick-and-the-galapagos-tortoises.

Conrad, Cyler, and Allen Pastron. "Galapagos Tortoises and Sea Turtles in Gold Rush-Era California." *California History* 91, no. 2 (2014): 20–39.

Conrad, Cyler, and James P. Gibbs. "The Era of Exploitation: 1535–1959." In *Galapagos Giant Tortoises*, edited by James P. Gibbs, Linda J. Cayot, and

Washington Tapia Aguilera, 63–81. London: Academic Press, 2020.

Conrad, Cyler, Kenneth W. Gobalet, Kale Bruner, and Allen G. Pastron. "Hide, Tallow and Terrapin: Gold Rush-Era Zooarchaeology at Thompson's Cove (CA-SFR-186H), San Francisco, California." *International Journal of Historical Archaeology* 19, no. 3 (2015): 502–51.

Darwin, Charles. *Journal of Researches into the Natural History and Geology of the Various Countries Visited by H.M.S. Beagle etc.* London: John Murray, 1890.

Dawkins, Richard. "The Genetic Book of the Dead." In *This Idea Is Brilliant: Lost, Overlooked, and Underappreciated Scientific Concepts Everyone Should Know*, edited by John Brockman, 8–10. New York: Harper Perennial, 2018.

Delano, Amasa. *A Narrative of Voyages and Travels in the Northern and Southern Hemispheres: Comprising Three Voyages Round the World Together with a Voyage of Survey and Discovery in the Pacific Ocean and Oriental Islands.* Boston: E. G. House, 1817.

Edwards, Danielle L., Edgar Benavides, Ryan C. Garrick, James P. Gibbs, Michael A. Russello, Kirstin B. Dion, Chaz Hysenia, et al. "The Genetic Legacy of Lonesome George Survives: Giant Tortoises with Pinta Island Ancestry Identified in Galápagos." *Biological Conservation* 157 (2013): 225–28.

Falcón, Wilfredo, and Dennis M. Hansen. "Island Rewilding with Giant Tortoises in an Era of Climate Change." *Philosophical Transactions of the Royal Society of London. Series B: Biological Sciences* 373, no. 1761 (2018). https://doi.org/10.1098/rstb.2017.0442.

FitzRoy, Robert. *Narrative of the Surveying Voyages of His Majesty's Ships* Adventure *and* Beagle *between the Years 1826 and 1836, Describing Their Examination of the Southern Shores of South America, and the* Beagle's *Circumnavigation of the Globe. Volume 2: Proceedings of the Second Expedition, 1831–1836, under the Command of Captain Robert Fitz-Roy, R.N.* London: Henry Colburn, 1839.

Foote, Nicola, and Charles W. Gunnels. "Exploring Early Human-Animal Encounters in the Galápagos Islands Using a Historical Zoology Approach." In *The Historical Animal*, edited by Susan Nance, 203–20. New York: Syracuse University Press, 2015.

Galápagos Conservancy. "Giant Tortoise Restoration in the Galápagos Islands." Accessed September 13, 2022. https://www.galapagos.org/conservation/giant-tortoise-restoration/.

———. "Breaking: Female Tortoise Found on Fernandina Island." February 19, 2019, accessed September 13, 2022. https://www.galapagos.org/newsroom/breaking-female-tortoise-found-on-fernandina-island/.

Gibbs, James P., Eleanor J. Sterling, and F. Javier Zabala. "Giant Tortoises as Ecological Engineers: A Long-Term Quasi-Experiment in the Galápagos Islands." *Biotropica* 42, no. 2 (2010): 208–14.

Gray, Alistair. "From Windfall to Copra: Trading Contacts in the Bismarck Archipelago During the Whaling Era, 1799–1884." Honors diss., University of Otago, 1989.

Hansen, Dennis M., C. Josh Donlan, Christine J. Griffiths, and Karl J. Campbell. "Ecological History and Latent Conservation Potential: Large and Giant Tortoises as a Model for Taxon Substitutions." *Ecography* 33 (2010): 272–84.

Hatt, Jean-Michel, Marcus Clauss, Ricarda Gisler, Annette Liesegang, and Marcel Wanner. "Fiber Digestibility in Juvenile Galapagos Tortoises (*Geochelone nigra*) and Implications for the Development of Captive Animals." *Zoo Biology* 24 (2005): 185–91.

Hennessy, Elizabeth, and Amy L. McCleary. "Nature's Eden? The Production and Effects of 'Pristine' Nature in the Galapagos Islands." *Island Studies Journal* 6, no. 2 (2011): 131–56.

Holdaway, Richard N., Morten E. Allentoft, Christopher Jacomb, Charlotte L. Oskam, Nancy R. Beavan, and Michael Bunce. "An Extremely Low-Density Human Population Exterminated New Zealand Moa." *Nature Communications* 5, no. 1 (2014): 1–8.

Horton, Travis W., Richard N. Holdaway, Alexandre N. Zerbini, Nan Hauser, Claire Garrigue, Artur Andriolo, and Phillip J. Clapham. "Straight as an Arrow: Humpback Whales Swim Constant Course Tracks During Long-Distance Migration." *Biology Letters* 7, no. 5 (2011): 674–79.

Jørgensen, Dolly. "Endling, the Power of the Last in an Extinction-Prone World." *Environmental Philosophy* 14, no. 1 (2017): 119–38.

Kroeber, Theodora. *Ishi in Two Worlds: A Biography of the Last Wild Indian in North America*. Berkeley: University of California Press, 2004.

MacArthur, Robert H., and Edward O. Wilson. *The Theory of Island Biogeography*. Princeton: Princeton University Press, 2001.

McBride, George McCutcheon. "The Galapagos Islands." *Geographical Review* 6, no. 3 (1918): 229–39.

Melville, Herman. "The Encantadas; or, Enchanted Isles." In *The Piazza Tales*, 181–252. London: Constable and Company, 1923.

———. *Moby-Dick; or, The Whale*. New York: Harper & Brothers, 1851. Reprinted with introduction by Andrew Delbanco and commentary by Tom Quirk. New York: Penguin Classics, 1992.

Nicholls, Henry. *Lonesome George: The Life and Loves of a Conservation Icon*. New York: Macmillan, 2006.

Porter, David. *Journal of a Cruise Made to the Pacific Ocean, by Captain David Porter, in the United States Frigate* Essex, *in the Years 1812, 1813, and 1814*. Vol. 1. Philadelphia: Bradford and Inskeep, 1815.

Pritchard, Peter C. H. *The Galápagos Tortoises: Nomenclatural and Survival Status*. Lunenburg: Chelonian Research Foundation, 1996.

Pugh, Jonathan. "The Relational Turn in Island Geographies: Bringing Together Island, Sea and Ship Relations and the Case of the Landship." *Social & Cultural Geography* 17, no. 8 (2016): 1040–59.

Russell, Lynette. *Roving Mariners: Australian Aboriginal Whalers and Sealers in the Southern Oceans, 1790–1870*. New York: SUNY Press, 2012.

Smith, Bernard. *The Spectre of Truganini*. Sydney: Australian Broadcasting Commission, 1980.

Sulloway, Frank J. "Darwin and His Finches: The Evolution of a Legend." *Journal of the History of Biology* 15, no. 1 (1982): 1–53.

Tønnessen, Johan Nicolay, and Arne Odd Johnsen. *The History of Modern Whaling*. Berkeley: University of California Press, 1982.

Townsend, Charles Haskins. *The Galápagos Tortoises in Their Relation to the Whaling Industry: A Study of Old Logbooks*. New York: New York Zoological Society, 1925.

Turvey, Samuel T., and Anthony S. Cheke. "Dead as a Dodo: The Fortuitous Rise to Fame of an Extinction Icon." *Historical Biology* 20, no. 2 (2008): 149–63.

Wells, Herbert George. *The War of the Worlds*. London: William Heinemann, 1958.

Whitehead, Hal, Jenny Christal, and Susan Dufault. "Past and Distant Whaling and the Rapid Decline of Sperm Whales off the Galápagos Islands." *Conservation Biology* 11, no. 6 (1997): 1387–96.

Whitehead, Hal, and Patricia L. Hope. "Sperm Whalers off the Galápagos Islands and in the Western North Pacific, 1830–1850: Ideal Free Whalers?" *Ethology and Sociobiology* 12, no. 2 (1991): 147–61.

Wicks, Deidre. "Silence and Denial in Everyday Life: The Case of Animal Suffering." *Animals* 1, no. 1 (2011): 186–99.

Wilme, Lucienne, Patrick O. Waeber, and Joerg U. Ganzhorn. "Human Translocation as an Alternative Hypothesis to Explain the Presence of Giant Tortoises on Remote Islands in the South-Western Indian Ocean." *Journal of Biogeography* 44, no. 1 (2017): 1–7.

Wilson, E. O., and Robert H. MacArthur. *The Theory of Island Biogeography*. Princeton: Princeton University Press, 1967.

CHAPTER 2

SHIPWORMS AND MARITIME ECOLOGY IN THE AGE OF SAIL

Derek Lee Nelson and Adam Sundberg

Introduction

"We must run all risque," Captain James Cook scribbled into his logbook, knowing that his options were limited. In June 1770, Cook rammed his ship the *Endeavor* into a reef off the coast of Australia and spent the next seven weeks overseeing repairs. By August, the *Endeavor* could sail, though not entirely to his liking. The ship's wooden "sheathing," which shielded the hull from stern to bow, had been rent beyond repair. "This alone," he feared, "will be sufficient to let the worm into her bottom, which may prove of bad consequence."[1] Cook was referring to wood-boring animals known variously as "shipworms," "teredo," or "cobra," and so on—the bane of seamen in the age of sail. With further repairs "impractical in our present situation," Cook set sail despite the danger. By November, he and his crew had made it all the way to Batavia (now Jakarta), where they discovered that shipworms had riddled the *Endeavor* so thoroughly that "it was a matter of surprise to everyone who saw her bottom how we had kept her above water."[2] Cook's risk was rewarded; countless others would not be so lucky.

The "worms" that Cook battled are an enigma to modern readers, for they are not worms at all—they are actually related to clams.

Shipworms belong to a family of marine mollusks that feed mostly on plankton. In an evolutionary quirk, shipworms learned to eat wood. They also live *outside* their shells, which are tiny and used to bore into driftwood and wooden ships, thus their nickname. Dozens of species of shipworms inhabit the ocean. Some are only a few centimeters long, while others grow to a meter or more. Most start out as minuscule larvae before burrowing deep into wood for food and shelter. Once inside, their bodies elongate, giving them their signature worm-like appearance.[3] While hundreds of shipworms can inhabit a single plank, they often went undetected by seamen like Cook, who lived in constant fear, never knowing if the ships below their feet were hollowed-out hulks.

For centuries, shipworms were among the most dangerous organisms in the sea. Yet the harrowing tales left behind by Cook and others are largely absent from history books, which is all the more striking given the sea change in maritime historiography over the past three decades. In recent years, scholars have rescued maritime history from antiquarianism and reinterpreted ships as social and cultural spaces, integral components of shipping networks, and prime movers of globalization.[4] Shipboard life, however, has remained stubbornly disconnected from the living sea. Even marine environmental historians have overlooked animals on ships, preferring instead to focus on the historical demise of commercial fisheries.[5] All of these trends have unwittingly contributed to a hardening of the conceptual boundaries between the ship (as a space of culture) and the ocean (a natural environment). Shipworms muddle these artificial boundaries and encourage us to see ships for what they really are: ecosystems.

Maritime ecology offers a way to conceptualize the interplay between ships, people, and animals. Shipworms are hardly alone in being overlooked or dismissed as mere shipboard exotics. Logbooks and journals contain frequent descriptions of rats, dogs, cows, maggots, and other animals. Whether enlisted on voyages to serve as companions or food, or reviled as pests and stowaways, sailors understood they lived in a mobile menagerie only partly of their own creation. Maritime ecology serves as a corrective by exploring the ship as a unique hybrid ecosystem, populated by communities of organisms—including animals and people—that participated in complex and historically contingent relationships. Reframing the ship in these terms has the potential to make animal histories, which have thrived on land in recent years, more central to the history of seafaring too.[6] Animals were not just on ships, they were part of them in fundamental ways, and remain so today.

Nowhere is this clearer than with shipworms, which played a crucial role in maritime ecology throughout the age of sail. While humans and woodborers have cohabited on wooden ships ever since antiquity, the expansion of interoceanic travel in the early modern period posed existential threats to people like Cook, who spent more time at sea in between stops for maintenance. Edible ships were increasingly at odds with globalization. Consequently, between the sixteenth and eighteenth centuries, shipbuilders tried to banish woodborers from the ship's ecology by delimiting the sea and the ship with metal plating and, later, metal hulls. Of course, shipworms were by no means the lone factor in this long and tortuous technological shift, but they were central to it.[7] This interpretation of the interplay between ecology and technology, and between shipworms and people, which builds on Etienne Benson's work on the "unexpected agency" of "invisible" animals in technological systems, can help re-center the history of seafaring around animals.[8] Cook's dilemma, then, is an invitation to rethink maritime history and to produce more inclusive interpretations of the sea—with people *and* animals.

Adapting to Marine Ecology

As early as the 1490s, dramatic tales about shipworms wrecking ships, marooning explorers, and forcing seamen to bail for their lives made their way through the seaports and courts of Europe. Most notably, Christopher Columbus's ill-fated fourth voyage gave Europeans a jarring introduction to shipworms. "With three pumps, pots and cauldrons and all hands at work," he writes, "I still could not keep down the water that entered the ship, and there was nothing we could do to meet the damage done by the shipworm." His ships ultimately sank, leaving him marooned for a year on the island of Jamaica.[9] Even though shipworms came across as exotic in records left by Columbus, Oviedo, and Balboa, woodborers were not wholly unknown in northern Europe prior to the age of discovery. Ancient Greek and Roman texts clearly document shipworms in the Mediterranean, where borers were still active when Columbus first set sail. Shipworms may even have nibbled at the wooden infrastructure that lined the coast of northern Europe as well, though the evidence is not straightforward.[10] Regardless, the tenor of early travel narratives suggests that shipworms were novel animals, at least in a practical sense.

Throughout the sixteenth century, explorers and traders documented shipworms and tried to map their biogeography. Were shipworms at home in the Arctic or primarily in the tropics? Were shipworms freshwater or saltwater species? Spanish and English records suggest that seamen exchanged anecdotes and debated these kinds of questions for most of the century. Clouding this discourse, unfortunately, is the likelihood that oceangoing vessels redistributed woodborers around the world, as Francis Drake's *Golden Hind* may have done when it brought shipworms back to London.[11] By and large, Europeans overlooked the invasiveness of shipworms for more than two centuries, so the true extent of their original distributions and subsequent spread around the globe may never be fully understood. Regardless, by the start of the seventeenth century, Europeans had distilled their knowledge down to a workable (though flawed) paradigm: shipworms were saltwater animals that thrived in warmer waters, especially the tropics.

While travel to the tropics was risky, the imperatives of empire building overrode fear of shipworms. European seafarers had to live with shipworms, but they did not have to die by them. With that in mind, sailors tried to protect their ships by zoning the ocean, with mixed results. The King of Portugal, for instance, "expressly under a great penalty," forbade travel to infested parts of Brazil in the late sixteenth century "because of the wormes," recounted the Dutch merchant Jan Huygen van Linschoten. The king's orders, however, proved unenforceable, since ships in distress chose to anchor in Brazil rather than accept the alternative.[12] By contrast, the British advised seasonal travel to North America. To avoid spawning shipworms, captains arrived in tropical and subtropical waters during the fall and headed back to the presumed safety of northern Europe by late spring or early summer.[13] This strategy was far from perfect. In 1700, when the Board of Trade requested an unseasonal departure, Maryland Governor Nathaniel Blakiston protested that it was "not practicable, for there are few or no ships goes out of this Province but from Feb. to June." After that date, "the worm begins to molest them, and no ship comes in but by great chance from the middle of March till October or November."[14] In short, temporal and spatial adaptations did not always mesh with biological and imperial necessities.

If mariners could not wield ecological knowledge to avoid risk, they still might weaponize environments against shipworms. Freshwater tributaries, which the British colloquially referred to as the "freshes," were prized havens for incoming ships because they suffocated borers. This strategy was described by Robert Beverley, a prominent colonist and historian of Virginia, who recommended "running up into the Freshes" for five or six weeks where the worms "never bite, nor do any Damage." While this was an effective remedy in theory, not every destination had a convenient or plentiful source of fresh water. What is more, it could take weeks or even months to kill borers in this fashion. This left ships idle and undermined the imperatives of fast-moving imperial rivalries, further limiting the effectiveness of this deterrent.[15]

For sailors unable to avoid infested waters, race back to northern Europe, or reach the "freshes," there was still another place to go. In 1770, naturalist Joseph Banks, who accompanied Captain Cook, spied a harbor in Australia, which appeared "almost providential." With the *Endeavor* badly leaking, Banks breathed a sigh of relief after finding "just the place we wanted, in which the tide rose sufficiently and there was every natural convenience that could be wished for either laying the ship ashore or heaving her down."[16] What he had found was the perfect place to "careen," the primary method of cleaning hulls of shipworms and other fouling organisms in the age of sail. Careening entailed the partial exposure of the ship's hull above the waterline and often involved laying the craft aground for extended periods of time.[17] Once careened, sailors scrubbed, scraped, and burned the hull in a process called "breaming." They then replaced rotten or worm-infested timbers and removed any other fouling organisms.

Careening, like other shipworm adaptations, came with significant risk. Safe careening required sheltered waters, often estuaries with sandbars or shingle banks. In uncharted territory, these could be difficult to come by. During his voyage with the *Golden Hind* along the western coast of North America in 1569, Francis Drake spent three days searching for an appropriate spot.[18] The English might have been slower to establish trade and imperial networks in the East Indies owing to the "want of a good Haven" to careen and spare ships from being "eaten by worms," as the Frenchman Jean-Baptiste Tavernier observed in the seventeenth century.[19] Careening was also time-consuming, expensive, and labor-intensive. In an effort to lighten the ship, sailors carefully moved or unloaded ballast to ensure the ship did not tip over. If improperly sited, careening exposed ships to dangerous rocks. Shipworm-infested timbers might buckle under their own weight, and ships risked toppling over and submerging. Also, breaming occasionally engulfed entire ships. In 1615, for instance, the Dutch ship *Hoorn* caught fire and was destroyed along the present-day Argentinian coast.[20] Careening was a delicate process that offered provisional benefits at best. It delayed, rather than solved, the problem of shipworms and only temporarily altered the oceans' role in molding ships' maritime ecologies.

Refashioning Maritime Ecologies

Throughout the early modern era, mariners yearned for security in the form of insulation from their marine surroundings. Managing woodborers through natural controls, maintenance, and avoidance were stopgap measures. It was imperative that ships sail into marine environments and remain unaffected by shipworms after passing through them. So, shipbuilders moved beyond risk avoidance and maintenance and physically refashioned ships' hulls to make them impervious to marine borers. Impenetrability was a broadly shared goal, but getting to that destination would lead Europeans in many directions.

Europeans kept their eyes peeled for trees unpalatable to the tastes of worms. In spite of nationalistic prejudice towards domestically grown trees, the oft-alleged resistance of European stands to shipworms never matched the rhetoric.[21] The need for truly resistant trees was so great that Europeans were willing to learn from people they considered inferior. In the 1510s, the Spanish conquistador Vasco Nunez de Balboa, for instance, learned of a tree too bitter for worms to eat from Careta, an Indigenous leader from what is now Panama. Careta offered up the information after the Spaniards entertained him with music and horses. A century later and half a world away, the French navigator Francois Pyrard commended shipbuilders in India for identifying timber he believed was harder than European varieties and "not so easily pierced by worms."[22] Although some Europeans may have interpreted these exchanges in reciprocal terms, they were at their core exploitative.

Europeans used non-Western knowledge and labor to build ships and shipyards in an effort to expand imperial networks around the globe.[23] Ironically, claims about resistant trees were not borne out; no tree is impervious to all shipworms. The optimism that Europeans initially felt about exotic trees usually faded and they were forced to look elsewhere for solutions. There would be no easy answers.[24]

In the absence of impervious timber, shipbuilders tried to slow the rate at which shipworms gnawed at their hulls by "sheathing" them. While "sheathing" is a loose descriptor for a variety of techniques, it typically involved layering light, pliable boards onto the bottom of a ship to protect its inner hull. During long months at sea or at anchor, shipworms devoured this sacrificial layer of wood, leaving the watertight hull (hopefully) intact. In the late sixteenth century, the British inventor John Hawkins developed a popular form of sheathing. His son, Sir Richard Hawkins, described the process as smearing planks with "tarre halfe a finger thicke, and upon the tarre, another halfe finger thicke of hayre." Sometimes these sheaths were covered with a shield of closely driven nails, a process known as "scuppering."[25] Strangely, no one agreed on how the sheaths worked. Some believed that the tar poisoned the borers, while others (including Richard) thought that the hair entangled and choked the worms. Regardless, the competing theories underscore just how carefully seamen considered the nature of shipworms. For the next two hundred years, "sheathing," in the British parlance, became synonymous with the Hawkins method.

Outside of the British Empire, shipbuilders experimented with different methods of sheathing, which included lime, whale oil, glass, and all sorts of resinous coatings. The Dutch shipwright Cornelius van Yk advised that builders apply sheaths made from *harpuis* (a boiled resin) and pine before ships traveled south toward the Cape of Good Hope or west to the Americas.[26] But even these hybrid sheaths suffered flaws. Their cost could be enormous, especially if the work took place in colonial shipyards. From his base in Batavia, Jan Pieterszoon Coen, the governor-general of the Dutch East Indies, complained to the Dutch India Company (VOC) that outfitting two ships with "doubling" at their shipyards in Japan cost the company upwards of 30,000 guilders—or 15 percent of the total cost of the ship. Applying sheathing also took time. In foreign waters, without easy access to timber and carpenters, these delays increased.[27] In spite of these drawbacks, the Dutch adopted sheathing on all VOC ships in the seventeenth and eighteenth centuries. Sheathing may have been expensive, but its costs paled in comparison to the loss of a ship.

Besides sheathing, Europeans experimented with a variety of strategies to make hulls less palatable, and resistant to biofouling more generally. One strategy was to apply paints. The English pioneered the use of anti-fouling paints, and the first patented composition dates to 1625. A number of patents for "gravings against the worm" followed in the seventeenth and eighteenth centuries, involving an array of compounds that included cement, copper, arsenic, iron, and turpentine.[28] Several compositions were systematically tested at Portsmouth in 1737, and a compound developed by a master caulker comprising pitch, tar, and brimstone appeared the most promising. Trials lasting two years indicated resistance to shipworms, and this "graving" method went into general use.[29] The Dutch likewise experimented with paints. In his 1671 treatise on shipbuilding, the Dutch politician and author Nicolaes Witsen advised mariners to apply a dressing made from "*harpuis*, refined resin, whale oil, and sulfur: it is thought no worm penetrates this."[30]

Paints and other "graving" strategies suffered several limitations, however. Their perceived efficacy partly depended on their toxicity to shipworms, but also on their durability. Compounds thus included strong adhesives such as pitch, tar, resin, or beeswax. Even then, paints needed to be continually reapplied. Painting hulls, like other maintenance work, required ships be dry-docked, laid ashore, or careened. The risks and costs of these cleaning strategies, therefore, extended to painted compounds. Critics argued that most paints that limited shipworms often failed to prevent the growth of barnacles, algae, and other biofouling. Focusing on one dimension of the larger maritime ecology was insufficient. Perhaps most troublingly, paints seemed only partly efficacious in the tropics, where critics continued to note the impacts of shipworms in such places as the Caribbean.[31]

Into the eighteenth century, Europeans employed a bewildering array of cleaning strategies, anti-fouling techniques, sheathing technologies, and oftentimes a mixture of each. The popularity of these adaptations waxed and waned, and although some strategies became widespread within specific shipbuilding traditions, centuries of use and refinement resulted in little consensus and no permanent solutions. Ships remained permeable throughout this period. Although adaptations increasingly emphasized technologies that slowed shipworms, none promised the control seafarers desperately sought. Until ships could be hardened against the influence of woodborers, ships remained a season away from ruin.

Hardening Maritime Ecologies

Between 1730 and 1761, the range of shipworm adaptations narrowed as shipbuilders slowly realized that sheathing with metal offered distinct advantages. While metal sheathing was not new (it dates back to antiquity), it was largely ineffective throughout much of the age of sail before it was finally subjected to systematic experimentation. By the start of the nineteenth century, after much trial and error, metal plates eclipsed wood, tar, exotic timber, and paints, thus hardening and insulating ships from the surrounding sea and excluding shipworms from maritime ecologies.

The Spanish may have been the first to cover their ships with lead in the early modern era. In 1514, Pedro Arias Davila sheathed his ship the *Santa Ana* with metal before sailing to the Caribbean.[32] By midcentury, the Portuguese and English were experimenting with this process as well.[33] Lead, however, proved ill-suited to the task because it was costly to manufacture and heavy. The weight and softness of lead increased the likelihood it would become dislodged—or purposely torn off and stolen, as Africans in Guinea would do.[34] Lead sheathing became fouled and required frequent and costly maintenance. Into the seventeenth century, the use of lead spread, but so did dissatisfaction with the process. VOC policy mandated lead sheathing in 1602, for instance, but had discontinued the practice by 1606, perhaps due to these limitations.[35] Likewise, the English soured on lead after discovering that iron bolts corroded the sheaths, forcing shipbuilders to revert to wooden sheathing.[36] Shipwrights continued to experiment with lead sheathing into the eighteenth century, but another metal would shortly displace it.

During the seventeenth and eighteenth centuries, copper attracted attention. In addition to its anti-shipworm qualities, copper prevented the growth of barnacles and other organisms that slowed and/or degraded ships. Copper looked to be a panacea, were it not for a couple of flaws. Its expense often limited its application to the most vulnerable parts of the ship, such as sternposts and stems. Even though copper effectively blocked shipworms, it created an entirely new maritime ecology with its own challenges, which the British Navy Board discovered in 1708 after encountering a startling drawback: corrosion. Ordinarily, shipbuilders hammered copper sheathing to ships' hulls using iron nails. In salt water, contact between iron and copper produced galvanic corrosion. This ultimately degraded copper plating, rendering it useless. For these reasons, the British abandoned copper and reverted to sacrificial sheathing.[37]

Copper caught the attention of the Dutch Republic during the 1730s after shipworms ate through the wooden revetments that lined coastal dikes, threatening to flood the lowlands.[38] The proliferation of shipworms in northwest Europe undermined existing paradigms about woodborers. Shipworms were not limited to the tropics, as long believed. The crisis catalyzed the first sustained interest by natural historians and also prompted a series of experiments with anti-shipworm and anti-fouling strategies. Unsurprisingly, the officials tasked with saving the dikes borrowed ideas from shipbuilders. They tested paints and chemical concoctions, and experimented with a variety of supposed shipworm-proof timbers, just as shipbuilders had done for centuries. Dike officials requested, and received, new strategies to combat shipworms from the public, and some submissions pointedly advertised how their benefits extended to ships. They also experimented with copper plating, lead sheathing, and *wormspijkers* (a type of scupper nailing), the latter achieving widespread use in the southern province of Zeeland as well as parts of Flanders to the south.[39] Dutch dike officials thus recapitulated over two centuries of maritime experimentation in three years. Although the Dutch finally opted for a capital-intensive strategy to rebuild dikes with shallower slopes lined with stone, the ordeal generated scientific interest in rigorous experiments into shipworm deterrence.[40]

By the 1760s, copper gained renewed interest and was subjected to tests. Although Dutch dike officials in the 1730s had balked at its expense, copper remained promising because of its combination of hardness and anti-fouling qualities. The British Navy experimented with the material again in 1761 after outfitting the hull of the HMS *Alarm* with copper plating "for an experiment of preserving it against the worm." After a sixteen-month voyage to the West Indies, the plates were checked. The results were heartening, though not entirely positive. Where they remained intact, copper sheets demonstrated not only resilience to shipworms, but also barnacles, "weeds, or any other cause" of degradation. Some sections of copper were completely gone, however, and shipworms took advantage of the exposed wood. The problem remained galvanic corrosion. According to their report, "the Nails and Staples that fastened [the copper plates] were found dissolved into a kind of rusty paste."[41] Fortunately, the British copper industry had matured since 1708, and as production dramatically increased, barriers to the use of copper decreased.[42] Ignoring corrosion—or perhaps trusting it would be solved—the British Navy proceeded to copper (as this process came to be called) nearly all of its ships within twenty years.

Copper sheathing was arguably the most important technological innovation in European shipping during the eighteenth century. Coppering allowed ships to sail faster, remain longer at sea, and make more frequent voyages. Ships had longer working lives and fewer were lost in transit. This presented strategic advantages for warships, competitive advantages for merchant fleets, and security for explorers.[43] Recent studies have demonstrated that the British East India Company enjoyed steep declines in the price of shipping goods to Asia between 1760 and 1830, a change largely attributed to coppering.[44] During long voyages to the Pacific, copper sheathing also limited or negated the need to careen ships. Whereas Captain Cook's ship *Endeavor* was sheathed in pine and careened twice, the crew of the copper-hulled HMS *Dolphin* never careened the ship during its two circumnavigations (1764–66 and 1766–68).[45] In the context of imperial rivalries, where commerce, warfare, and communication relied on speed and security, copper presented revolutionary advantages.

Copper altered not only the ship's exterior ecologies but its interior ecologies as well. British slavers are a perfect example. By the 1790s, coppering was almost universal throughout the British Atlantic slave trade. Slavers spent less time repairing damages caused by shipworms and benefited from increased speeds and shortened voyages. Faster transatlantic crossings reduced dampness below deck and limited the time enslaved people remained chained tightly together. Therefore, modifications made to the hulls of ships, in an effort to combat shipworms and biofouling, likely contributed to a reduction in mortality among enslaved people. In the eyes of slavers, these benefits translated into profit, and indeed the broader profitability of the trade itself. In their own small way, shipworms influenced the material conditions of the Middle Passage and in doing so insinuated themselves into the brutal history of chattel slavery.[46]

The introduction of iron hulls in the mid-nineteenth century signaled the beginning of the end for shipworms in ships. Up to this point, even the best copper sheathing could crack and allow shipworms to enter. But iron and, later, steel removed any semblance of the habitat that shipworms once enjoyed aboard ships. As during prior periods of technological innovation in shipping, however, this transformation was more a process than an event. The shift to iron and steel was slow, incremental, and uneven.[47] Wood and iron hybrids, called "composite ships," made their debut in the mid-nineteenth century and promised the benefits of both materials. In a semi-reversal, composite ships sometimes attached a "doubling" hull of wood to the outside of iron ships, which allowed shipbuilders to continue using copper. More often, shipbuilders simply attached wooden planking to iron frames. Copper or copper alloy could then be nailed to the wooden hull. By the 1830s, shipbuilders began using "composite metals" as well. A new copper alloy called "Muntz metal," which consisted of 60 percent copper and 40 percent zinc, revolutionized sheathing. Muntz metal was more durable than pure copper, lighter, and retained its anti-shipworm and anti-biofouling properties. Composite ships clad with composite metals were noted for their lightness, durability, and speed. Composite "clipper" ships like the *Cutty Sark* became icons of shipbuilding in the age of sail, renowned for their speedy voyages to Asia. That speed was due, in part, to its Muntz metal sheathing.[48]

The transition to iron and steel was a major turning point. Indeed, the impermeability of iron and steel hulls to woodborers was an important advantage that observers noted at the time. In his 1842 communication to the Polytechnic Society of Liverpool, the English engineer John Grantham extolled the benefits of iron as a material for shipbuilding, noting multiple advantages such as durability and the fact that it required "no such metallic sheathing to protect it from the ravages of worms." These benefits would be particularly advantageous for ships traveling to the tropics.[49] Grantham's enthusiasm was warranted. Although the transition out of the age of wood and sail and into the age of steel and steam would last decades longer (navies and merchant fleets continued to innovate new methods to limit the impact of shipworms and biofouling in wooden ships into the twentieth century), ships grew increasingly impermeable to woodboring assaults.

Iron and steel hulls diminished the role that shipworms played in maritime ecologies, and, by the mid-twentieth century, the animals had all but receded from maritime awareness. If the battle to ensure security from woodborers was won, however, the campaign to ensure impermeability from hostile marine environments was far from resolved. Iron and steel presented new frontiers for biofouling. Fully hardened metal steamers continued to accumulate organisms during their voyages and suffered declines in shipping speed and reliability as a result. Copper had proven itself to be a useful material to prevent biofouling, but it could not be applied to these metal hulls. Muntz metal slowed, but did not stop, galvanic corrosion—and it remained expensive. Shipbuilders, chemists, and engineers developed new nonmetallic sheathings and anti-fouling paints, each with unique weaknesses and limitations.[50] Hardening the ship with metal seems at first glance to be a story of progress. But in reality, shipworm adaptations simply modified the ecology of the ship. Although increasingly unfavorable to shipworms, maritime ecologies evolved and continued to influence the history of life at sea.

Conclusion

Every day, gigantic metal ships cruise the seas unhindered by shipworms. It is all too easy, and quite understandable, to overlook how massive ships and minuscule shipworms share a common history. But they do. Throughout the early modern era, European seamen accepted (reluctantly) that shipworms were part of the maritime experience. Nature was not just out there in the deep blue. The ship itself was an ecosystem in constant flux, forcing sailors to tend it like a garden by weeding out shipworms to prevent decay; that is, until the imperatives of globalization forced a reimagining of the relationship between man and worms. Shipbuilders banished shipworms, first with tar, hair, and hides, and later with copper sheaths and steel hulls. To be sure, shipworms were not the sole catalyst for technological change, but they were a constant throughout the age of sail. It took over three centuries to evict woodborers from the ecology of the ship, but what is striking is how unresolved this story remains from a larger standpoint. Steel hulls resist shipworms, but they nevertheless accumulate entire communities of organisms on their hulls and in their ballast tanks, and steel bulkheads created novel environments that fostered new risks for human health and well-being. Shipworms were merely one part of a maritime ecology that humans could not completely control, eradicate, wall off, or escape. Shipworms' role in our maritime past may be largely forgotten, but every time a non-native species is jettisoned from a ballast tank, or a novel virus circulates among passengers, we are reminded of this long history.

Notes

1. Cook, *Captain Cook's Journal*, 281.
2. Ibid., 359.
3. For biological overviews of shipworms, see Nair and Saraswathy, "Biology of Wood-Boring," 335–509; Turner, *Survey and Illustrated Catalogue*; and the many works by James T. Carlton, such as "Molluscan Invasions," 439–54.
4. Broeze, *Maritime History*, 1–14; O'Hara, "'Sea Is Swinging Into View.'"
5. Bolster, "Opportunities."
6. Ritvo, "On the Animal Turn"; Specht, "Animal History"; for recent general surveys into animal history and geography, see Nance, ed., *Historical Animal*; and Wilcox and Rutherford, eds., *Historical Animal Geographies*.
7. Russell and Vinsel, "After Innovation."
8. Benson, "Generating Infrastructural Invisibility."
9. Cohen, ed., *Four Voyages*, 293–95.
10. Nelson, "Shipworms," 25–38, 59–61.
11. Muffet, "Theatre of Insects," 1083.
12. Van Linschoten, *Itinerarium*, 154.
13. Hoagland, "Effects of Temperature," 94–96.
14. "America and West Indies: February, 1700, 1–5," in *Calendar of State Papers*, 46–59.
15. Beverley, *History and Present State of Virginia*, 2:5–6; Nair and Saraswathy, "Biology of Wood-Boring," 459.
16. Banks, "Banks Journal: Daily Entries, 13 June 1770," *South Seas*.
17. Barker, "Careening."
18. Cassels, "Where Did Drake Careen?," 263–67.
19. Tavernier, *Collection of Several Relations*, 51.
20. Elkin, "Managing Historic Shipwrecks," 165.
21. Albion, *Forests and Sea Power*, 11. While Albion's focus is on English oak, other Europeans held similar unfounded views.
22. Martyr d'Anghera, *De Orbe Novo*, 355; Pyrard, *Voyage*, 181.
23. Wing, *Roots of Empire*, 102–3, 115.
24. Southwell and Bultman, "Marine Borer Resistance."
25. Hawkins, *Observations*, 118–21.
26. Van Yk, *De Nederlandsche*, 91.
27. Van Duivenvoorde, *Dutch East India*, 198–99, 203; Van Duivenvoorde, "Use of Copper," 351.
28. Woodcroft, *Subject-Matter Index*, 520–21.
29. Goodwin, "Influence of Industrial Technology," 47.
30. Witsen, *Aeloude en hedendaegsche*, 267.
31. Fincham, *History of Naval Architecture*, 95.
32. Artíñano y de Galdácano, *Arquitectura Naval Española*, 130–31.

33. *Hakluyt's Collection*, 1:270–71; Hawkins, *Observations*, 118–21.
34. Waters, *Art of Navigation*, 92; *Golden Coast*, 71.
35. Van Duivenvoorde, "Use of Copper," 350–51.
36. Woods Hole Oceanographic Institution, *Marine Fouling*, 19.
37. Cock, "'Finest Invention'"; Staniforth, "Introduction and Use of Copper," 22.
38. Sundberg, "Uncommon Threat," 122–38.
39. Serruys, "Societal Effects," 108.
40. Sundberg, *Natural Disaster*, 122–64.
41. Woods Hole Oceanographic Institution, *Marine Fouling*, 220.
42. Burt, "Transformation," 28, 35–42.
43. Harris, "Copper and Shipping"; Solar, "Opening to the East"; Solar and De Zwart, "Why Were Dutch East Indiamen So Slow?"
44. Solar and Hens, "Ship Speeds."
45. Cock, "Precursors of Cook," 47.
46. Solar and Rönnbäck, "Copper Sheathing"; Haines and Shlomowitz, "Explaining the Mortality Decline," 263.
47. Mendonça, "'Sailing Ship Effect,'" 1726.
48. McCarthy, *Ships' Fastenings*, 115–16, 121.
49. Grantham, *Iron*, 26, 63.
50. Woods Hole Oceanographic Institution, *Marine Fouling*, 215.

Bibliography

Printed Primary Sources

Banks, Joseph. *South Seas Voyaging Accounts*. Accessed June 12, 2020. National Library of Australia Web Archive. https://webarchive.nla.gov.au/awa/20040411204152/http://southseas.nla.gov.au/index_voyaging.html.

Beverly, Robert, *The History and Present State of Virginia, in Four Parts*. Vol. 2. London: R. Parker, 1705.

Calendar of State Papers Colonial, America and West Indies: 1700. Vol. 18. Edited by Cecil Headlam. London: His Majesty's Stationery Office, 1910.

Cohen, J. M., ed. *The Four Voyages of Christopher Columbus*. London: Harmondsworth, 1969.

Cook, James. *Captain Cook's Journal During His First Voyage Round the World Made in H.M. Bark "Endeavour" 1768–71*. Edited by W. J. L. Wharton. London: Elliot Stock, 1893.

Fincham, John. *A History of Naval Architecture: To Which Is Prefixed, an Introductory Disertation on the Application of Mathematical Science to the Art of Naval Construction*. London: Whittaker and Company, 1851.

The Golden Coast, or, A description of Guinney. London: S. Speed, 1665.

Grantham, John. *Iron, as a Material for Ship-Building: Being a Communication to the Polytechnic Society of Liverpool*. London: Simpkin, Marshall, and Company, 1842.

Hakluyt, Richard. *Hakluyt's Collection of the Early Voyages, Travels, and Discoveries of the English Nation*. London: Evans, Mall, Mackinlay, Strand, & Holborn, 1809.

Hawkins, Richard. *The Observations of Sir Richard Hawkins, Knt, in His Voyage Into the South Sea in the Year 1593*. Edited by C. R. Drinkwater Bethune. London: Hakluyt Society, 1847.

Martyr d'Anghera, Peter. *De Orbe Novo: The Eight Decades of Peter Martyr d'Anghera*. Vol. 1. Translated by Francis Augustus MacNutt. New York: G. P. Putnam's and Sons, 1912.

Muffet, Thomas. "The Theatre of Insects." In *The History of Four-Footed Beasts and Serpents*. Vol. 3. Edited by Edward Topsel, 889–1026. London: E. Cotes, 1658.

Pyrard, Francois. *The Voyage of Francois Pyrard of Laval to the East Indies, the Maldives, the Moluccas and Brazil*.

Vol. 2. Translated by Albert Gray. London: Hakluyt Society, 1888.

Tavernier, Jean-Baptiste. *A Collection of Several Relations and Treatises Singular and Curious of John Baptista Tavernier, Baron of Aubonne*. London: A. Godbid and J. Playford, 1680.

Van Linschoten, Jan Huygen. *Itinerarium, ofte schip-vaert naer Oost ofte Portugaels Indien. Inhoudende een beschrijvinghe dier landen, zee-kusten, havens, riuieren, hoecken ende plaetsen, met de gedenck-weerdighste historien der selver. . . / alles beschreuen door Ian Huyghen van Linschoten*. Amsterdam: Everhardt Cloppenburch, 1644.

Van Yk, Cornelis. *De Nederlandsche Scheepsbouw Konst Open Gestelt. Vertoonende naar wat regel of eventedenheyd, in Nederland messt alle scheepen werden gebouwd mitsgaders masten, Zeylen, Ankers en Touwen, enz. Daar aan gepast*. Amsterdam: Andries Voorstad, 1697.

Witsen, N. C. *Aeloude en hedendaegsche scheeps-bouw en bestier: waer in wijtloopigh wert verhandelt, de wijze van scheeps-timmeren, by Grieken en Romeynen: scheeps-oeffeningen, strijden, tucht, straffe, wetten en gewoonten: beneffens evenmatige grootheden van schepen onses tijts, ontleet in alle hare deelen: verschil van bouwen tusschen uitheemschen en onzen landaert: Indisch Vaertuygh: Galey-bouw: hedendaegsche Scheeps-plichten: verrijckt met een reex verklaerde Zeemans spreeck-woorden en benamingen*. Amsterdam: C. Commelijn & J. Appelaer, 1671.

Woodcroft, Bennet. *Subject-Matter Index of Patents of Invention, from March 2, 1617 (14 James I.) to October 1, 1852 (16 Victoriae)*. Commissioners of Patents' Sale Department. London: George Edward Eyre and William Spottiswoode, 1857.

Secondary Sources

Albion, Robert Greenhalgh. *Forests and Sea Power: The Timber Problem of the Royal Navy, 1652–1862*. Cambridge: Harvard University Press, 1926.

Artíñano y de Galdácano, Gervasio de. *La Arquitectura Naval Española*. Madrid: Self-published, 1920.

Barker, Richard. "Careening: Art and Anecdote." *Mare Liberum* 2 (1991): 177–207.

Benson, Etienne. "Generating Infrastructural Invisibility: Insulation, Interconnection, and Avian Excrement in the Southern California Power Grid." *Environmental Humanities* 6 (2015): 103–30.

Bolster, W. Jeffrey. "Opportunities in Marine Environmental History." *Environmental History* 11, no. 3 (2006): 567–97.

Broeze, Frank. *Maritime History at the Crossroads: A Critical Review of Recent Historiography*. Oxford: Oxford University Press, 1995.

Burt, Roger. "The Transformation of the Non-Ferrous Metals Industries in the Seventeenth and Eighteenth Centuries." *The Economic History Review* 48, no. 1 (February 1995): 23–45.

Cassels, Simon. "Where Did Drake Careen the *Golden Hind* in June/July 1579? A Mariner's Assessment." *The Mariner's Mirror* 89, no. 3 (August 2003): 260–71.

Carlton, James T. "Molluscan Invasions in Marine and Estuarine Communities." *Malacologia* 41 (1999): 439–54.

Cock, Randolph. "'The Finest Invention in the World': The Royal Navy's Early Trials of Copper Sheathing, 1708–1770." *The Mariner's Mirror* 87, no. 4 (November 2001): 446–59.

———. "Precursors of Cook: The Voyages of the *Dolphin*, 1764–8." *The Mariner's Mirror* 85, no. 1 (February 1999): 30–52.

Elkin, Dolores. "Managing Historic Shipwrecks in Argentina: Challenges to

Reach the Public." In *Between the Devil and the Deep: Meeting Challenges in the Public Interpretation of Maritime Cultural Heritage*. Edited by Della A. Scott-Ireton. New York: Springer, 2014.

Goodwin, Peter. "The Influence of Industrial Technology and Material Procurement on the Design, Construction and Development of HMS Victory." PhD diss., University of St Andrews, 1998.

Haines, Robin, and Ralph Shlomowitz. "Explaining the Mortality Decline in the Eighteenth-Century British Slave Trade." *Economic History Review* 53, no. 2 (May 2000): 263–83.

Harris, John R. "Copper and Shipping in the Eighteenth Century." *The Economic History Review* 19, no. 3 (December 1966): 550–68.

Hoagland, K. "Effects of Temperature, Salinity, and Substratum on Larvae of the Shipworms *Teredo bartschi* Clapp and *T. navalis* Linnaeus (Bivalvia: Teredinidae)." *American Malacological Bulletin* 4, no. 1 (1986): 89–99.

McCarthy, Mike. *Ships' Fastenings: From Sewn Boat to Steamship*. College Station: Texas A&M University Press, 2005.

Mendonça, Sandro. "The 'Sailing Ship Effect': Reassessing History as a Source of Insight on Technical Change." *Research Policy* 42, no. 10 (December 2013): 1724–38.

Nair, N. Balakrishnan, and M. Saraswathy. "The Biology of Wood-Boring Teredinid Molluscs." *Advances in Marine Biology* 9 (1971): 335–509.

Nance, Susan, ed. *The Historical Animal*. Syracuse: Syracuse University Press, 2015.

Nelson, Derek Lee. "The Ravages of Teredo: The Rise and Fall of Shipworm in US History." *Environmental History* 21, no. 1 (January 2016): 100–124.

———. "Shipworms and the Making of the American Coastline." PhD diss. University of New Hampshire, 2018.

O'Hara, Glen. "'The Sea Is Swinging Into View': Modern British Maritime History in a Globalised World." *The English Historical Review* 124, no. 510 (2009): 1109–34.

Ritvo, Harriet. "On the Animal Turn." *Daedalus* 136, no. 4 (2007): 118–22.

Russell, Andrew L., and Lee Vinsel. "After Innovation, Turn to Maintenance." *Technology and Culture* 59, no. 1 (2018): 1–25.

Serruys, Michael-W. "The Societal Effects of the Eighteenth-Century Shipworm Epidemic in the Austrian Netherlands (c. 1730–1760)." *Journal for the History of Environment and Society* 6 (2021): 95–127.

Solar, Peter M. "Opening to the East: Shipping Between Europe and Asia, 1770–1830." *The Journal of Economic History* 73, no. 3 (September 2013): 625–61.

Solar, Peter M., and Luc Hens. "Ship Speeds During the Industrial Revolution: East India Company Ships, 1770–1828." *European Review of Economic History* 20, no. 1 (February 2016): 66–78.

Solar, Peter M., and Klas Rönnbäck. "Copper Sheathing and the British Slave Trade." *The Economic History Review* 68, no. 3 (August 2015): 806–29.

Solar, Peter M., and Pim de Zwart. "Why Were Dutch East Indiamen So Slow?" *International Journal of Maritime History* 29, no. 4 (November 2017): 738–51.

Southwell, C. R., and J. D. Bultman. "Marine Borer Resistance of Untreated Woods over Long Periods of Immersion in Tropical Waters." *Biotropica* 3 (1971): 81–107.

Specht, Joshua. "Animal History After Its Triumph: Unexpected Animals, Evolutionary Approaches, and the Animal Lens." *History Compass* 14, no. 7 (June 2016): 326–36.

Staniforth, Mark. "The Introduction and Use of Copper Sheathing—A History." *Bulletin of the Australian Institute for Maritime Archaeology* 9, no. 1/2 (1985): 21–48.

Sundberg, Adam. "An Uncommon Threat: Shipworms as a Novel Disaster." *Dutch Crossing* 40, no. 2 (2016): 122–38

———. *Natural Disaster at the Closing of the Dutch Golden Age: Floods, Worms, and Cattle Plague*. Cambridge: Cambridge University Press, 2022.

Turner, Ruth Dixon. *A Survey and Illustrated Catalogue of the Teredinidae (Mollusca: Bivalvia)*. Cambridge: Museum of Comparative Zoology, Harvard University, 1966.

Van Duivenvoorde, Wendy. *Dutch East India Company Shipbuilding: The Archaeological Study of Batavia and Other Seventeenth-Century VOC Ships*. College Station: Texas A&M University Press, 2015.

———. "The Use of Copper and Lead Sheathing in VOC Shipbuilding." *International Journal of Nautical Archaeology* 44, no. 2 (September 2015): 349–61.

Waters, David Watkin. *The Art of Navigation in England in Elizabethan and Early Stuart Times*. London: Hollis and Carter, 1958.

Wilcox, Sharon, and Stephanie Rutherford, eds. *Historical Animal Geographies*. London: Routledge, 2018.

Wing, J. T. *Roots of Empire: Forests and State Power in Early Modern Spain, C. 1500–1750*. Leiden: Brill, 2015.

Woods Hole Oceanographic Institution. *Marine Fouling and Its Prevention*. Annapolis: U.S. Naval Institute, 1952.

CHAPTER 3

SHEEP FROM COWES

Using a Shipboard Diary to Explore Animal Mobilities

Nancy Cushing

On the second of June 1826, the brig *Fairfield* encountered very rough seas as it made its way from the Isle of Wight on Britain's south coast to Sydney in southeastern Australia. The ship was carrying French Merino ewes for the Australian Agricultural Company, and the man charged with ensuring their safe passage, James White, was worried. He watched through the night as the sheep pen on deck filled with water several times, knocking the sheep down and leaving some seriously injured. White picked out the weakest ewe and carried her belowdecks to join the rest of the flock sheltering there. But there was no safety to be had, and one of the lower pens collapsed as the sheep were thrown against it by the heaving vessel. The storm continued for two days, during which one sheep was killed, the ewe moved belowdecks died, and those who remained on deck became sodden and very weak.

Most animals transported en masse at sea disappear from sight during the voyage, rendering their experiences of mobility unrecorded and unknowable. This voyage is a partial exception because White maintained a "Journal of Occurrences on board the ship *Fairfield* from Cowes to N.S.W." each day of the 12,500-nautical-mile, four-and-a-half-month-long journey. While the animal experience is elusive, the journal captures a human perspective on the interlinked mobilities experienced by the sheep as they made their intercontinental voyage, including the conditions of travel, the movements imposed by their keepers, and the buffeting of the ship by the elements. Their remaining mobilities, the autonomous movements through which the sheep attempted to make bearable the strange conditions in which they found themselves, remained undocumented. By exploring the human-mediated mobilities of these sheep, this chapter seeks to shed new light on the establishment of settler colonial Australia, by insisting on the significance of the voyage out for the imperial animals drafted to support this project.[1] Further, it argues that the shared experience of the journey did little to shift the views of animals as live stock—that is, living commodities. They were not fellow travelers but instead particularly fragile commodities demanding great attention if they were to retain their value at their destination.

The nonhuman animals designated as desirable in colonies for the food, fiber, and power they would produce were extracted from their former environments, loaded onto ships, and carried to new worlds. While at sea, they were subjected for varying periods of time to what Sadie E. Hale has characterized, using Rachel Carson's phrase, as a "not quite fatal" existence of pain, deprivation, and dissatisfaction in a strange and unnatural setting.[2] For the sheep on the *Fairfield*, severance from their past lives was permanent, but those who survived the voyage were released into an environment that, while novel, enabled them to reconnect with natural systems in which most would thrive. While they had the opportunity to regain and even increase their agency in Australia, the forced movement of these sheep by sea can also be seen to foreshadow both the trend to reduce productive animals to passivity over time, culminating in high-intensity animal husbandry practices on land, and the live export industry in which Australia plays a leading role. By drawing attention to the nature of past animal mobilities at sea, I hope to follow Susan Nance in being a "historical whistle blower . . . tell[ing] those stories that people want to forget," as a counter to the triumphal tales about the origins of the wool industry in Australia and ongoing justifications for live animal export.[3]

Animal Mobilities

Mobilities have been of increasing scholarly interest in the current century across fields including geography, sociology, cultural studies, and history. From 2003, the late John Urry and his Centre for Mobilities Research at the University of Lancaster developed the "new mobilities paradigm" as a means of understanding human mobilities. Applying this paradigm to imperial histories, Tony Ballantyne argues that "mobility was the life-blood of empire," and that viewing the past from "fixed vantage points . . . [can] occlude or marginalise the importance of [economic and cultural] linkages and the multiple forms of mobility that underwrote both the routine operation of empires and the production of nation states."[4] Ballantyne's focus was on the mobilities of humans, goods, and paper-based communications, but, more recently, other animals have become the subject of mobilities scholarship, demonstrating an awareness that, as Tim Cresswell observed, "human mobilities [are] in an entangled web of 'other' mobilities."[5] The introduction of favored animals was a key element of initiating extractive colonial economies. An examination of these animal mobilities serves a fuller understanding of the colonialism that depended on them.

In exploring animal mobilities, one of the great challenges is the limitations of human-generated sources in conveying animal experience. Animal historians have long grappled with our capacity to capture and convey animal perspectives, restricted as we are by our own embodied identities as humans and the human origins of almost all of our source materials. While some limit their aims to seeking to understand human representations of animals, Sandra Swart suggests an approach she terms "animal sensitive history." This does not seek to represent animal experience or to "ventriloquize the subject," as might have been the case had I attempted to write this chapter's opening paragraph from the sheep's perspective. Instead, it adds species to race, class, and gender as a key analytic category, drawing attention to the animal just as the other categories have insisted that people of color, workers, and women had meaningful roles in the past and must be taken into consideration in the writing of history.[6] In the case of the transportation of herd animals, the challenges of writing animal-sensitive history are amplified.

As this current volume shows, there has been considerable interest in studying animal life at sea. The ships in and on which many of those animals traveled are also important to mobility studies because they are places on the move that become mobile sites for the creation and consumption of meaning.[7] However, the focus of such studies has tended to be on individuated animals like racehorses and circus animals, and on exotic species taken to sea in small numbers. The much larger and more regular movements of animals establishing populations of familiar domesticates in the New World, and the return voyages often for immediate consumption, have attracted less attention. Prior to the animal turn, in the 1970s, Richard Perren studied nineteenth- and early twentieth-century live animal exports from North America to Britain.[8] I have considered imports and exports from colonial New South Wales, and there has been some work on late twentieth-century, shorter-haul transport from an animal rights perspective.[9] Other scholars interested in the global movement of sheep and cattle including Elinor G. K. Melville and Rebecca J. H. Wood have focused their attention on matters of breed, place, and impacts at the destination rather than on journeying.[10] As will be discussed in the next section, the availability of sources undoubtedly plays a role in this passing over of animal voyages.

Sources

One of the typical characteristics of long-distance animal transport by sea is its invisibility and a corresponding lack of written or other accounts of it. Packed into holds of ships, animals disappear for the duration of the voyage, and those who die between ports do not reach the other end. Instead, they are discarded into the sea, an even more poorly documented realm. Breaking this silence is difficult, and can be dangerous, as when workers secretly filmed footage of thousands of sheep dying on the *Awassi Express* on a voyage from Western Australia to the Middle East in August 2017. Their bravery led to public outrage in Australia, followed by the cancellation of the exporter's license.[11] In the early nineteenth century, passengers, crew, and visitors found the presence of parrots, penguins, and lions remarkable and literally note (or sketch) worthy, and dogs and cats inserted themselves into daily life onboard ships, but few wrote about less charismatic and more anonymous species. In any event, passenger ships generally carried only a small number of goats, cattle, sheep, and chickens to provide fresh milk, eggs, and meat during the voyage. Commercial shipments of these animals traveled on dedicated voyages, and even then, the people working on board paid little attention to the animals, especially if they were housed below decks or in areas off-limits to human seafarers.

Turning specifically to sheep in the Australian context, their importance to the economy has meant that they have attracted a great deal of attention from contemporaries and from historians. These studies approach them en masse and not as individuals. As the title of one volume from 2007, *The Australian Merino: The Story of a Nation*, suggests, sheep are used in these histories as a device through which narratives focusing on the settler-colonist struggle with the vicissitudes of the Australian climate and biota, the business of pastoralism, and the development of a national identity can be told.[12] Such studies do not allow for the subjectivity of sheep, regarding them instead as commodities, or what Josh Specht labels "economic or agricultural inputs, rather than meaningful actors."[13] Just as some individual sheep were literally swallowed as chops, roasts, or in stews after having enriched humans by producing fleeces throughout their lives, sheep are swallowed up in these histories.[14] A contemporary account written about sheep at sea, where their invisibility is usually amplified, could be expected to help to reposition them as highly mobile actors operating within a complex network of relations.

Merinos on the Move

James White's "Journal of Occurrences" is just such a document, and it holds even greater significance in the Australian context because of the high visibility of sheep in the continent's settler-colonial landscape and how they have been used as symbols of the advance of colonization within Australian historiography. The sheep he wrote about were part of a historical movement that was an antipodean echo of the Columbian Exchange, although one that was largely unidirectional as far as live animals went, with the exception of some kangaroos and native birds. Animals were transported in parallel with convicted British and Irish men and women, conscripts rather than volunteers in the colonization project. Spreading across the continent from their ports of arrival, they helped to displace the original inhabitants, both human and nonhuman, while laying the foundation of a new economy and society. As the producers of the fine wool that would become Australia's staple export, Merino sheep like those on the *Fairfield* had a special place in the hierarchy of introduced species.

Mobility played a central role in the making of the Merino breed. Their characteristic fine wool was attributed to the practice of transhumance in their native Spain. There they were walked in an annual cycle between lowland winter pastures and summers in the Alpine regions of Leon, Castille, and Aragon, under the oversight of the Mesta, a powerful council of sheep-owners.[15] Having been closely held by the Spanish monarchy and nobility, only from the mid-eighteenth century were small numbers of sheep gifted or sold to other European nations, including Saxony and France. In Britain, they were initially not well received, with one critic decrying them as "deformed, unthrifty, diminutive sheep."[16] It was predicted that relocation of Merinos out of Spain and into areas with different soils, climates, and environments would lead to a deterioration of the breed and, in particular, its highly valued fine wool.[17]

Despite these concerns, the need for reliable fiber to support Britain's production of fine woolen cloth made some graziers support expanding local Merino flocks and, further, to suggest using them to establish wool production in the new Australasian colonies, honoring mercantilist principles by freeing Britain from reliance on imported Spanish and German wool. Merinos began to arrive in New South Wales in 1797, being purchased from a herd at the Cape of Good Hope (in present-day South Africa) by military officers hoping to set themselves up as pastoralists. These sheep were descended from Merinos given by Carlos III of Spain to Prince William of Orange and introduced to the Cape with the intention of establishing a fine wool industry there.[18] Given the exigencies of the voyage from Britain to Australia, many of the continent's first imported species were sourced from colonies in the region, including the Cape of Good Hope and India. In Sydney, fractious pastoral entrepreneur John Macarthur purchased some of the South African Merinos and, with his wife Elizabeth, built up both the local reputation of the breed and their family's fortunes. The Macarthurs exported the colony's first commercial shipment of wool in 1812, and by 1825, their reputation was such that young rams culled from their flock sold for up to thirty-three guineas a head, more than twice the annual wages of a shepherd employed to look after them.[19]

Merinos came to be accepted by most as the variety best suited to growing fine wool in the generally hot and dry Australian conditions. Once the animals had made the difficult voyage, it was said that even the degraded "English Merino improves considerably in the quality of the fleece every shearing after arrival in this climate."[20] This message was heard by a group of investors in London who in 1824 secured an Act of Parliament and Royal Charter to form the Australian Agricultural Company (AACo) to produce fine wool on what were considered the wastelands of the empire. The company was granted one million acres (404,685 hectares) of land in exchange for the investment of one million pounds in this enterprise and, in 1826, set up their headquarters around a harbor in Worimi country north of Sydney that had been given the name Port Stephens.[21] The AACo had shipped over 1,000 Merino sheep to Sydney in three voyages in 1825 and 1826, before the *Fairfield* arrived, and another 1,300 in five shipments by the end of the decade.[22] The sheep under White's management had been selected, like the others, by the Company's agent, Robert Dawson, who traveled through Europe purchasing Merinos in Britain, Saxony, and France.[23] France then had the largest national flock of the breed, descended from those acquired by Louis XVI in 1786 and reared at Rambouillet outside Paris, together with the Merinos taken as spoils during the Peninsular War of 1807–14.[24] Having crossed the English Channel to be loaded at Cowes on the Isle of Wight, the French Merino sheep on the *Fairfield* were part of an ovine aristocracy, with ancestral, familial, and personal experience of mobility.

The "Journal of Occurrences"

Exactly why White wrote his journal is not known but as it remained in his possession rather than becoming part of the AACo's records, and subsequently its substantial archives, it appears not to have been an official document.[25] Most likely, it was White's personal record of the voyage written as an aide-mémoire upon which he could draw to report on how he discharged his shipboard role. Almost four decades after the colonization of Australia began, knowledge of how to successfully convey animals over long distances by sea was accumulating, although it was not always clear that it was applied. White's report could serve as a way to pass on information about the hazards faced and remedies attempted to those making such voyages in the future. As the younger son of a yeoman farmer family from the sheep-rearing county of Somerset, who had worked as a wool classer and been hired as a bailiff to oversee the Company's flocks, he might have thought he had something significant to say.[26]

For the historian of animal-human relations, the journal contains evidence that, in this case, limited space and shared experiences of mobility did little to reduce the accustomed social distance between humans and other animals. There is no evidence that White's sense of the sheep as a barely differentiated mass, lacking intelligence and agency, was challenged as they undertook a life-changing journey together. Even with his future prospects tied to their survival, and while committed to using all available resources to keep them alive, White revealed little empathy for the sheep as they struggled with the effects of a restricted diet, disease, and confinement. Indeed, the "Journal of Occurrences" contains none of the personal revelations that are found in writing by many oceanic voyagers. The focus is firmly on the sheep, and only on sheep as inputs into an agricultural enterprise.

This character of the journal is in contrast with one kept by an earlier diarist, Lieutenant Ralph Clark of the Royal Marines, who traveled to Australia with the "First Fleet" of convicts in 1787–88. Having gained thirty sheep as shipmates at the Cape of Good Hope, Clark became emotionally invested in their individual welfare, recording their diet and well-being, celebrating the birth of lambs and sorrowfully reporting their deaths.[27] Almost two months after they left the Cape, he declared that he longed for the journey to end for the sake of the sheep as much as for himself and bemoaned another "terrible night and day for the poor sheep" on the final approach to Botany Bay.[28] For Clark, traveling away from his wife and son to found a colony in an unknown land, the sheep were surrogate objects of genuine affection and the diary an emotional outlet. White was able to confide in his wife Sarah (née Crossman) as she traveled beside him to what was by then a much better-known destination. His journal had only to serve as a more matter-of-fact working document.

Reflecting its nature, White's journal is made up of entries that are regular and concise. For many days, the neat writing extends to only two lines and on only a very few days more than five. The whole account takes up only half of the notebook, the rest of it being left unused. The language is similarly spare. White deployed a very limited vocabulary to track the health of the sheep, conditions at sea, and what he did to try to ensure their survival. He repeated simple phrases such as "sheep as usual," "sheep very weak," and, rarely, "sheep very well." The writing is certain, with few crossings out, even when his care of the sheep was full of uncertainties.[29] Any expectations that someone who had lived with a group of animals in the close quarters of a 250-ton brig for four and a half months would have written about the personalities amongst them, odd happenings along the way, instances of agency, or a reciprocated connection with them, are bound to be disappointed. What is clear from the journal is that White understood the sheep to be experiencing mobility passively. His simple words demonstrate that while Merinos as a breed were shaped by the need to undertake self-propelled movement between their Spanish summer and winter pastures, and the French Merinos had already been moved across the English Channel, they were poorly equipped for travel on the open sea. This new form of mobility threw up multiple challenges, of which I will consider food, disease, and micro-mobilities within the ship.

Food

Providing sufficient food for the animals during the voyage was a logistical challenge. Sheep are better able to adjust to life at sea if they are transitioned from grazing on pasture to dry fodder or pelletized foods prior to departure.[30] The deaths in the first weeks of travel suggest that this was not done in this case and that the hay, bran, and corn they were offered was not eaten by inappetent sheep or could not be digested. For sheep who were struggling, White produced gruel and brewed what he called a bran tea, which he administered from a bottle.[31] The quality of the bales of hay varied, with White judging some to be coarse and bad. The bran became very musty.[32] White was cautious about running out of food. Like those transporting convicts, he allocated a set ration of food and water per animal per day, and like the convicts, many of the sheep eagerly ate their whole allowance and wanted more.[33] Having eked out supplies in this way, White was able to increase the hay ration by half a pound on June 13 as the end of the voyage approached. He noted that this was in response to the sheep's robust appetites, but it was possible because by this stage there were thirteen fewer mouths to feed.[34]

As soon as the ship docked in Hobart, the first Australian port of call, White went to the government mill to purchase fresh bran for the sheep.[35] This did not protect the sheep from what White termed inflammation on the final leg from Hobart to Sydney. He attributed this disorder to the dry diet having taken a heavy toll on the older sheep.[36] This was a particular issue because, as was the case for humans on long sea voyages, access to fresh water was limited. White rationed water for the sheep to one pint (half a liter) a day each for most of the voyage, with more during hot weather.[37] Considering that current practice requires that sheep are provided with four liters of water per day during live export, and six liters if the temperature rises above 95°F (35°C), the sheep of the *Fairfield* would have experienced their journey in a state of constant dehydration.[38] The change from fresh to dry food and limited access to water were challenging conditions to which the sheep had to adjust during the voyage. This left them uncomfortable, disoriented, and as will be explored in the following section, more vulnerable to disease.

Disease

While both humans and sheep suffered from seasickness in the initial days of the *Fairfield*'s voyage and again in times of rough weather, the damp conditions of life at sea took a particular toll on the sheep.[39] White was disappointed by the condition in which he received his charges, noting on the day after they were loaded that they were all seasick and twenty-five were very lame with footrot, to which Merinos are particularly susceptible.[40] Footrot is a bacterial disease caused by *Dichelobacter nodosus* that easily spreads between animals in damp conditions as experienced on board ship. While the primary damage is to the feet, the pain, burden of chronic infection, and reluctance to move about it causes are generally debilitating, resulting in slow growth, infertility, and reduced wool production.[41] The sheep were also affected by scab, the common term for psoroptic mange, which is now recognized as an allergic reaction to infestations of the *Psoroptes ovis* mite. When White sheared the sheep over the course of a week at the beginning of April, with the aim of making them more comfortable in the equatorial heat, the extent to which they were affected by scab became more obvious to him. As the mite moves from one animal to another, scab is highly contagious and creates great discomfort, leading to scratching, restlessness, open wounds, and general poor condition. The mite and the bacterium are reminders that the sheep did not travel alone, but brought with them their biological familiars, extending the reach of the life-forms to which they played host in defiance of the notional quarantine function of the long voyage.

It was known at the time that keeping sheep in airy and dry conditions would help to minimize the incidence of both footrot and scab.[42] This was not achievable at sea, where long-distance mobility required that the sheep forfeit their accustomed spacing and freedom of bodily movement. White noted that being "so much confined" was contributing to the incidence of scab in particular.[43] Contemporary treatments for scab included making ointments from combinations of green broom, brimstone (sulfur), quicksilver (mercury), saltpeter, salt, tobacco, balsam of sulfur (sulfur in turpentine), and hog's lard to apply topically to the affected areas, but White could only wash the scabby sheep and those with footrot in salt water.[44]

Being seriously unwell was the only way in which an individual sheep drew White's notice and entered the written record. In a regular pattern, he singled out a ewe as being sick one day, described her as being very weak the second day, and generally by the third day, the sheep had died. He became pessimistic about the prospects of the sheep who boarded the ship with footrot, often recording that they were "as well as I can expect" and quickly giving up hope that they would recover during the voyage.[45] White logged the deaths of sheep as they occurred. The focus on tallying deaths in transit is something that current animal rights advocates have objected to in their critiques of live animal export, as a very incomplete measure of how animals were affected by the conditions of transport.[46] Any given death toll signals that many more animals were subsisting in a "not quite fatal" state.

One of the forms of distress for which sheep are now monitored during live export from Australia is heat stress. Along with respiration rate, panting, neck position, and stance, reduced movement is a recognized sign of moderate heat stress. Severe heat stress can be manifested in either a reluctance to move or in greater activity as sheep jostle and climb on one another in efforts to access vents and railings where the air is slightly cooler.[47] White did not include any references to the movements undertaken by the sheep of their own volition, but he did record heat stress during a rare period of reduced mobility when the ship was in the calm waters and still air of the equatorial region. White observed that the heat was overpowering the sheep, who were already in a weakened condition.[48] White's silence about autonomous movement suggests that he read no significance in it, focusing only on how the sheep were moved by the sea, the wind, the ship, or by humans.

Except in cases of seasickness, oceangoing mobility did not cause illness in sheep, but it did exacerbate it. The toll of illness left animals weakened and more vulnerable to the final types of mobilities that can be read from White's journal: micro-mobilities within the ship.

Micro-Mobilities

Just as food restrictions and exposure to living conditions that encouraged the development of disease were side effects of mobility at sea, so were the micro-mobilities to which the sheep were subjected by their keepers. Underlying all of these were the movements caused by the elements of sea and air.

Humans and other animals on the *Fairfield* shared distinct but overlapping spaces left over after the loading of a cargo of casks, trunks, hogsheads, and bundles of goods ranging from china and linen to hats, soap, and seeds.[49] The sheep were confined in pens both on and below deck. White, as has been noted, had his quarters in the cabin on deck, with just four other passengers of the gentry class. The two men traveling to take up positions as shepherds with the AACo, Richard Merchant and William May, were accommodated belowdecks with other Company staff and the crew, within range of the sounds and smells of the sheep.[50] The shepherds had trouble adjusting to life on board ship. In much the same terms as he used for the sheep, White noted that Merchant and May were "[sea]sick," "very sick," "better," and then "nearly well," rendering them initially unable to attend to the sheep, more prolonged in the case of Merchant by a serious injury to his arm.[51] While White said little about their roles in the day-to-day work of feeding, watering, mucking out, and managing the sheep, it can be assumed that they shared these duties with him while he undertook higher-order tasks, including shearing fleeces, varying the allocation of food and water, inspecting for footrot and scab, bottle feeding with bran tea, and postmortem examinations. Had Merchant or May kept a journal, their greater immersion in the lives of the sheep might have led them to offer a different perspective on animal-human relationships forged by mobilities.

Spatial arrangements were not fixed, and both keepers and sheep moved horizontally and vertically around the ship. White favored having the sheep belowdecks, but there was insufficient space for all of them there, and so some had to remain on the deck. In fine weather, there were benefits to being in the open air, where the sheep could breathe freely and footrot and scab could be better managed. When storms struck, rain and waves left the sheep sodden, caused damage to their pens, and posed the risk of individuals being lost overboard.[52] Belowdecks, sheep encountered oxygen-depleted air and near darkness. To address these shortcomings, White engineered a third space by erecting a pen immediately below the main hatchway that received better light and airflow. This space was not available in the worst weather, when sails were stowed there and the hatches tightly shut. White regularly recorded the micro-mobilities associated with shuffling the sheep between decks, to bring weaker sheep under cover and to separate those most affected by scab from the rest.[53] Carrying a sheep down a companionway as the ship pitched beneath them would have been a challenging task. Ultimately, only the strongest sheep remained on deck, to face events like the storm with which this chapter opened.[54]

Above or belowdecks, storms were a serious hazard of mobility for the sheep. Rough seas knocked animals off their feet, into the sides of their pens and into one another. White noted that the sheep who were already weak were most hurt by the pitching and rolling of the ship, from which it took them days to recover.[55] In the worst cases, the pens were damaged, as in early May when White reported that one on deck had collapsed, harming the most vulnerable sheep and leading him to move them below.[56] While, in contrast with Clark, there is generally little evidence in White's journal that their shared journey and intertwined fortunes endeared the sheep to him, there were some hints of empathy during these storms, when he was also being made uncomfortable and perhaps fearful for his own life. In a very rare recording of any type of emotion, he wrote on the third day of one episode of rough seas in June, "I am afraid [the weather] will seriously injure those sheep on deck."[57] We are left to conjecture about whether he was afraid for the sheep or for what their injuries or deaths would mean for him.

Being carried through a hatchway by a shepherd or knocked over by the pitching of the ship, sheep were subjected to involuntary and sometimes harmful micro-mobilities that were far from their familiar practices of walking and grazing. Their voyage was a confused mixture of having their mobility constrained by the encircling pens and having human and natural interventions forced upon them.

The End of the Voyage

As the ship approached Australia, White's commitment to the journal waned. Many of the final week's entries indicate only "sheep as usual." The burden on the sheep of dry food, limited drinking water, disease, and the movement within the ship had been steady and substantial, and deaths had mounted. White recorded the date of each death, showing an irregular but relentless toll of no more than two on any single day, and never more than three weeks without a death. The first sheep died on March 16 and the last on July 14. With the weakest of the sheep gone, White was able to record over the final eight days of the voyage that although the sheep started off very sick in rough seas, from day to day, they became "rather better" and "continued better," and then were "quite well" and "all well," until he could report that he had safely landed fifty-seven of the initial seventy-nine sheep on Gadigal land in Sydney.[58] The death rate of 28 percent was higher than on other AACo voyages, and much more than the 1 percent mortality rate that would now trigger a government enquiry on an Australian live export vessel, but it was not the worst outcome for the period.[59] In 1825, forty-eight Merino ewes and five rams, all affected by scab and otherwise in a distressing "thin, bare, sickly looking state" arrived from England on the *William Shand* as the survivors of a larger flock.[60] The *Medora* left London with 112 Merinos in May 1826 and arrived in Sydney in September with none.[61] The loss of so many sheep points to the challenges they faced at sea, not least of which was the willingness of settler-colonists to risk animal lives in pursuit of profit.

For the sheep on the *Fairfield*, arrival in Sydney did not mean that their journeying was at an end. They were walked some 40 miles

(70 km) west to the Company's rented property in Dharawal country near Camden, to recover from the voyage. Once fit, they were again taken to the road, progressing overland 155 miles (250 km) north to the company's huge Port Stephens grant.[62] At their destination, the scale of their mobility was curtailed, but they continued on the move, grazing in flocks of three hundred during the day, under the watch of one of the immigrant shepherds or a convict assigned to the task, and being herded into temporary hurdles at night.[63] Once a year, around October, they were sheared of the year's growth of wool. Through importation, local purchases, and natural reproduction, the Company had amassed 32,000 sheep by 1832.[64]

James White served as the AACo's assistant superintendent of sheep until March 1829, when a member of the Company's local committee, Dr. James Bowman, offered him the position of sheep manager on his Ravensworth Estate, in Wonnarua country in the Hunter Valley. White remained in this role for ten years while developing his own 1,280-acre (518-hectare) land grant on the nearby Isis and Page Rivers.[65] With the advantages of cheap stolen land, the wool grown by the sheep who grazed on it, and the free labor of assigned convict-shepherds, the White family became a wealthy and influential wool dynasty. When James White died in 1842, aged just forty-one, he left an estate worth £15,000 and four pastoral properties to his nine children, several of whom continued their father's work.[66] The first James lived on in family and community lore, forever identified with his contribution to ovine mobilities.[67] The White family historian claimed that James White's tenacity, discipline, and "deep sense of responsibility with a genuine care for the stock in his charge" enabled him to land the sheep safely in Sydney, omitting any mention of the loss of over one-quarter of the animals.[68]

When the *Fairfield* left Sydney for the return voyage to London in mid-October 1826, it was laden with goods for Britain.[69] There was a mix of products derived from trees (slabs, planks, treenails, and bark) and components of animal bodies: casks of seal skins and sperm whale oil, and salted bullock hides. There were no live animals recorded on this voyage, although there were four consignments of curiosities that likely included preserved specimens of native animals. The bulk of the cargo was over one hundred wool bales, reflecting the purpose for which the ewes had been sent.

Conclusion

The title of this chapter draws attention to the happenstance that the sheep at the center of this story left Great Britain through a port named after the supposed resemblance of nearby hills to another domesticated animal, the cow. I will close with another instance of not taking language for granted. The ship on which this voyage was made was the *Fairfield*. Had the sheep been cognizant of human language they might have been comforted that their voyage was to take place on a fair field. A field was a familiar and hospitable environment for them and one that provided the opportunity for self-directed movement. But the ship proved to be a very poor facsimile of a field. On board, the sheep's lives were much more closely determined by humans than they had been on land. Fresh food was replaced with fodder that was dried and processed, and their water was rationed. They were subject to diseases that were exacerbated by shipboard conditions, and to the attempted cures White was able to administer. They were simultaneously forced into various scales of mobility—journeying ever further from their birthplaces, being knocked about by the movement of the ship and the sea, and being shifted between the open deck and the hold—and restricted to near immobility by enclosing pens. This voyage and the thousands of others that carried large numbers of animals to destinations around the world are of significance to the imperial project and should not be omitted from reckonings of the balance sheet of colonization.

This history of the passage of a flock of Merino sheep from Britain to Australia has been based on an animal-sensitive reading of the single remaining account of the voyage. It has shown that the sheep's experience of mobility subjected them to challenges associated with diet, disease, and the violent movement of the ship during storms, and that the humans charged with their care responded as best they could to try to keep the sheep alive in a hostile setting. I have been unable to venture beyond these topics to a more intimate account of the voyage from the perspective of the sheep, because White had little interest in the sheep as sentient beings and left no record of their autonomous movement. His attitude, which still permeates the thinking of those who support live animal export, is summed up in the final entry in his journal. In it, he recorded his delivery to the AACo's stores of the seventy-seven fleeces of wool that he had sheared during the voyage.[70] There was one fleece for each of the fifty-seven sheep who survived the voyage and twenty more from sheep who died en route, with two unaccounted for. Wool, the commodity for which these ewes had been imported, was what mattered. The fleeces of the missing were empty shells that once surrounded the living, breathing sheep. In contrast with the usually total absence of animals who died at sea, in this instance, these specters completed the journey, making their contribution to the imperial economy even after the sheep's lives ended. They serve as a reminder of the sometimes fatal effect of imperial mobilities, and of the lives sacrificed and swallowed up by history, when sheep were shipped from Cowes.

Notes

1. Historians have paid attention to the human experience of the voyage. See Haines, *Life and Death*; Hassam, *Sailing to Australia*; Hassam, ed., *No Privacy for Writing*; Pietsch, "Bodies at Sea," 209–28.
2. Hale, "What Does It Mean?"
3. Nance, in Way et al., "Roundtable," 448. The currency of this issue was emphasized at the time of writing, in September 2020, when the *Gulf Livestock 1* carrying 5,800 cows from New Zealand to China sank off the coast of Japan, with only two human lives saved. See Mari Yamaguchi, "Coast Guard Resumes Search," *Sydney Morning Herald*, September 8, 2020, accessed April 12, 2021, https://www.smh.com.au/world/asia/coast-guard-resumes-search-for-missing-cattle-ship-crew-off-japan-20200908-p55tjc.html.
4. Ballantyne, "Mobility, Empire, Colonisation," 7–8.
5. Cresswell, "Mobilities III," 713.
6. Swart, in Way et al., "Roundtable," 454–55.
7. Woolford and Dunn, "Micro Mobilities," 115.
8. Perren, "North American Beef"; Perren, *Meat Trade in Britain*.
9. Cushing, "Animal Mobilities"; Cushing, "'Few Commodities'"; Howkins and Merricks, "'Dewy-Eyed Veal Calves.'"
10. Melville, *Plague of Sheep*; Woods, *Herds Shot*; Woods, "From Colonial Animal."
11. Australian Government, "Department's Investigation."
12. Massey, *Australian Merino*.
13. Cushing, "'Few Commodities,'" 457–58; Specht, in Way et al., "Roundtable," 446.
14. Drawing on Alain Corbin, Erica Fudge wrote about animals being swallowed up by history. See Fudge, "Milking," 15, n.10.
15. Woods, *Herds Shot*, 56.
16. "Practicus," in *Agricultural Magazine* (June 1802), quoted by Woods, *Herds Shot*, 53.
17. Woods, *Herds Shot*, 66.
18. Of these first twenty-nine Merinos shipped from the Cape, only ten or fewer survived the voyage. See Library Committee, *Historical Records*, ser. 1, vol. 2, no. 4 (1914): 707–8.
19. "Sydney," *Sydney Gazette and New South Wales Advertiser*, November 28, 1812, 2; Massey, *Australian Merino*, 220.
20. "The Third Anniversary Address to the Agricultural Society of New South Wales by the President of That Body," *Australian*, February 23, 1826, 2.

21. Pemberton, *Pure Merinos*, 1.
22. Ibid., 46–51; Bairstow, *Million Pounds*, 157.
23. Campbell, "First Decade," 119.
24. Woods, *Herds Shot*, 57.
25. The Australian Agricultural Company's records are held in the Noel Butlin Archives Centre, Australian National University, Canberra. Listing is at https://archivescollection.anu.edu.au/index.php/australian-agricultural-company.
26. Bairstow, *Million Pounds*, 39.
27. Cushing, "Animal Mobilities," 19; Clark, *Journal and Letters*, November 6, 1787.
28. Clark, *Journal and Letters*, January 5, 9, and 18, 1788.
29. Under the notebook's marbled cover is a printed document, apparently a bill of sale for stationery, bearing the year 1825, suggesting that if this is a fair copy, it was made shortly after the voyage.
30. Phillips and Santurtun, "Welfare of Livestock," 312.
31. White, "Journal," March 12–July 25, April 12, 1826.
32. Ibid., April 1 and April 19, 1826.
33. Ibid., May 22, 1826.
34. Ibid., June 13, 1826.
35. Ibid., June 28, 1826.
36. Ibid., July 6, 1826.
37. Ibid., March 17, 1826.
38. Australian Government, *Australian Standards*, 41.
39. White, "Journal," March 24, 1826.
40. Ibid., March 13, 1826.
41. NSW Department of Primary Industries, "Footrot."
42. For scab, see "Hobart-Town," *Hobart Town Gazette and Van Diemen's Land Advertiser*, January 4, 1823, 2.
43. White, "Journal," April 4, 1826.
44. R. B. "To the Editor," *Hobart Town Gazette and Van Diemen's Land Advertiser*, June 10, 1825, 3; "The Third Anniversary Address," *Australian*, February 23, 1826, 2; "Improved method for the management and increase of . . . Sheep," *Hobart Town Gazette and Southern Reporter*, May 23, 1818, 2.
45. White, "Journal," March 16 and March 28, 1826.
46. Royal Society for the Prevention of Cruelty to Animals (Australia) Knowledge Base, "What Are the Standards of Animal Welfare Onboard Live Export Ships?," accessed April 12, 2021, https://kb.rspca.org.au/knowledge-base/what-are-the-standards-of-animal-welfare-onboard-live-export-ships/#high-mortality-rates-and-heat-stress.
47. Carnovale and Phillips, "Effects of Heat Stress," 4.
48. White, "Journal," April 8–10, 1826.
49. "Shipping Intelligence," *Hobart Town Gazette*, July 1, 1826, 2.
50. Pemberton, *Pure Merinos*, 47.
51. White, "Journal," March 13, 1826.
52. Ibid., April 13, 1826.
53. Ibid., March 30 and May 3, 1826.
54. Ibid., June 2, 1826.
55. Ibid., March 24 and May 7, 1826.
56. Ibid., May 7–9, 1826.
57. Ibid., June 4, 1826.
58. Ibid., July 18–25, 1826.
59. Australian Agricultural Company, "Report read at the Third Annual General Court of Proprietors, King's Arm Yard, London, 26 Jan 1827," *Report for 1827*, 5. Of the 726 sheep carried on the AACo's chartered ships *Brothers* and *York* in 1825, 18, or 2.5%, died.
60. "The Third Anniversary Address," *Australian*, February 23, 1826, 2.
61. "Colonial Times," *Colonial Times and Tasmanian Advertiser*, October 27, 1826, 3.
62. Pemberton, *Pure Merinos*, 4.
63. Bairstow, *Million Pounds*, 65.
64. Pemberton, *Pure Merinos*, 8.
65. Campbell, "First Decade," 137; White, *White Family*, 27, 30.

66. Rutledge, "White, James."
67. Newspaper clipping recording the death of Francis John White, dated August 29, 1934, included with the "Journal of Occurrences." An article reproducing parts of the diary and mistakenly claiming that these sheep were the first brought out by the Australian Agricultural Company was published in two Hunter Valley papers in October 1934 ("The First Sheep, Story of a long voyage, Mr. James White's Diary," *Newcastle Morning Herald and Miner's Advocate*, October 5, 1934, 2; *Gloucester Advocate*, October 12, 1934, 4).
68. White, *White Family*, 29.
69. "Manifest of the Export Cargo of the Brig *Fairfield*, of Aberdeen, James Work, Commander, bound from Sydney, New South Wales, to London," *Sydney Gazette and NSW Advertiser*, 14 October 1826, 3.
70. White, "Journal," August 1, 1826.

Bibliography

Australian Agricultural Company. *Report for 1827*. London: CS Ruthven, 1827.

Australian Government Department of Agriculture, Water and the Environment. "Australian Standards for the Export of Livestock (Version 3.1)." Accessed April 12, 2021. Canberra: Commonwealth of Australia, 2020. https://www.agriculture.gov.au/sites/default/files/documents/asel-v3.1-a4.pdf.

———. "Media Statement: Department's Investigation into the *Awassi Express*." April 22, 2020. Accessed April 12, 2021. https://www.awe.gov.au/news/media-releases/media-statement-departments-investigation-awassi-express.

Bairstow, Damaris. *A Million Pounds, A Million Acres: The Pioneer Settlement of the Australian Agricultural Company*. Sydney: Self-published, 2003.

Ballantyne, Tony. "Mobility, Empire, Colonisation." *History Australia* 11, no. 2 (2014): 7–37.

Campbell, J. F. "The First Decade of the Australian Agricultural Company, 1824–1834." *Royal Australian Historical Society Journal and Proceedings* 9, no. 3 (1923): 113–60.

Carnovale, Francesca, and Clive J. C. Phillips. "The Effects of Heat Stress on Sheep Welfare During Live Export Voyages from Australia to the Middle East." *Animals* 10, no. 694 (2020): 1–22.

Clark, Ralph. *The Journal and Letters of Lt. Ralph Clark 1787–1792*. Sydney: Australian Documents Library in Association with the Library of Australian History, 1981.

Cresswell, Tim. "Mobilities III: Moving On." *Progress in Human Geography* 38, no. 5 (2014): 712–21.

Cushing, Nancy. "Animal Mobilities and the Founding of New South Wales." In *Visions of Australia: Environments in History*, vol. 2 of *RCC Perspectives: Transformations in Environment and Society*, edited by Christof Mauch, Ruth Morgan, and Emily O'Gorman, 19–26. Munich: Rachel Carson Center, 2017.

———. "'Few Commodities Are More Hazardous': Australian Live Animal Export, 1788–1880." *Environment and History* 24, no. 4 (2018): 445–68.

Fudge, Erica. "Milking Other Men's Beasts." *History and Theory* 52, no. 4 (2013): 13–28.

Haines, Robin. *Life and Death in the Age of Sail: The Passage to Australia*. Sydney: University of New South Wales Press, 2003.

Hale, Sadie E. "What Does It Mean to Live a 'Not Quite Fatal' Existence?" *Seeing the Woods* (blog). The Rachel Carson Center, September 10, 2020. Accessed

April 12, 2021. https://seeingthewoods.org/2020/09/10/what-does-it-mean-to-live-a-not-quite-fatal-existence.

Hassam, Andrew. *Sailing to Australia: Shipboard Diaries by Nineteenth-Century British Emigrants*. Manchester: Manchester University Press, 1994.

———, ed. *No Privacy for Writing: Shipboard Diaries 1852–1879*. Melbourne: Melbourne University Press, 1995.

Howkins, Alun, and Linda Merricks. "'Dewy-Eyed Veal Calves': Live Animal Exports and Middle-Class Opinion, 1980–1995." *Agricultural History Review* 48, no. 1 (2000): 85–103.

Library Committee of the Commonwealth Parliament. *Historical Records of Australia*. Melbourne, 1914.

Massey, Charles. *The Australian Merino: The Story of a Nation*. Sydney: Random House Australia, 2007.

Melville, Elinor G. K. *A Plague of Sheep: Environmental Consequences of the Conquest of Mexico*. Cambridge: Cambridge University Press, 1994.

New South Wales Department of Primary Industries, Animal Biosecurity and Welfare. *Footrot in Sheep and Goats*. 4th ed. Sydney, July 2017.

Pemberton, Pennie. *Pure Merinos and Others: The "Shipping Lists" of the Australian Agricultural Company*. Canberra: ANU Archives of Business and Labour, 1986.

Perren, Richard. *The Meat Trade in Britain, 1840–1914*. London: Routledge, 1978.

———. "The North American Beef and Cattle Trade with Great Britain, 1870–1914." *Economic History Review* 24, no. 3 (1971): 430–44.

Phillips, Clive J. C., and Eduardo Santurtun. "The Welfare of Livestock Transported by Ship." *Veterinary Journal* 196, no. 3 (June 2013): 309–14.

Pietsch, Tamson. "Bodies at Sea: Travelling to Australia in the Age of Sail." *Journal of Global History* 11, no. 2 (2016): 209–28.

Rutledge, Martha. "White, James (1828–1890)." *Australian Dictionary of Biography*. Carlton: Melbourne University Press, 1976. Accessed September 14, 2020. http://adb.anu.edu.au/biography/white-james-4837/text8073.

Way, Albert G., William Thomas Okie, Reinaldo Funes-Monzote, Susan Nance, Gabriel N. Rosenberg, Joshua Specht, and Sandra Swart. "Roundtable: Animal History in a Time of Crisis." *Agricultural History* 94, no. 3 (2020): 444–84.

White, James. "Journal of Occurrences on board the ship *Fairfield* from Cowes to N.S.W. 12 March to 25 July 1826." MLMSS1008. State Library of New South Wales, Sydney.

White, Judy. *The White Family of Belltrees*. Sydney: The Seven Press, 1981.

Woods, Rebecca J. H. "From Colonial Animal to Imperial Edible: Building an Empire of Sheep in New Zealand, ca. 1880–1900." *Comparative Studies of South Asia, Africa and the Middle East* 35, no. 1 (2015): 117–36.

———. *The Herds Shot Round the World: Native Breeds and the British Empire, 1800–1900*. Chapel Hill: University of North Carolina Press, 2017.

Woolford, Kirk, and Stuart Dunn. "Micro Mobilities and Affordances of Past Places." In *Past Mobilities: Archaeological Approaches to Movement and Mobility*, edited by Jim Leary, 113–28. Farnham, UK: Ashgate, 2014.

CHAPTER 4

WEAPONS, COMMODITIES, SUBJECTS

Stories of Horses at Sea

Donna Landry

Introduction

If animal studies theory today should be asking questions *of* a species that are of interest *to* that species, what might we ask, from an equine point of view, about horses and ships, horses and maritime existence?[1] Following Vinciane Despret, this question arises: "What can make maritime voyaging acceptable to horses?"[2]

This essay will investigate the evidence in accounts of horses being shipped for war in the Napoleonic and Crimean campaigns, and Arabian breeding stock being acquired from the Middle East. Horse-human relationships aboard are explored in relation to the way that an equine *Umwelt*, or "environment-world," is fundamentally at variance with being at sea.[3] As shipboard passengers, horses make for especially awkward customers. *Equus caballus* requires special provisions of space, fodder, water, and air, all of which encumber a ship rather than fitting in neatly with a maritime ecosystem. Aboard ships, even the "nature-cultures" of equine domestication are disrupted.[4] Nineteenth-century archives begin to accumulate stories of mishaps, tragic occurrences, sometimes heroic devotion or action displayed by humans, sometimes outrageous behavior or exceptional intelligence and cooperation exhibited by horses. The dedication of horsemen and -women, grooms, soldiers, and sailors resounds in these stories, as do the effects of class and military hierarchies. What is especially interesting, given the hardships of shipboard existence, is identifying what makes possible a less than melancholy outcome.

Before the nineteenth century, maritime history and the horse trade converged principally in the frequent comparisons between the relative value of horses and human slaves as reflected in their prices, treatment, and shipboard accommodation.[5] Horses came into their own as subjects of stories beginning in the nineteenth century.[6] Consequently, although horses were still figuring in shipboard accounts largely as valuable commodities and weapons of war, they were also now increasingly being represented as sentient beings with whom complex affective relationships could be established.[7] These accounts thus make a striking contrast with James White's journal on the transport of sheep, discussed by Nancy Cushing in chapter 3: however valuable sheep might have been to his enterprise, White regarded them as "a barely differentiated mass, lacking intelligence and agency," and revealed little empathy for them in their struggles on board.

The twentieth-century Estonian-German biologist and ethologist Jakob von Uexküll theorized living beings as inhabiting species-specific environments, or "environment-worlds," in Derek Ryan's formulation.[8] "All animal subjects, from the simplest to the most complex, are inserted into their environments to the same degree of perfection," according to Uexküll. "The simple animal has a simple environment; the multiform animal has an environment just as richly articulated as it is."[9] Each species inhabits its world in its own way:

> We must therefore imagine all the animals that animate Nature around us, be they beetles, butterflies, gnats, or dragonflies who populate a meadow, as having a soap bubble around them, closed on all sides, which closes off their visual space and in which everything visible for the subject is also enclosed.[10]

This bubble should be understood as constituted by sign-production—that is, meaning-making for and by the individual representatives of a species: "Everything a subject perceives belongs to its *perception world* [*Merkwelt*], and everything it produces, to its *effect world* [*Wirkwelt*].

These two worlds, of perception and production of effects, form one closed unit, the *environment*."[11] Ryan remarks how innovative it was for Uexküll to emphasize "all animals' creative and *meaningful* relations to their environment."[12] The consequence of all animals being engaged in signifying is that "there is no space independent of subjects."[13]

What environment-world do horses signify into being? How is their species' "bubble" affected by domestication? Horses' subjectivity, or "horse psychology" in trainers' parlance, can only be understood by recognizing, in the first instance, that horses are prey animals. Constantly vigilant against possible predators, horses avoid aggression or conflict and seek a peaceful coexistence. Establishing that humans might serve as protectors, rather than predators, delivering horses from threats and discomfort, has been a principle of horsemanship from antiquity onwards. Xenophon advised, circa 365 BCE, that horsekeepers contrive "that hunger and thirst and horseflies are associated by the colt with solitude, while eating and drinking and delivery from irritation come through man's agency. For in these circumstances a foal is bound not only to like men, but to hanker after them."[14] Thus the notion of a horse-human assemblage, grounded in companionship, care, and reciprocity, has served as the basis for *Equus caballus* and *Homo sapiens* to collaborate in war and peace.

Modern horsemanship practitioners suggest that the "four things that are important to horses" are: "1. safety, 2. comfort, 3. play, and 4. food."[15] Like Uexküll, in his close observations of species in the field, the ethologist Lucy Rees, who studies both feral and domestic horses, concludes that, above all, horses require an understanding of the "flight algorithm." This is her term for the factors that constitute horses' "social system, that of self-organizing bands": cohesion, synchrony of movement, and collision avoidance, or respect for individual space.[16] Living freely as feral horses in bands, competition for food or water, often a source of aggression amongst domestic horses, does not even register on horses' agendas because these "maintenance resources" are taken for granted.[17] Rees debunks the all-too-familiar "dominance hierarchy paradigm," which she reads as a projection of human preoccupation with dominance in all its forms.[18] Hers is a controversial stance in light of the competition for food so often observed in situations of domestication, especially if provisioning is far from ideal, or the mutual aggression likely to be manifested by domestic stallions in the presence of mares. Yet her understanding of equine sociality as more akin to anarchism rather than hierarchy, derived from her observations of feral horse herd behavior, illuminates strikingly the evidence of cohesion, synchrony, and shared enjoyment of free movement to be glimpsed in maritime narratives.[19]

Thus, there can be few environments more antithetical to what horses would choose than being confined on board ships. They cannot move about freely, feeding as they please, or lie down to sleep when they feel like it. Cohesion and synchrony are next to impossible. Group play is out of the question. However spacious the accommodations they are given, horses must be confined for their own safety, and if the sea is rough, confined in yet more restricted spaces, with partitions or slings to support them. Seasickness may affect them with painful digestive complaints, and the available rations, in the absence of grazing, may cause blockages, often with fatal consequences. Without constant vigilance on the part of dedicated horsekeepers, and certainly if weather conditions are bad, horses are as likely to die as to survive a journey by sea.

Fellow Comrades: Horses Transported for War

War horses are a walking contradiction: companion species in co-becoming: comrades in arms with humans, but also pieces of technology, both fellow sentient sufferers and implements of destruction. The Napoleonic Wars were the first to be so extensively written about, generating an "outpouring" of soldiers' letters, diaries, and memoirs that was unprecedented.[20] And for the first time, this writing was being produced by soldiers of all ranks.[21] Not many soldiers recorded incidents involving horses and ships. What emerges from the stories we *do* have are the unnaturalness of the horse-ship conjuncture, and its potential costliness in human as well as animal terms.

> April 1st, 1809. One squadron of the 16th Light Dragoons arrived at Falmouth and embarked yesterday, and the one to which I belonged this day marched in from Truro and immediately embarked. My bay horse (Bob), as he was in the slings, twice kicked himself out, and was near being lost. He stood on

> the deck of the vessel for some time, whilst they were putting a fresh pair of slings on him, and nearly killed the second mate of the vessel by knocking him overboard. The man fell the whole height of the vessel, there being no water near the quay at which we embarked, from the tide being out. He was left behind sick at Falmouth.[22]

So wrote the cavalry officer William Tomkinson, whose son, in posthumously editing his father's diary, speaks of his father's writing as offering, "by its directness and simplicity, a conviction of accuracy and absence of exaggeration," a judgment with which military historians, who continue to quote liberally from the *Diary*, concur.[23] Tomkinson and Bob endured "five campaigns" together, and in 1813, after "an absence of four years and a half," Bob "returned safe and sound to his old home, the servant reporting that he knew his way back to his stable at Dorfold perfectly. He lived for many years to carry his master with the pack of harriers kept by him."[24] Bob was a privileged horse, whose owner could afford to ship him home, even having a stall specially made.[25] His value was such that, despite his bad behavior in violently kicking himself out of the slings used to hoist horses aboard and support them on deck or below, the luckless second mate persists in trying to "put a fresh pair of slings on him"—and is thrown overboard for his pains and nearly killed.

There is a class hierarchy in which officers' chargers are worth saving, no matter how difficult they prove; such horses are worth accommodating even at the cost of a sailor's broken body. Tomkinson's taciturn prose records the facts, not judging his horse, and not mourning the sailor. Yet between the lines we can glimpse how this miserable scene reveals the difficulties posed by horse-ship assemblages. Bob resisted becoming a shipboard passenger as fervently as possible, venting his displeasure on a human he did not know—a sailor, who may not have had much experience with horses. A similar incident is recorded by Captain Alexander Cavalié Mercer of the Royal Horse Artillery. Setting sail in April 1815 for the Belgian coast from Harwich before the battle of Waterloo, a sailor is "somewhat hurt in endeavouring to recover a horse that had fallen overboard."[26] Mercer was thankful that this "accident" was not more "serious."[27] More than one kind of boat was often involved in getting horses aboard, doubling the chances of mishap.

Mercer tells us that the gunners' horses were first loaded "in flats to be taken off to the transports, not easily found in the fog."[28] A fogbound passage in shallow boats sounds distinctly hazardous, yet "by noon all were on board"—without any "serious accident," apart from the "somewhat hurt" sailor.[29] This seaman was much luckier than Tomkinson's second mate had been, and no harm had come to the horse. Tomkinson's report of embarking for the Waterloo campaign from Ramsgate in April 1815 describes the crossing as in "small colliers, holding from ten to thirty-five horses each. The horses were put loose in the hold, and it being fine weather we did not lose any from there being no bails [partitions]."[30] The importance of fine weather for horses and their keepers at sea cannot be overestimated.

Disembarking horses could be just as perilous, especially if urgency was required. Mercer observes a regiment of Light Dragoons "throwing their horses overboard" at Ostend, and then hauling them ashore by a long rope attached to their head-collars: "What a scene! What halloing, shouting, vociferating, and plunging! The poor horses did not appear much gratified by their sudden transition from the warm hold to a cold bath."[31] But worse is in store for Mercer and his artillery horses, because the Duke of Wellington has given orders that all troops and horses are to be got ashore as fast as possible. Mercer is incensed at this haste without a plan. When Captain Hill comes aboard to assist with "a gang of sailors,"

> [they] instantly commenced hoisting our horses out, and throwing them, as well as our saddlery, etc., overboard, without ever giving time for making any disposition to receive or secure the one or the other. . . . Bundles of harness went over the side in rapid succession, as well as horses. In vain we urged the loss and damage that must accrue from such a proceeding. "Can't help it—no business of mine—Duke's orders are positive," etc. etc. was our only answer. . . . The Dragoons and our men (some nearly, others quite, naked) were dashing in and out of the water, struggling with the affrighted horses, or securing their wet accoutrements as best they could. Some of the former were saddling their dripping horses. . . . Our poor shivering horses and heaps of wet harness could not remain on the sands much longer. . . . I got one of my horses saddled and rode into the town.[32]

Searching for the officer in charge to learn of his marching orders, Mercer finds chaos. The only orders are "that the troops of every arm should march for Ghent," without "halting a single day in Ostend."[33] A thunderstorm breaks, and Mercer, although missing "some two or three" horses "which had escaped altogether," sets out by lantern-light to find shelter for the night.[34] The missing horses are recovered the next day "at a barrier" on the road.[35] But the immersion in the sea and being drenched by the storm have caused all the horses considerable distress. Mercer is always attentive to horses' signifying; their appearance speaks louder than words:

> Our noble horses, yesterday morning so sleek and spirited, now stood with drooping heads and rough staring coats, plainly indicating the mischief they had sustained in being taken from a hot hold, plunged into cold water, and then exposed for more than seven hours on an open beach to such a tempest of wind and rain as we experienced last night. Here was a practical illustration of the folly of grooming and pampering military horses, destined as they are to such exposures and privations.[36]

Mercer sympathizes with the horses, fears for the coughs and colds that may well be forthcoming, and is upset on their behalf. As a professional soldier, however, he endeavors to be philosophical about the rigors of military service. He goes so far as to question the advisability of pampering horses and grooming them to perfection in order to turn out a "smart" troop when they may well be subjected to such harsh occurrences in the line of duty.

Sailing longer distances during the Crimean War (1853–56) posed greater challenges than Channel crossings or Iberian voyages had done during the Napoleonic Wars. Weather was everything, and the longer at sea, the greater the chance of adverse conditions. Frances Isabella Duberly's 1855 *Journal kept during The Russian War* presents the most vivid of all accounts of the unnatural equine environment-world to be found at sea. It is an elegy. The dying began within just three days out of port from Plymouth when a storm blew up. Masts were broken, a sailor had his leg "crushed to the bone," and two horses were killed.[37] Accompanying her husband Henry, paymaster to the 8th Royal Irish Hussars, Mrs. Duberly, as horsey as her husband, was seasick but could not help admiring how the ship "bounded over the huge waves like a wild hunter springing at his fences."[38] Three days later she reported the death of another horse "from inanition, having eaten nothing since he came on board."[39] Having passed Gibraltar and entered the Mediterranean after a week at sea, conditions were deteriorating badly, causing a fourth horse to revolt and die, and causing Mrs. Duberly anguish because she understands what the horses must be feeling:

> They tell me he went absolutely mad, and raved himself to death. The hold where our horses are stowed, although considered large and airy, appears to me horrible beyond words. The slings begin to gall the horses under the shoulder and breastbone; and the heat and bad atmosphere must be felt to be understood. Every effort to alleviate their sufferings is made; their nostrils are sponged with vinegar, which is also scattered in the hold. Our three horses bear it bravely, but they are immediately under a hatchway where they get air.[40]

The Duberlys' horses are the fortunate ones, with concerned owners and grooms on board to attend to them. Yet even this care is not enough to prevent mishap. The very next day is "a day of much sorrow and suffering to me,"

> as I was awoke by our servant (Connell) coming to our door at seven o'clock, and saying that the Grey Horse—"Missus's Horse"—my own dear horse, was very ill. Henry ran to him directly, and after examining him, fancied his attack was different from that of the others, and that he might live.
>
> How deeply one becomes attached to a favourite horse! Never was a more perfect creature, with faultless action, faultless mouth and faultless temper.[41]

It is "colic" almost certainly, a gastric upset that all too often leads to an intestinal blockage, since horses cannot regurgitate. This attack will not have been mitigated by the sea getting up during the following night—"a fresh wind and rolling sea" making even the well horses uncomfortable.[42] Two days later, the Grey Horse's suffering is over; he is buried at sea with due ceremony in the harbor at Malta:

> [W]hen the calm evening was dressed in all the gorgeous colours of a southern sunset, and whilst the military calls were sounding those stirring notes he loved to hear, my good horse was lowered to his rest among the nautili and wondrous sea-flowers which floated round the ship.[43]

Mrs. Duberly's grief is partly assuaged when she imagines her adored horse appreciating the "stirring notes" of a military send-off.

To add insult to injury, their ship is then becalmed close to an allied ship, "a small French brig" of "150 tons" containing "a detachment of the Chasseurs d'Afrique," which had lost none of its twenty-eight horses "although they provided no stalls for them, but huddled them into the hold as closely as they could stow them away."[44] We learn no more about why the French have been so much more successful in their shipping arrangements than the 8th Hussars. Were the North African horses themselves tougher, or more used to being crowded in confined conditions than were the English and Irish horses? They must have stood quietly packed together in the hold, without kicking or fighting. Perhaps they enjoyed a calmer sea voyage as well as a shorter one. Perhaps their attendants stayed with them in the hold. Reading between the lines one can detect indignant, if unvoiced, questions: "What justice is there—why is it so easy for the French?" The Duberlys' troubles are not yet over, for three days later hurricane conditions of rain and wind beset the ship, which heels over until her deck is under water. In the hold "every horse was down, one being pitched half over the manger."[45] Yet no injuries worth mentioning occurred.

Military shipping prized efficiency. There was no point in wasting troopers, sailors, or horses through preventable accidents. However unnatural the condition of horses at sea, or during embarking and disembarking, therefore, attention was paid to ameliorating these hazards. Captain Tomkinson observed that upon arrival at Lisbon, some of the vessels amongst his convoy "landed their horses by means of large boats on the river [Tagus], and others ran in close to shore, which was the best plan, as the horses then had water to stand in on coming down, and ran no chance of being injured."[46] His pride is palpable when he reports: "There was not, I think, a single accident."[47] Of the 640 horses of his regiment, the 16th Light Dragoons, he concludes, "the only horse I heard of as lost was one shot and thrown overboard in the harbour at Falmouth, being suspected of farcy."[48] If even suspected of carrying a highly contagious disease, or otherwise found unfit for purpose, warhorses met a quick (thought to be painless) death from a bullet. Pieces of technology, weapons of shock and awe, and sometimes mass destruction, yet also fellow creatures, and companions and comrades in arms, military horses occupied an ambiguous position on the spectrum between the natural and the technological that conditioned human perceptions of their subjectivity.

Equid Subjectivity: Horses as Exotic Cargoes

The question of horses' subjectivity would become newly foregrounded when Eastern bloodstock, primarily desert-bred Arabians, were imported to Europe and North America during the later nineteenth and early twentieth centuries. These turn-of-the-century importations from the Middle East were not the first. More than 250 stallions and mares had arrived in the British Isles between 1650 and 1750 from the territories of the Ottoman Empire.[49] There was, however, a renewed interest in the purebred Arabian for military as well as sporting purposes from the period of the Napoleonic Wars onwards.[50] The most famous English arrivals of the nineteenth century were the horses imported by Lady Anne and Wilfrid Scawen Blunt for their Crabbet Stud. By breeding purebred Arabian horses on English soil and re-exporting them, the Blunts initiated a global trade in the breed that continues to this day.[51] Horses were shipped from Aleppo via the port of Iskenderun, and from Cairo via Alexandria, though a few came via India. The published accounts of the stud reveal nothing of the conditions on these vessels. So when the American horseman and cartoonist Homer Davenport, inspired by the Blunts' endeavors, sought to acquire similar horses direct from the desert, he included details in his account of Arabian horses at sea that, so far as he knew, had never appeared in print before.

Davenport set out to be amusing to readers, portraying himself as a novice shipper, and relating how the Blunts and others never seemed to reveal the nitty-gritty of what such transport involved. In his chapter on "What One May Overlook in the Shipment of Horses," Davenport remarked:

> When you're at home sitting on the shady side of your porch and planning the exportation of Arab horses, there are some

> details which you overlook while seated in a comfortable rocking chair. Generally, when you are reading of the exportations which have been made into England, you read something like this:
>
> "We brought from Damascus, or Aleppo, a bay mare." Then follows a description of how this particular mare enjoyed the grass in the paddocks in England. So I had been careless and even ignorant of some of the things I afterward learned must have happened between the time that horse was purchased in the desert and when you hear of it again in the English paddocks.[52]

Those English paddocks were those of the Crabbet Stud in Sussex. In *Bedouin Tribes of the Euphrates* (1878), the aftermath of the Blunts' first journey to Syria was described as follows: "half-a-dozen Arabian mares grazing in the park outside," including the bay horse Hagar, who had carried Wilfrid during the journey and is portrayed as enjoying "galloping and jumping hurdles on English ground."[53] Davenport corresponded with Lady Anne before undertaking his own journey in 1906, during which he succeeded, in a little over three weeks, in acquiring and shipping from Iskenderun not the half-dozen horses for which he had previously obtained a permit from the Ottoman authorities, but twenty-seven.[54]

Unlike the military shipment of horses for war, the shipping of these rare commodities was both a commercial proposition and an amateur undertaking. Usually, some diplomatic intervention was necessary to enable the proper infrastructure for horses to be shipped to be put in place—in Davenport's case, it was the American consul at Aleppo, J. B. Jackson, who helpfully intervened.[55] "Buccaneers"[56] such as Davenport were open about the need for improvisation.

One important factor that emerges in Davenport's account is the horses' own attitude towards such ventures, and how this attitude was bound up with the horses' relationships with the Bedouin, their previous keepers. These relationships were legendary.[57] Arabians expected a certain kind of understanding. As beings who were born and brought up in very close proximity to humans, thus acquiring many "humanized" characteristics, the Arabian horses were accustomed to being treated as intelligent fellow creatures. They were, we might say, reared to be recognized as subjects with more human awareness of their capacities than were most other horses. As Lucy Rees puts it, "horses do think about responsiveness. They read each other's signals constantly, and they are very good at it."[58] Treated with kindness and leniency, living in steppe, desert, or other open-horizon conditions, side-by-side with humans who prize and depend upon her, the horse "is likely to become more sensitive, more intelligent, and more interested in life if we adopt her attitude rather than forcing her against the grain to adopt an alien one."[59] Bedouin horsekeeping, adapted to horses' *Umwelt,* like other forms of desert and steppe horsemanship, led over the centuries to horses being "more sensitive, more intelligent, and more interested in life," to their having a repertoire of signifying actions that the humans around them were accustomed to "reading" and respecting.

Davenport's improvisations were aided by Bedouin intervention. Davenport had ordered, with Consul Jackson's help, wooden box stalls to be made for the "boat," the steamer upon which the horses were to travel as far as Naples before being transferred to a bigger steamship to the United States, but had forgotten how the horses would actually be boarded.[60] Having entered a box, the first "stall" they would ever have seen, they would be hoisted into the air, lowered into a lighter, trundled to the ship, and then hoisted again from the lighter onto the deck. Davenport chose to begin with a stallion of the Maneghi strain whose "broad forehead" promised the wisdom of experience:

> The Maneghi approached the box. With five hundred curious town Arabs looking on, he stopped for a moment to gaze at it, and then at the first asking he walked in with a majestic swing that characterised all his motions. The door was closed behind him and fastened by an iron bar.[61]

The Maneghi possessed both dignity and sagacity. Then Davenport made a nearly fatal mistake, suggesting that a bandage be tied over the horse's eyes before he was lowered into the lighter: "At the first move of the box he nearly got out of it. When he made one real effort, the box that had looked so stout, bound as it was with iron, seemed as frail as a chicken coop."[62] The quick thinking of Faiot, the son of the Anazeh sheikh who has befriended Davenport, saved the situation, because "he knew the stallion better than we did" and tore off the bandage from the horse's eyes: "The horse never moved after his bandages were taken off.

He was calmer by 50 per cent. than I was during the whole operation."[63] The next to board, a playful two-year-old colt, also "walked into the box, and without a bandage over his eyes he was perfectly quiet, looking over the landscape as they swung him up into the air, and down into the small boat, without even a move."[64] Since nothing further is said, the other twenty-five horses must have followed quietly.

This episode makes clear how it is only with the willing collaboration of the horses themselves that such ventures were even possible. Davenport learned to learn from the Bedouin how to anticipate what the horses required, which was often quite different from the ways horses were handled at home, where bandaging the eyes in such situations was the norm.

Horse-human collaboration in desert society was exemplified when Wadduda, one of the mares Davenport had acquired, was secretly accompanied aboard by her groom Said Abdullah ("whose name translated means 'The Happy Servant of God'"); Said is introduced as a "slave" belonging to Faiot's father, Sheikh Akmet Haffez.[65] The sheikh declared that "as the boy had been brought up with the mare," and as "[t]he mare was going with me [Davenport]," "so was Said":

> The logic seemed perfectly clear to his mind. He dismissed the subject at once and considered the incident closed. As his guest I could do no more than follow suit and Said as a faithful servant (both of us had forgotten the word slave) has followed the fortune of Wadduda ever since.[66]

Said stowed away until out of reach of the authorities; his interventions proved crucial for the horses' safe transport.

Said's story testifies to how essential human mediation was in the assemblage of horse and ship. At Naples, in the transfer from boat to shore, when the horses were bursting with energy and excitement after a calm two weeks at sea and plenty of food on board, "Said was a wonder. He had got hobbles from the barges and at the risk of his life secured the horses, and eventually we got the animals all ashore. It took all of Said's skill to quiet them and there was much kindling wood left on the docks. The horses had kicked their boxes to pieces."[67] Learning from Said, Davenport's friend Jack Thompson became an ever more skillful horseman, taking charge of the cargo for the Atlantic crossing. Arriving in Hoboken, New Jersey, on October 8, in "perfect condition and health," the horses, having been on their feet since August 28, never able to lie down, "played and pranced, with legs free from any swelling whatever."[68] According to Said (and Thompson agreed), it was Allah, lover of horses, who assured their safe passage,[69] but humans dedicating themselves to the horses' comfort were clearly essential for the successful workings of the horse-ship assemblage.

Coda

A final brief example: The title of Apsley Cherry-Garrard's book *The Worst Journey in the World* (referring in particular to his winter journey to Antarctic Cape Crozier in search of emperor penguins' eggs), also aptly describes Scott's *Terra Nova* expedition from the point of view of the nineteen Manchurian ponies on it. All would perish in the end because hauling on ice towards the South Pole proved even more lethal than the raging seas in a leaking ship on the voyage from New Zealand. (The seven mules that were subsequently sent out by the Indian government to replace the ponies—"beautiful animals" and, unlike the ponies, "most carefully trained and equipped"—would also perish during Antarctic hauling because they were improperly fed.[70]) The ponies were housed on deck rather than in the hold because there was no room below.[71] Those in the bows of the ship were more exposed to rough weather than those amidships:

> Under the forecastle fifteen ponies close side by side, seven one side, eight the other, heads together and groom between—swaying, swaying continually to the plunging, irregular motion. One takes a look through a hole in the bulkhead and sees a row of heads with sad, patient eyes come swinging up together from the starboard side, whilst those on the port swing back; then up come the port heads, whilst the starboard recede. . . . There are four ponies outside the forecastle and to leeward of the fore hatch, and on the whole, perhaps, with shielding tarpaulins, they have a rather better time than their comrades.[72]

Two of those under the forecastle died during the gales. With the Antarctic Ocean continuing to do her worst, Scott later comforted himself with the thought that horses had often been at sea before: "One felt quite free from anxiety as to the ship, the sails. . . . One thought of the ponies, but after all, horses have been carried for all time in small ships, and often for very long voyages."[73] The seventeen that survived the voyage were unloaded by means of a horse-box, and as soon as their feet touched the ice floe, they were, Cherry-Garrard reported, seen "rolling and kicking with joy."[74] Thus we may glimpse their signifying of their preferred *Umwelt—terra firma*—even if it is ice: a space of play, freedom of movement, and synchrony. Humans put horses to sea; ships are only endurable with the attunement of human attendants; even then these human-equid communities may easily not survive the rift in *Umwelt* created by the sea.

Notes

1. See Haraway, "Cosmopolitical Critters," vii–xiv, note 6.
2. Despret, *What Would Animals Say?*
3. Uexküll, *Foray*.
4. "Situated naturecultures" is Haraway's formulation for the mutual imbrications of "nature" and "culture" within which interspecies collaborations might be recognized as such. Haraway, *When Species Meet*, 25. Haraway also argues that human practices are never entirely human, being regularly tested by horses themselves in ongoing processes (or ecologies of practice) of "co-becoming." Haraway, *When Species Meet*, 222–23; Despret, "The Body We Care For," 116, 122.
5. See Landry, "Rewriting the Sea"; Jardine and Brotton, *Global Interests*, 148, 208n51; Thomas, *Slave Trade*, 807.
6. Landry, "Horses at Waterloo."
7. For more on the importance of human care for equids during transport by sea, see Clarence-Smith, "Equids Across the Indian Ocean." Clarence-Smith has pioneered the study of the economics of trade and transport of equids and other animal laborers; see, for example, his articles "Donkey Trade"; "Mules in the 'English World'"; and "Horses, Mules and Other Animals."
8. Ryan, *Animal Theory*, 103–5.
9. Uexküll, *Foray*, 49.
10. Ibid., 54.
11. Ibid., 42. Via Thomas Sebeok, Uexküll's concept of environment-worlds has been influential for "anthroposemiotics, zoosemiotics and endosemiotics." See Brantari, *Jakob von Uexküll*, 227, citing Sebeok, *The Sign and Its Masters*, 26.
12. Ryan, *Animal Theory*, 105.
13. Uexküll, *Foray*, 70.
14. Xenophon, *Art of Horsemanship*, 307.
15. Bird, *Keeping a Horse*, 41.
16. Lucy Rees, *Horses in Company*, 66–76.
17. Ibid., 91–92, 133–36.
18. Ibid., 120–44.
19. Ibid., 76, 145–54.
20. Neil Ramsey describes as an "outpouring" the soldiers' writing that Charles Oman first identified. Ramsey, *Military Memoir*, 1. See also Oman, *Wellington's Army*, 2–3.

21. Oman, *Wellington's Army*, 4–5; and White-Spunner, *Of Living Valour*, xix.
22. Tomkinson, *Diary*, 1.
23. J. Tomkinson, "Editor's Preface," *Diary*, viii–ix, viii.
24. Tomkinson, *Diary*, 272n1.
25. Ibid., 272.
26. Mercer, *Journal*, 50.
27. Ibid.
28. Ibid.
29. Ibid.
30. Tomkinson, *Diary*, 273–74.
31. Mercer, *Journal*, 53.
32. Ibid., 54.
33. Ibid., 56.
34. Ibid.
35. Ibid., 61.
36. Ibid., 58.
37. Duberly, *Mrs. Duberly's War*, 4.
38. Ibid.
39. Ibid.
40. Ibid., 5–6.
41. Ibid., 6.
42. Ibid.
43. Ibid., 7.
44. Ibid.
45. Ibid., 8.
46. Tomkinson, *Diary*, 1–2.
47. Ibid., 2.
48. Ibid. Farcy was "a highly contagious disease of the lymphatic system" in horses, mules, and donkeys caused by "the *Pfeifferella mallei*, formerly called *Bacillus mallei*, or glanders bacillus," and transmitted through "ingestion of the organism in food or water which has become contaminated with nasal discharge." See Hayes, *Veterinary Notes*, 229–33.
49. Landry, *Noble Brutes*.
50. Derry, *Horses in Society*, 32–33, 101–20.
51. Archer, Pearson, and Covey, *The Crabbet Arabian Stud*; Derry, *Bred for Perfection*.
52. Davenport, *My Quest*, 197–98.
53. Blunt, *Bedouin Tribes*, vol. 2, 160.
54. Blunt, *Journals and Correspondence*, 457–65.
55. Davenport, *My Quest of the Arab Horse*, 198.
56. Blunt, *Journals and Correspondence*, 465.
57. For stories of individual horses' subjectivity and Bedouin veterinary medicine, see, for example, Raswan, *Drinkers of the Wind*.
58. Rees, *Horse's Mind*, 169.
59. Ibid., 169.
60. Davenport, *My Quest*, 210.
61. Ibid., 200.
62. Ibid., 201.
63. Ibid.
64. Ibid., 201–202.
65. Ibid., 202.
66. Ibid., 203.
67. Ibid., 214.
68. Ibid., 221–22.
69. Ibid., 216. In the United States, Said worked for Davenport, learned English, and overcame his homesickness for the desert so long as he had Wadduda to care for and could pray in the direction of Mecca. Ibid., 225–32.
70. Cherry-Garrard, *Worst Journey*, vol. 2, 416, 439. The mules could not eat the high-protein diet they were given (oats and oilcake), went off their feed, and became "terrible rope-eaters, cloth-eaters, anything to eat, though they are not hungry." Ibid., 472, 474. That the mules were desperate for carbohydrates—fodder such as hay—seems not to have been recognized by Cherry-Garrard or anybody else. See Harrowfield, "Mules of the British Antarctic."
71. Carrying horses on deck rather than in the hold was customary in calmer seas. See Clarence-Smith, "Equids."
72. Cherry-Garrard, *Worst Journey*, vol. 1, 96; Scott, *Last Expedition*, vol. 1, December 1, 1910.
73. Scott, *Last Expedition*, vol. 1, December 27, 1910.
74. Cherry-Garrard, *Worst Journey*, vol.1, 128.

Bibliography

Archer, Rosemary, Colin Pearson, and Cecil Covey. *The Crabbet Arabian Stud, Its History and Influence*. Northleach, UK: Alexander Heriot, 1978.

Bird, Jo. *Keeping a Horse the Natural Way: A Natural Approach to Horse Management for Optimum Health and Performance*. Foreword by Pat Parelli. Dorking, UK: Interpret Publishing, 2002.

Blunt, Lady Anne. *Bedouin Tribes of the Euphrates. Edited with a Preface and Some Account of the Arabs and Their Horses, by W. S. B.* 2 vols. London: John Murray, 1879. Reprint, London: Frank Cass, 1968.

———. *Journals and Correspondence 1878–1917*. Edited by Rosemary Archer and James Fleming. Northleach, UK: Alexander Heriot, 1986.

Brantari, Carlo. *Jakob von Uexküll: The Discovery of the Umwelt Between Biosemiotics and Theoretical Biology*. Dordrecht: Springer, 2015.

Cherry-Garrard, Apsley. *The Worst Journey in the World: The Story of Scott's Last Expedition to the South Pole*. 2 vols. 1922. London: Penguin, 1937.

Clarence-Smith, William Gervase. "The Donkey Trade of the Indian Ocean World in the Long Nineteenth Century." In *Animal Trade Histories in the Indian Ocean World*, edited by Martha Chailklin, Philip Gooding, and Gwyn Campbell, 147–79. Cham, Switzerland: Palgrave Macmillan for Springer Nature, 2020.

———. "Equids Across the Indian Ocean c. 1800–1918." In "Animals at Sea," edited by Kaori Nagai. Special issue, *Journal for Maritime Research* 22, nos. 1–2 (2020): 41–57.

———. "Horses, Mules and Other Animals as a Factor in Ottoman Military Performance, 1683–1918." Paper presented at the War Horses of the World Conference, School of Oriental and African Studies (SOAS), London, May 3–4, 2014.

———. "Mules in the 'English World': Cultural Rejection Versus Practical Utility." In *Gallery 8: Animals and Empire Exhibition*. Los Angeles: Animal History Museum, 2014.

Davenport, Homer. *My Quest of the Arab Horse*. 1909. Reprint, Chicago: Arabian Horse Club of America, n.d.

Derry, Margaret E. *Bred for Perfection: Shorthorn Cattle, Collies, and Arabian Horses Since 1800*. Baltimore: Johns Hopkins University Press, 2003.

———. *Horses in Society: A Story of Animal Breeding and Marketing Culture, 1800–1920*. Toronto: University of Toronto Press, 2015.

Despret, Vinciane. "The Body We Care For: Figures of Anthropo-zoo-genesis." *Body & Society* 10, nos. 2–3 (2004): 111–34.

———. *What Would Animals Say If We Asked the Right Questions?* Translated by Brett Buchanan. Minneapolis: University of Minnesota Press, 2016.

Duberly, Frances Isabella. *Mrs. Duberly's War: Journal and Letters from Crimea*. Edited by Christine Kelly. 1855. Oxford: Oxford University Press, 2007.

Haraway, Donna J. "Cosmopolitical Critters: Preface for *Cosmopolitan Animals*." In *Cosmopolitan Animals*, edited by Kaori Nagai, Karen Jones, Donna Landry, Monica Mattfeld, Caroline Rooney, and Charlotte Sleigh, vii–xiv. Houndmills, UK: Palgrave Macmillan, 2015.

———. *When Species Meet*. Minneapolis: University of Minnesota Press, 2008.

Harrowfield, D. L. "Mules of the British Antarctic Expedition, 1910–1913." *Polar Record* 27, no. 160 (1991): 23–28.

Hayes, M. Horace, Captain, FRCVS. *Veterinary Notes for Horse Owners: A Manual of Horse Medicine and Surgery*. 1877. Revised by J. F. Donald Tutt,

FRCVS. 1968. Reprint, London: Stanley Paul, 1974.

Jardine, Lisa and Jerry Brotton. *Global Interests: Renaissance Art Between East and West.* Ithaca: Cornell University Press, 2000.

Landry, Donna. "Horses at Waterloo, 1815." In *Equestrian Cultures: Horses, Human Society, and the Discourse of Modernity,* edited by Kristen Guest and Monica Mattfeld, 26–38. Chicago: University of Chicago Press, 2019.

———. *Noble Brutes: How Eastern Horses Transformed English Culture.* Baltimore: Johns Hopkins University Press, 2009.

———. "Rewriting the Sea from the Desert Shore: Equine and Equestrian Perspectives on a New Maritime History." In *Trade and Cultural Exchange in the Early Modern Mediterranean: Braudel's Maritime Legacy,* edited by Maria Fusaro, Colin Heywood, and Mohamed-Salah Omri, 253–77. London: I. B. Tauris, 2010.

Mercer, Alexander Cavalié. *Journal of the Waterloo Campaign.* Edited by Andrew Uffindell. 1870. Barnsley, UK: Pen & Sword Military, 2012.

Oman, C. W. C. *Wellington's Army, 1809–1814.* 2nd impression. London: Edward Arnold, 1913.

Ramsey, Neil. *The Military Memoir and Romantic Literary Culture, 1780–1835.* Farnham, UK: Ashgate, 2011.

Raswan, Carl R. *Drinkers of the Wind.* New York: Creative Age Press, 1942.

Rees, Lucy. *The Horse's Mind.* London: Ebury, 1997.

———. *Horses in Company.* Ramsbury, UK: J. A. Allen, 2017.

Ryan, Derek. *Animal Theory: A Critical Introduction.* Edinburgh: University of Edinburgh Press, 2015.

Scott, Robert Falcon. *Scott's Last Expedition.* 2 vols. London: Smith, Elder, and Co., 1913. http://www.gutenberg.org/cache/epub/11579/pg11579-images.html

Sebeok, Thomas. *The Sign and Its Masters.* Austin: University of Texas Press, 1979.

Thomas, Hugh. *The Slave Trade: The History of the Atlantic Slave Trade: 1440–1870.* London: Picador, 1997.

Tomkinson, William. *The Diary of a Cavalry Officer in the Peninsular War and Waterloo Campaign 1809–1815. By the Late Lieut.-Col. Tomkinson 16th Light Dragoons. Edited by his Son James Tomkinson.* 1894. Reprint, London: British Library, 2002.

Uexküll, Jakob von. *A Foray into the Worlds of Animals and Humans: With a Theory of Meaning.* 1934, 1940. Translated by Joseph D. O'Neil. Introduction by Dorion Sagan. Minneapolis: University of Minnesota Press, 2010.

White-Spunner, Barney. *Of Living Valour: The Story of the Soldiers at Waterloo.* London: Simon and Schuster, 2015.

Xenophon. *On the Art of Horsemanship.* In *Scripta Minora,* 296–363. Translated by E. C. Marchant. Cambridge: Harvard University Press, 2000.

CHAPTER 5

REPATRIATING CASTAWAYS

Travel Tales of the Tuatara

Anna Boswell

"Maritime Animals"

Scattered across the archival records of the Zoological Society of London (ZSL), the submerged crest of a story starts to surface: between 1868 and 1895, a total of 109 live tuatara (*Sphenodon punctatus*) were accessioned by Regent's Park Zoo in London. These small terrestrial reptiles—colloquially known as "spiny-backed lizards" and named by Māori for their dorsal resemblance to mountain ridges—had been transported across the waters of the globe from Aotearoa / New Zealand, and they were highly prized possessions for what was, at that time, the world's premier zoological society (figure 5.1).[1]

Notably, the three-decade-long period of the tuatara's marooning and display in Regent's Park Zoo is bookended by two key shifts in understanding. First, the tuatara was internationally feted as the sole survivor of an order of reptiles with an evolutionary history spanning nearly a quarter of a billion years. The sensational discovery of the tuatara's status as the planet's so-called "living fossil" was made in 1867 by Albert Günther of the British Museum, following initial confusion and misclassification arising from examination of the un-prepossessing tuatara specimens first brought to London. And second, in the closing

Figure 5.1 Tuatara (*Sphenodon punctatus*) in front of its burrow. Michael Hamilton, February 28, 2006 (CC BY-SA 3.0).

decade of the nineteenth century, ZSL made special mention of the tuatara as a species requiring urgent and active intervention to secure its survival from threatened extinction. The Society's plea for preservation of the tuatara—recorded in its annual report of 1893—stands as its first proactive expression of a species-level conservation agenda.[2] As such, the tuatara pinpoints a watershed in the conception of the zoo, occasioning its shift from colonial-scientific showcase to bastion of conservation.[3] The tuatara is pivotal, then, in the sense of being one of the very oldest evolved species on earth and the very first species recognized as requiring active conservation measures. The timespan of that pivot is the timespan of London Zoo's acquisition of those 109 live specimens.

As suggested by the contours of this sketch, tuatara have, in the past century and a half, become renowned as time travelers.[4] They are "other-worldly" in the sense that they have lived in worlds radically foreign to us, surviving through millennia and across geological epochs that have claimed all other species of the Rhynchocephalian order. As such, they endure as "ghosts of Gondwana,"[5] the planet's ancient southern supercontinent, and as relics of what J. R. H. Andrews has termed "the Southern Ark."[6] Yet tuatara are not typically disposed to geographical ranging. Endemic to Aotearoa / New Zealand, they have inhabited the islands of that place since the fracturing of Gondwana, and—having adapted to the often cold and windswept conditions of the isolated landmasses and archipelagos of southern climes—they are notorious for being sedentary and slow. Tuatara do not readily exert themselves and they are able to reduce their respiratory rate to a single breath per hour. Under their own steam, in the ordinary course of their daily activities, individual tuatara may only venture as far as twenty meters from their burrows—in a lifetime that may span more than a century. Indeed, recorded observations of tuatara held in captivity indicate that individual creatures may not move at all for periods of up to six weeks, confining themselves entirely within the boundaries of penciled outlines drawn around them.[7] In alignment with this tendency, academic research to date has tended to focus on the tuatara's biological habits and physiological quirks—such as the so-called "third eye" that is present on the top of its head and may be seen to emblematize the role of the species as a "seer" into other realms. The relevant scholarly discourse has been slow-moving and has, itself, emerged from the stasis of normative observational practices and paradigms of knowledge that take the "captive" lives of tuatara as given.

To chance upon the archival footprints of tuatara in the Northern Hemisphere, then, is to encounter traces of a story that bespeaks dramatic and unprecedented mobility, while to think of the tuatara as a geographic traveler is to set its story and its associated knowledges in motion. Given the tuatara's antiquity and its natural distribution, the vectors and reversals conjured by the information embalmed in the ZSL records are particularly arresting. It appears that without warning, in the latter half of the nineteenth century, tuatara found themselves completing trans-hemispheric voyages, adjusting to shipboard life, dwelling in terrariums, partaking of new diets, recalibrating their diurnal and seasonal patterns, and washing up in "other worlds": strange institutional environments (zoos, museums, private collections, and networks of exchange) in parts of the globe hitherto unknown to them.

Because the tuatara has not conventionally been understood as a maritime voyager, however, the task of outlining the ridges and fleshing out the fragments of its travel story—encompassing new surfaces, new circles, and new conditions of circumscription—presents distinct methodological difficulties. Prior to my approach in 2019 to share the preliminary information that I had gleaned from the ZSL archives, the

Ngāti Koata tribal authorities who are custodians of the largest surviving populations of tuatara—as well as knowledges about this *taonga* (or treasured) species—were unaware that live tuatara had been transported to the Northern Hemisphere in the nineteenth century, and they were stunned by this news.[8] The information preserved in the ZSL records, however, appears frustratingly scant, merely comprising dates of acquisition, the numbers of tuatara, and the names of individual donors (mostly sea captains).

Moreover, factors beyond my control have prevented my return to the United Kingdom and Europe to further this research through on-the-ground investigation. Unanticipated global conditions in the second and third decades of the twenty-first century have imposed limits on international travel, blocking access to the journeying of the tuatara that began roughly 150 years ago. Indeed, this strange COVID-era turn of events means the knowledge held in international repositories is arguably less accessible nowadays than it was in the nineteenth century, during the era of the tuatara's own period of extensive voyaging. The most that can be done at this time is to glean, sift, and piece together tentative shards of the tuatara's travel tale from available resources. However, the sources that yield this information present distinct challenges. Notably, the shipboard aspects of the tuatara's transnational venturing remain to be uncovered—and may prove unrecoverable. Due to its camouflaged appearance, its small stature, its relative quietness and stillness, and its inclination for subterranean living, this creature may well have evaded the notice and record of observational processes and knowledge practices that were applied by mariners to other faunal cargo. For this reason, to dig up burrows or repositories or gravesites—both in literal and metaphorical senses—in order to flush out hard evidence of the tuatara's forced emigration seems the wrong way to approach this subject. Rather, attunements of a more oblique order seem to be required in order to catch glimpses of how the tuatara has been moved by people on-the-move; what this creature has seen through its shifts, passages, and trafficking; and how this information in turn may move us.

I turn, then, to submerged stories as a means of making preliminary contributions to what may be known about the travel tales of the tuatara. My interests in stories and storytelling are, in part, pragmatic, but they are also motivated by links to scholarly work and Indigenous knowledge practices. In methodological terms, narratives may be understood as having distinct informational value, transmitting a range of learnings, while stories and anecdotes are particularly helpful as devices or provocations for *thinking with*. Yet stories and their frameworks may hinder understanding, too. When animals are storied or cast as "maritime," for instance, they risk inhabiting an erased kind of "no-place," such that the contained, self-enclosed world of the ship becomes the horizon line of the tale. While it is true that maritime stories may highlight (and tell compelling stories about) local politics, it is also possible that localities and local knowledge practices may be erased in the circumstances of these stories' telling, with the result that the politics of possession and invasion (whose boats, in whose waters, to what purposes or ends, with what impacts) evaporate—particularly in circumstances of colonial activity. "Mare nullius" is the term applied by the Māori scholar Dan Hikuroa to this phenomenon, meaning "empty sea" or "available sea" (no-one's sea; sea-for-the-taking).[9] Moreover, to cast tuatara as maritime "animals" risks confining them to the traditional roles prescribed by a hierarchized and European-conceived lifeworld, precluding the possibility that they can be seen as kin and as spiritual guardians (as they are in *te ao Māori* [the Māori world]). It is notable that in tribal lore in Aotearoa / New Zealand, tuatara and people are understood as being descended from common ancestors. Tuatara are charged with guarding difficult places and difficult knowledges, and they are considered to possess access to realms of wisdom and spirituality that are beyond those perceivable by humans—and thus are not able to be described or recorded. For these reasons, tuatara pose challenges to conventional academic practices and necessitate nuanced forms of storytelling.

In seeking to recover facets of the travel tales of the tuatara, then, I proceed with caution—both with and against the grain of the term "maritime animal." I work from the premise that the tuatara's travel tale is a story that we only stand to discover by conversing, listening, and learning, by taking it places and setting it in motion. In what follows, I look to a late nineteenth-century text by the Austrian taxidermist and amateur naturalist Andreas Reischek (1845–1902)—itself a difficult source—in an attempt to recover fragments of the story of how and why tuatara came to be transported so far from their home ranges and in such numbers in the second half of the nineteenth century, and what might be learned from these tales. Reischek was a known collector of lizards and other reptiles, and his extensively documented journeying in Aotearoa / New Zealand embodies (or perhaps "re-bodies" for us) the European practices and epistemologies that produced new conditions of life and motion for the tuatara from the nineteenth century onwards. As I hope to show in recovering this source, which has long since been abandoned for its controversial content (such that it is now an obscure and effectively proscribed archival relic), storytelling is, itself, a conservation activity, just as conservation work is reliant on the workings and modalities of stories. I conclude the chapter by tracing Reischek's activities back to his homeland, where a tuatara specimen transported by ship in the nineteenth century, and now held in the Natural History Museum in Vienna, can unquestionably be identified and attributed as a representative trans-hemispheric voyager. The present-absences or palpable spaces and gaps that emerge in and around this creature's story seem particularly apt with respect to the elusiveness of the tuatara and its status as a guardian of thresholds of understanding.

Castaway Knowledges

Andreas Reischek arrived in Aotearoa / New Zealand from Austria in 1877 with the original intention of taking up a fixed-term two-year residence. He ended up staying until 1889, traveling the length and breadth of the country in search of zoological, botanical, ethnographic, and mineral specimens. "Highlights" of Reischek's twelve-year sojourn—encompassing a volatile mix of ecological and ethnographic observations, accounts of specimen collection and preservation, and blow-by-blow recountings of self-heroicized feats of adventure, survival, and cunning—comprise the texture and substance of his 300-page book *Yesterdays in Maoriland* (1902), while two short but highly significant scientific papers published in the *Transactions and Proceedings of the Royal Society of New Zealand* in 1881 and 1885 also document the findings of the research that Reischek conducted into the habits and physiology of the tuatara. Reischek's writings make it clear that he was intrigued by the tuatara. More than any other creature, this species formed the backbone of his most significant contributions to the nascent scientific discourse of the era.

The fact that Reischek has become a difficult figure in the history of Aotearoa / New Zealand is perhaps prefigured by the troubled emergence of *Yesterdays in Maoriland.* Already backward-glancing—as a retrospective account of his time in Aotearoa/New Zealand, and as a record of "vanished times" in that country's history[10]—it was based on diaries, notebooks, and a manuscript written by Reischek in the period 1877–1889. The book was compiled by Reischek's son and first published in German after Reischek's death in 1902; it was not translated into English until 1930. These publication delays meant Reischek's story was already in lag at the time when it emerged, and the book itself is tinged with Reischek's disappointment that he had failed to attract acclaim in scientific scholarly circles in own lifetime—as well as being shaped and scarred by the financial instability he faced during his career as a technical contractor. H. E. L. Friday, the translator and editor of the 1930 English edition of *Yesterdays in Maoriland*, expressed concerns that Reischek was a "forgotten" figure whose work had been "practically neglected."[11] In this sense, Reischek's book can be understood as the "castaway" tale of a "castaway" traveler: its own marooning was effectively redoubled.

Despite Friday's salvage efforts, the events of *Yesterdays in Maoriland*—and Reischek's reputation more generally—have traveled exceptionally badly through time to our present age. The book glorifies activities and attitudes with which it is difficult for contemporary audiences to identify. As a European man of his era, Reischek might be partially excused for the "ordinary" colonial sentiments that he expresses, for his racialized (and at times openly racist and xenophobic) views,[12] for the imported sublime and romantic imaginary that he lays thickly over the country he traverses, and for his "just" sense of the inevitable destructiveness of European settlement: "It seems that wherever the white man goes," he matter-of-factly explains, "a part of Nature must die."[13] Yet, as a memoir or travelogue, his book bespeaks a rapacity that seems grotesquely excessive, and it is filled with self-importantly heroic escapades that go far beyond the bounds of what might nowadays be understood as acceptable conduct; it reads as self-incriminating testimony, the basis for a charge sheet of unscrupulous acts. Reischek enjoys hospitality from Māori communities and accepts from them multiple prestigious (and extremely valuable) *huia* tails as gifts, yet he repeatedly robs gravesites and hoards human remains, conceiving of *pā* (hilltop fortifications), *kāinga* (villages), and *urupā* (burial places) as collection grounds for looting;[14] he vandalizes and desecrates *taonga* (precious objects), sawing the heads off carved posts where he deems this necessary for transportation purposes;[15] he deliberately conceals the objects that he plunders, slipping this so-called "booty" onto ships bound for European collections and institutions;[16] he befriends the Māori king and then dupes him into allowing his passage through territories forbidden to European travelers in order to further his searches for human remains; and he engages in casual yet concerted violence against nature. Conducting shooting sprees targeting endemic fauna known to be rare and on the verge of extinction, he pictures these living creatures as trophy specimens that will enhance his own standing and reputation. A biography of Reischek, published by the New Zealand historian Michael King in 1981, sealed his reputation for duplicity and villainy; King openly struggles with Reischek's actions and attitudes, questioning his taste and judgment throughout his account.

To disengage from what is disturbing and offensive about Reischek's book presents distinct challenges, and it is by no means my intention to portray Reischek as a "simple, sympathetic foreigner," to use Friday's terms.[17] Yet to disavow or dismiss *Yesterdays in Maoriland* for the outright difficulty of its content is to risk overlooking the valuable information freighted within it. The book itself survives as a taxidermied specimen or mount of sorts: flea-bitten, timeworn, and shabby (and emanating a certain kind of toxic stench), but nevertheless preserving the forms and shapes of a world otherwise inaccessible to us. I would also add that, in the context of a settler-colonial history, which is itself "ugly" in parts, shying away from the ugliness of such texts is a strategy of avoidance that necessarily produces new forms and conditions of difficulty. Given the paucity of information available about the nineteenth-century travel tales of the tuatara too, I proceed in the hope that repatriating the insights of this castaway text will provide a foundation for furthering present-day knowledges.

First, Reischek immerses us in a maritime or "water world." Traveling by boat, he presents vivid descriptions of extraordinary-yet-mundane events of shipboard life: he copes with overcrowded conditions that turn humans into sardine can–like captives; he endures plagues of red ants and infestations of rats who play hide-and-seek over the passengers' sleeping bodies at night and gnaw on their clothing and shoes; he experiences seasickness to the point of vomiting blood, and so on.[18] In part, the maritime world that Reischek describes has global compass, involving transoceanic traveling, voyaging, shipping, and specimen dispatching—as well as border control, quarantining, and disease-management protocols. Yet Reischek's maritime world is a localized one too. He catches steamers and riverboats around Aotearoa / New Zealand and rows himself by dinghy to otherwise inaccessible stretches of coast, presenting waterways as the country's main highways. Through this portrait, moreover, he teaches us about the patternwork of European settlement in so-called "new" countries. The Aotearoa / New Zealand of Reischek's travels is largely "trackless" in the sense that it has little in the way of internal roading infrastructure.[19] It comprises European rim or edge settlements—ports and harbor towns in general—and is roadblocked in its interior by Māori, who are resistant to European presence and penetration. In this sense, the book's maritime outlook reminds the reader of a time before cross-country travel was possible, when the interior remained to be mapped, when different proximities and units of measure for distances prevailed, and when the writers of such accounts—travelers, officials, and so on—were primarily itinerant water-bound outsiders peering in.

Second, Reischek captures a world in a state of turbulent transition set in motion by European shipborne activities. In his account, colonialists were subjecting Aotearoa / New Zealand to a makeover in the image of a European landscape. As a newly destabilized "docking-ground" for imperialist agendas swept in from the seas, it is war-torn in several senses: Reischek documents uneasy relations between tribal communities and European newcomers, the after-effects of escalating intertribal tensions, and a full-scale European-driven assault on the environment. In his account, this transformation of the country is not shorn or cleansed of its associated devastations and violence: the large-scale hacking and razing of ancient kauri forests whose valuable timber was being converted into materials for international industries centered on ship repair and mast building, for instance, is recounted in unflinching detail.[20] While waves of upheaval surface prominently in various meetings, events, and patterns of guest-host relationship, they also find their way into "micro-" moments in Reischek's text, particularly in regard to shipborne faunal introductions. At Taylors Mistake (a desolate bay situated some distance from the busy port in Lyttelton Harbour), for instance, Reischek tracks a "good-sized" mammal and is astonished that it turns out to be a European rat "of exceptional size," later finding "continual opportunities of observing the ravages of the brown rat (*Mus decumanus*), one of the great plagues of New Zealand."[21]

At Lake Brunner, he encounters Australian black swans, a species that had been deliberately acclimatized in Aotearoa / New Zealand between 1864 and 1870 for ornamental purposes,[22] and on Kawau Island he hunts and eats possums and wallabies imported for Governor George Grey's menagerie. As he provides insights into the turbulent, mixed-up ecology of a settler-colonial place, Reischek repeatedly offers views of the border between cultivated land and so-called "virgin mountain world";[23] he comes across sheep grazing amongst tussock instead of pasture, pointing up the crude incompleteness of the conversion of forested lands into agronomic patchwork;[24] he feasts with local tribes on wild pigs and cattle, whose established feral populations are already found throughout the country; and he catches sight of horses, newly adopted by Māori as working animals, being ridden with flax-plaited stirrups.[25]

Third, following on from this, if Reischek's story is dedicated to settler-colonial lifeworld transformation, the world that Reischek documents abounds with animals. Indeed, *Yesterdays in Maoriland* is populated with animals more than it is by humans, and people (station-owners, run-holders, shepherds, gold and gum diggers, guides, Māori hosts, museum officials, and so on) are conceived of as conduits for Reischek's faunal encounters. Reischek supplies detailed descriptions and vignettes of various endemic species found in the course of his travels, marveling at the creatures he comes across and lamenting the destructiveness of "those parasites of European invasion" (rats, cats, and so on) that have caused the extinction of the Māori dog (*kūri*) and the threatened extinction of the Māori rat (*kiore*).[26] He is also sensitive to the pressures that endemic nature faces in an era of settler-colonial disturbance. As this suggests, if his descriptions contribute to the world of amateur (that is, pre-professionalized) science, they also provide a window onto late nineteenth-century understandings of extinction. The issue of "rarity" surfaces repeatedly in the course of his book: for instance, with this term meaning difficult-to-come-by because the species in question lives in remote and inaccessible conditions and/or because it is on the brink of extinction (such that there are few remaining specimens to locate). In this sense, Aotearoa / New Zealand itself emerges in Reischek's writings as an "ark-place" or a "country-as-ark"—a globally significant repository for remnant species salvaged from earlier tides of evolutionary history.

And fourth, as this suggests, as a dedicated and determined collector, Reischek provides a window onto the nineteenth-century world of collecting, as well as metropolitan modes of colonial acquisition. His account offers insights into the intensity and appetite of individuals, networks, and institutions for amassing animal specimens as well as knowledges about animals. During his travels, Reischek collects many hundreds of kilograms of animal matter to sell or export on consignment, and he sets up makeshift laboratories in the bush for skinning and preparing specimens—poisoning himself at one point when he forgets to wash the toxic preserving chemicals from his hands. Reischek closes *Yesterdays in Maoriland* with the observation that he is set to return to Austria with "an abundance of specimens" as well as "a rich treasure of observations and discovery."[27] Indeed, the collection of ethnological and natural history specimens that he had amassed (approximately 14,000 items, including 8,000 fish and reptile specimens) was the single largest ever taken to Europe from Aotearoa / New Zealand.[28]

Death-Work

As his "dirty-handedness" serves to remind, if Reischek is a collector, an aspiring amateur naturalist, and an accomplished tradesman, he is also, importantly, a death-worker. As King observes, Rieschek's writings and activities reveal that he was obsessed with human remains and the paraphernalia of death,[29] along with documenting Māori death rituals, observances, and practices. In accordance with his taxidermist's eye view, live animals seem to be pictured in Reischek's account as already dead; they appear pre-frozen and mounted in poses, viewed in terms of their "afterlives"[30] as scientific specimens, commodities, and/or objects of curiosity. Throughout his account, Reischek hunts and shoots an astonishingly wide array of birds and animals; he describes preparing skins and skeletons; he arranges museum displays and dioramas of dead animals; and he traffics in specimens, supplying these to private collectors, museum officials, and sea captains.[31] In documenting his specimen collection practices, however, Reischek makes it clear that he does not confine himself to already deceased animals. Reischek is known to have curated menageries of animals in his youth[32] and during his time in Aotearoa / New Zealand he keeps domesticated, or "pet," specimens, including live weka, rats, kiwi, albatrosses, and penguins. At one point in his account, several live kakapos (a critically endangered ground-dwelling, flightless parrot) escape from their cages on board the ship and climb the rigging, falling to their deaths in the ocean. At another point, Reischek recounts:

> At the farm I found the Maori chief and the prophet, to whom Wilson introduced me. Both of them displayed almost excessive signs of friendship, and said they were curious to examine my gun and the contents of my pack. Under different circumstances such curiosity would have been inconvenient [i.e., because Reischek's pack contains looted burial objects and human remains], but on this occasion I was only too willing for them to look. In the tins I had poisonous spiders, centipedes, and lizards, of which the Maoris are greatly afraid. These specimen tins I now opened, carelessly letting their contents fall at the feet of the tohunga. The live creatures clung to the legs of the holy man, and full of fear and fright, both natives dropped their dignified bearing and took to their heels. The prophet cried out: "He has let the devil run loose at me!"[33]

As his actions suggest, Reischek is, at times, capable of demonstrating clear-sighted understandings of Māori beliefs and knowledge practices. Lizards and other reptiles—including tuatara—appear in his account at telling moments, and they are closely associated with trepidation and death. In one burial ground, for instance, Reischek finds a human bone carved with the image of a lizard, understanding this to be a sign of *tapu* (proscription or taboo).[34] On another occasion, Rieschek recounts a Māori legend of "a giant lizard, Ngarara, [who] lived in a great cavern, and he ran out upon and devoured every one who came by his lair."[35] Later in his account, Reischek notes:

> Naturally the Maoris were very superstitious; they had so many good and bad demons whom they must not offend. Their greatest dread was of lizards, especially the tuatara. If a lizard ran out at a Maori and he did not immediately kill it, he thought he must die. This superstition, which, as the excavation of lizard bones in old Maori cooking-places shows, could only be of recent origin, worked so suggestively in many cases that Maoris were known to die from auto-suggestion through fear of the tapu.[36]

On this particular occasion, Reischek mistakes or misinterprets the evidence: lizards, including tuatara, were ingested by Māori in ritualized ways in recognition of the fear and awe that pertain to them, as a sign of bravery or as a means of increasing the *mana* of a warrior. More generally, however, the pervasive pattern of tales about lizards and tuatara in his account serves as acknowledgment that tuatara have long held special status as a potent *taonga* (treasured species) in Māori epistemologies, and that they, too, are associated with realms of death.

Reischek's firsthand observations of tuatara—culminating in a trip to Karewa Island in February 1885 with two university professors to study this species—are presented in *Yesterdays in Maoriland* as well as in the two articles that he published in the 1880s. These observations are thickly overlaid with Reischek's characteristic romanticism and his penchant for melodramatic storytelling: tuatara are introduced in *Yesterdays in Maoriland* as "the rare and singular fringe-back lizard, and the last remaining offspring of the Saurians," while Reischek's personal introduction to tuatara is to be bitten by one, having shoved his hand into the animal's burrow.[37] This gives rise to his discovery of the tuatara's symbiotic cohabitation with sea birds on the Hen and Chicken Islands, a thesis that he substantiates through careful observation.[38] It seems clear that Reischek was seizing an opportunity to stake his reputation as a naturalist in documenting and exporting, for publication and circulation, this "remarkable" stumbled-upon fact of the tuatara's "sociable" living.[39] What Reischek does not consider is that this adaptation has been brought about by the tuatara's conditions of confinement on small offshore islands; having survived across millennia and geological epochs, tuatara populations on the mainland of Aotearoa / New Zealand were unable to withstand the impacts of settler-colonial expansion, leading tuatara to be marooned in remote and scattered locations. Indeed, their lives had been profoundly shaken up in the end-to-end lifespans of just one or two of their kind. Further details reveal that as well as dismembering tuatara specimens and recovering tuatara bones from middens, Reischek kept live tuatara in order to study their habits. In *Yesterdays in Maoriland* he explains: "On all the larger islands they live principally on insectivorous foods, such as beetles, grubs, wetas [*sic*], grasshoppers, flies, etc., which I found on dissecting. I think where such food—which they prefer even in confinement—is plentiful, they will not prey on birds."[40]

These details are fleshed out in Reischek's scientific articles, in which he notes that tuatara run fast and defend themselves against capture by biting and scratching, and that nighttime is the best time to catch tuatara.[41] He also describes obtaining tuatara eggs and hatchlings, and reports that "even in confinement, in my possession, they burrow."[42] Recent changes to the distribution and abundance of animals and people are also documented by Reischek. Chicken Island is said to contain archaeological evidence of relatively recent occupation by Māori, while Reischek describes searching "in vain" for tuatara on Little Barrier Island: "The large quantities of feral pigs living upon that island may easily account for their absence."[43] Further wide-ranging changes in tuatara distribution under the pressure of European settlement are also recorded by Reischek, who laments that this species had become extinct on the mainland by the time of his sojourn.[44] In this sense, Reischek's encounters with tuatara—and his failures to encounter them—point to the settler-colonial enterprise as a "deathworlding" one.[45]

That European-wrought deathworld, however, does not lay sole and terminal claim to the trajectories of the tuatara's tale—or, to put it another way, there is a further horizon line to perceive here. In Māori storytelling traditions, the spirits of the dead travel to the northern tip of Aotearoa (Te Rerenga Wairua, or "the Leaping-Off Place") before commencing their journey to the distant Pacific homeland of Hawaiki.[46] As already noted, according to Māori worldviews, animals and people are genealogically related and their lives are inter-implicated. Moreover, Aotearoa / New Zealand itself is understood in Māori traditions as a floating world rather than an anchored landmass: it comprises a canoe (Te Waka-a-Māui, the South Island) from which Māui, the legendary ancestor-hero, fished up Te Ika-a-Māui (the North Island, or literally the fish of Māui). Tuatara were already known by Māori as "boat creatures," or cast as "guardians of the canoe," and in this sense, the exiled tuatara netted by Reischek can be understood as completing a shadow or ghost voyage—"departing" from Aotearoa / New Zealand another kind of way. Even as their physical bodies were loaded into the holds of European ships, and as their stories were remitted to foreign knowledge-worlds of paper and print, tuatara spirits were simultaneously undertaking a "third" voyage of return from their "canoe-home" in Aotearoa / New Zealand across Te Moana-nui-a-Kiwa (the Pacific Ocean) to their Polynesian place of belonging.

Repatriating Knowledges

If Reischek provides us with tantalizing glimpses into the world of tuatara in the late nineteenth century, unanswered (and perhaps unanswerable) questions begin to surface. Given that Reischek's observations of tuatara were informed by holding specimens in captivity, it is tempting to speculate that the materials shipped overseas by Reischek included live eggs of various creatures, including tuatara, for incubation and hatching. It remains unclear from reading his accounts what specific volume of tuatara material Reischek amassed during his time in Aotearoa / New Zealand, whether he was commissioned by overseas collectors to fill crates with tuatara for shipment to the Northern Hemisphere, and/or whether these specimens were freighted alive or dead. A surviving account written by one of Reischek's contemporaries notes that on a single excursion to Moritiri Island in 1881, Reischek "collected for the market some 30 or 40 [tuatara], many of them of a very large size."[47] It also remains unclear whether or how Reischek (or his business associates) may have sold, traded, and exchanged tuatara specimens, cared for them (or not), or preserved and mounted them once they had arrived in the northern world. The matter of what collectors, curators, and publics may have made of these tuatara is also obscure, although the tuatara's *mana* (privileged status) as a so-called "living fossil" suggests there would have been considerable prestige surrounding these specimens—at least at the time of their arrival.

In a certain sense, it does not strictly matter how much or how little of this information proves recoverable; the questions themselves provide new angles and ridgelines of enquiry. And, moreover, since tuatara guard realms that humans cannot access, we might expect that the knowledges these castaway tuatara hold or protect cannot be recovered in full (or can only be recovered in fragments). It is tempting to speculate that Reischek may have been responsible for sending tuatara to London—perhaps even to the collections of ZSL—although at this stage I have been unable to verify the extent of the networks of exchange traversed by the specimens that he collected. At least one surviving tuatara specimen marooned in the Northern Hemisphere can, however, definitively be traced to Reischek.

In Exhibition Hall XXVII of the Natural History Museum (NHM) in Vienna, a tuatara occupies a special place, selected to feature in the "Top 100" specimens displayed in that institution. The tuatara is mounted in a traditional wood-and-glass case. It is dated "circa 1885" and is described as follows:

> Tuataras [*sic*] are now found only on about 30 small islands off the coast of New Zealand. The Sphenodon collection at NHM Vienna is one of the largest collections outside New Zealand. . . . Tuatara are the only surviving members of the Sphenodontia order, which was widespread in the Mesozoic age more than 200 million years ago. They differ very little from their ancestors and are, therefore, described as "living fossils." Besides tuataras [*sic*], crocodiles are the only other animal to have complete temporal arches. Like other primal vertebrates, the tuatara has a third eye on the top of its head, which does not supply an image, but serves only to determine differences in brightness. Today these ancient lizards are strictly protected. The specimen at the museum was mounted in the 19th century and comes from the collection of the famous Austrian taxidermist Andreas Reischek. The director at that time of the royal and imperial Natural History Museum gave Reischek the opportunity of working for twelve years at the Museum of Christchurch, New Zealand. He took advantage of this time to collect and preserve thousands of plants and animals. A subspecies of tuatara, *Sphenodon punctatus reischeki*, was named after him.[48]

The specimen on display is set at the entrance to a burrow, in company with a petrel—highlighting Reischek's contribution to understanding the sociality of the tuatara in its confinement on Hauturu / Little Barrier Island.

A number of specific observations emerge from consideration of this singular specimen. The first is an issue of scale: in metonymic terms, the single tuatara on display stands in for a much larger volume of specimens, producing a part-for-whole or tip-of-the-iceberg effect. To look at the Reischek tuatara in the Natural History Museum is to see countless other "invisible" tuatara specimens—perhaps stored in basement or off-site facilities dispersed across Europe and the United Kingdom, perhaps degrading in condition and luster, perhaps already decomposed altogether. Moreover, these tuatara can be pictured as having new "burrow-mates" (that is, new creatures in whose proximity they live), given the strange forms of taxonomic sociality produced by museum collections and their associated display practices.

Second, this specimen focalizes issues of extinction—both of species and knowledges. The fact that the looming extinction of tuatara was widely anticipated in the nineteenth century is poignantly ironic: these creatures were shipped and deposited in overseas institutions so that they would not become "lost" to knowledge, yet what has become lost is the very knowledge of how they came to be there and what emerged as a result of this maritime history. Because the tuatara on display in Vienna maintains its connection to Reischek's activities in Aotearoa / New Zealand, it stands out as a "storied" animal with a (comparatively) well-known provenance.

Third, the tuatara in Vienna raises questions about repatriation, which is a term that I deliberately borrow from museum studies discourse. Typically, this term is applied to ethnographic materials that have been taken from tribal owners unethically or without permission—including human remains and funerary items that have come to be considered inappropriate for public display. And, indeed, human remains plundered by Reischek and deposited in the Imperial Museum in Vienna (the precursor to the Natural History Museum) in the late nineteenth century have been subject to repatriation requests dating back to World War II. These *taonga* began being returned to Aotearoa / New Zealand in 1985 by the late Māori queen, Te Arikinui Dame Te Atairangikaahu, in accordance with *iwi* (tribal) wishes and following extensive diplomatic efforts.[49] In 2015, a further delegation from the Museum of New Zealand Te Papa Tongarewa visited Vienna to receive further remains to be laid to rest in accordance with *tikanga* (prescribed protocols). Those remains included one of the so-called "Kawhia mummies" stolen by Reischek, along with "nine human vertebrae, a coffin with skeletal remains from three different individuals and a *toi moko* or mummified and tattooed head."[50] While the preserved materials themselves are deeply significant, charged with "political, evidentiary, and emotional meanings,"[51] as well as spiritual ones, it seems clear that preservation and repatriation apply to stories as much as they do to things; or, to put it another way, to bring home the stories of what has happened to these things, and to reverse their maritime voyaging trajectories through the process of *hokinga* (return), is an equally significant undertaking. These same considerations apply in considering what it might mean to repatriate the travel tales of the tuatara, and in understanding why repatriation in this context will necessarily involve more than the physical return of preserved specimens. The tuatara teaches that stories are, themselves, precious artifacts that must be cared for and guarded if they are to survive.

Fourth, the presence of tuatara in the Natural History Museum's collection raises the prospect of tuatara as so-called "working animals." Māori are known to have stationed tuatara in the landscape to keep watch over burial grounds and battle sites; in accordance with tribal protocols and knowledge practices, it seems highly likely that living tuatara were historically charged with watching over the very same places that Reischek raided in Aotearoa / New Zealand. It also seems possible to imagine that throughout the course of their maritime and captive lives, the tuatara transported from Aotearoa / New Zealand in the nineteenth century, whether living or dead, have protected the sacred possessions (including human remains and funerary items) taken by collectors such as Reischek. To remove tuatara from their home ranges and freight them across oceans and hemispheres may place at risk the long and deep streams of place-based knowledge for which tuatara stand (and stand guard). Yet the surviving fragments of the tuatara's travel tale suggest new ways of picturing this creature as the guardian of a further suite of difficult places, repositories, and tales, and as the patron of delicate modes of recovery work and storytelling. In this sense, as keepers of alternate realms of knowledge, tuatara fracture and overturn the taxonomic certainties of the museum, which evolved as "an expression of the western conviction in the onward march of the rational" and as an institution exerting power, protection, and control.[52]

As a final note or postscript, one further detail associated with Reischek's activities stands out. According to King, Reischek was one of the main agitators for the establishment of a sanctuary on Hauturu / Little Barrier Island, an offshore island on which he had unsuccessfully searched for tuatara in the 1880s. King explains that Reischek petitioned colonial officials and government administrators in December 1886, proposing "a reserve in which rare native birds would be protected from general poaching, but from which specimens could be taken for museums in a controlled and conserving manner by the curator," and putting himself forward as the candidate for the role.[53] While this attempt failed at the time, in 1894, Hauturu / Little Barrier Island was declared a sanctuary—five years after Reischek had returned to Austria, and one year after ZSL had publicly endorsed the establishment of conservation measures in Aotearoa / New Zealand to protect the country's remaining avifauna as well as its tuatara. Tuatara were subsequently reintroduced to the sanctuary in 1913, translocated from Stephens Island / Takapourewa, whose tribal custodians are Ngāti Koata.[54] King notes that the setting aside of the sanctuary on Hauturu / Little Barrier Island "could have been the end result of Reischek's earlier submissions."[55] In this sense, Reischek's mixed and contentious legacy may be seen to encompass tuatara preservation as well as tuatara destruction, and to travel—and work—as a story that crosses spatial, temporal, cultural, and ethical boundaries. This makes it particularly apt as a means of approaching the travel tales of a creature enduringly associated with keeping watch over thresholds to tricky realms and fraught border zones.

Notes

1. According to European classification practices, tuatara are "reptiles," not "lizards," although they are frequently referred to as such. Māori culture does not make this distinction; tuatara are considered to be lizards (*ngarara*) within the Māori universe.
2. ZSL, *Report*, 5–6; Boswell, "Climates of Change."
3. This coincided with strict legal protection of tuatara in Aotearoa / New Zealand. See Cree, *Tuatara*, 13–14.
4. In *te reo Māori* (the Māori language), "tuatara" is both the singular and plural form of the noun, as with other animals as well (e.g., "weka" and "kiwi").
5. Gibbs, *Ghosts of Gondwana*.
6. Andrews, *Southern Ark*.
7. Cree, *Tuatara*, 14
8. I wish to express my sincere thanks to Louisa Paul, Oliver Sutherland, and the Ngāti Koata Tuatara Committee for their keen and generous interest in this research.
9. Hikuroa, "Mare Nullius."
10. Friday, "Preface," 7.
11. Ibid., 7, 10.
12. The terms used may be translator's terms (see p. 14).
13. Reischek, *Yesterdays in Maoriland*, 63.
14. Ibid., 50. Reischek describes kea (a large alpine parrot native to the South Island) as "robbers," which is ironic, given his own propensity for taking stuff.
15. Reischek, *Yesterdays in Maoriland*, 65, 168.
16. Ibid., 172.
17. Friday, "Preface," 7.
18. Reischek, *Yesterdays in Maoriland*, 13–14.
19. Ibid., 45.
20. Ibid., 68.
21. Ibid., 43, 251.
22. Ibid., 35. See also Long, *Introduced Birds*, 34, 38–39.
23. Reischek, *Yesterdays in Maoriland*, 45.
24. Ibid., 47.
25. Ibid., 153.
26. Ibid., 77.
27. Ibid., 304.

28. King, *Collector*, 142. See also O'Hara, "Andreas Reischek Collection," 1–2; Prebble, *Dictionary of New Zealand Biography*, Te Ara—the Encyclopedia of New Zealand, s.v., "Reischek, Andreas," accessed December 30, 2020, https://teara.govt.nz/en/biographies/2r14/reischek-andreas.
29. Ibid., 91.
30. Alberti, *Afterlives of Animals*.
31. See, for example, Reischek, *Yesterdays in Maoriland*, 61, 66.
32. King, *Collector*, 17.
33. Reischek, *Yesterdays in Maoriland*, 66–67; see also 104.
34. Ibid., 62.
35. Ibid., 176.
36. Ibid., 201–2.
37. Ibid., 98.
38. Ibid., 98, 108.
39. Reischek, "Notes," 275; Reischek, "Observations," 108. It is notable that in Māori lore, the tuatara is generally considered to be a loner rather than a sociable being.
40. Reischek, *Yesterdays in Maoriland*, 100; see also p. 110 in the same book.
41. Reischek, "Notes," 276.
42. Reischek, "Observations," 108.
43. Reischek, "Notes," 277.
44. Reischek, "Observations," 108.
45. Rose, *Wild Dog Dreaming*, 12. Rose glosses "death world" or "death space" as meaning "where worlds and lives are un-made." The term is used to describe the destructions wrought through settler-colonial expansion; Rose also points towards understandings of the Holocaust ("where genocide is practiced and both time and becoming are extinguished") and the overarching context of extinctions ("where the 4-billion-year history of life on Earth is being terminated").
46. See, for instance, Pomare and Cowan, *Legends of the Māori*, 48–52.
47. Buller cited in Turbott, *Buller's Birds*, 213.
48. Natural History Museum [NHM] Vienna, *NHM Top 100*, 167.
49. See Smallman, "Kawhia"; O'Hara, "Andreas Reischek Collection"; Prebble, *Dictionary of New Zealand*, s.v., "Reischek."
50. Smallman, "Kawhia."
51. Cassman et al., *Human Remains*, 1.
52. Mackenzie, *Museums and Empire*, 1.
53. King, *Collector*, 121.
54. Cree, *Tuatara*, 453.
55. King, *Collector*, 121.

Bibliography

Alberti, Samuel J., ed. *The Afterlives of Animals: A Museum Menagerie*. Charlottesville: University of Virginia Press, 2011.

Andrews, J. R. H. *The Southern Ark: Zoological Discovery in New Zealand, 1769–1900*. Auckland: Century Hutchinson, 1986

Boswell, Anna. "Climates of Change: A Tuatara's-Eye View." *Humanities* 9, no. 2 (2020): 38. Accessed November 22, 2020. https://doi.org/10.3390/h9020038.

Cassman, V., Odegaard, N., and Powell, J., eds. *Human Remains: Guide for Museums and Academic Institutions*. Lanham, MD: Altamira Press, 2007.

Cree, Alison. *Tuatara: Biology and Conservation of a Venerable Survivor*. Christchurch, NZ: Canterbury University Press, 2014.

Friday, H. E. L. Preface to *Yesterdays in Maoriland: New Zealand in the 'Eighties*, by Andreas Reischek, 7–10. Translated and edited by H. E. L. Friday. London: Jonathan Cape, 1970 [1930].

Gibbs, George. *Ghosts of Gondwana: The History of Life in New Zealand*. Nelson, NZ: Craig Potton, 2008.

Hikuroa, Daniel. "Mare Nullius: Mai Tikapa Moana ki te Moana Nui a

Kiwa." Paper presented at Department of Anthropology seminar, University of Auckland, July 28, 2016.

King, Michael. *The Collector.* Auckland: Hodder & Stoughton, 1981.

Long, John H. *Introduced Birds of the World.* Sydney: A. H. & A. W. Reed, 1981.

Mackenzie, John M. *Museums and Empire: Natural History, Human Cultures and Colonial Identities.* Manchester: Manchester University Press, 2009.

Natural History Museum [NHM] Vienna. *NHM Top 100.* Vienna: Natural History Museum Vienna, 2012.

O'Hara, Coralie. "The Andreas Reischek Collection in Vienna and New Zealand's Attempts at Repatriation." In *The Routledge Companion to Indigenous Repatriation: Return, Reconcile, Renew,* edited by Cressida Fforde, C. Timothy McKeown, and Honor Keeler, 438-451. London: Routledge, 2020.

Pomare, Sir Maui, and James Cowan. *Legends of the Māori.* Vol. 1. Auckland: Southern Reprints, 1987. Accessed May 20, 2022. https://nzetc.victoria.ac.nz/tm/scholarly/tei-Pomo1Lege-t1-body-d9-d1.html.

Prebble, Ray G. "Reischek, Andreas," *Dictionary of New Zealand Biography,* first published in 1993, updated October, 2022. Te Ara—the Encyclopedia of New Zealand. Accessed December 30, 2020. https://teara.govt.nz/en/biographies/2r14/reischek-andreas.

Reischek, Andreas. "Notes on Zoological Researches Made on the Chicken Islands, East Coast of the North Island." *Transactions and Proceedings of the Royal Society of New Zealand* 14 (1881): 274–77.

———. "Observations on *Sphenodon punctatum,* Fringe-Back Lizard (Tuatara)." *Transactions and Proceedings of the Royal Society of New Zealand* 18 (1885): 108–10.

———. *Yesterdays in Maoriland: New Zealand in the 'Eighties.* Translated and edited by H. E. L. Friday. London: Jonathan Cape, 1970 [1930].

Rose, Deborah Bird. *Wild Dog Dreaming: Love and Extinction.* Charlottesville: University of Virginia Press, 2011.

Smallman, Elton. "Kawhia the Final Destination for Mummified Child 100 Years On." *Stuff,* May 21, 2015. Accessed 30 December, 2020. https://www.stuff.co.nz/national/68728079/kawhia-the-final-destination-for-mummified-child-100-years-on.

Turbott, E. G., ed. *Buller's Birds of New Zealand.* Christchurch: Whitcoulls, 1979.

Zoological Society of London [ZSL]. *Report of the Council and Auditors of the Zoological Society of London.* Vol. 44. London, 1893.

CHAPTER 6

RATTUS-HOMO-MACHINE

Rats as Seafarers in the Nineteenth Century

Kaori Nagai

Joseph Conrad, in his short story "Youth: A Narrative" (1898), gives a vivid description of rats abandoning a ship. The ship in question is the *Judea*, which was commissioned to transport coal from Newcastle to Bangkok. However, the ship is old and leaky, and, after being badly damaged by winter storms and a series of accidents at sea, it has to stop in Falmouth, Cornwall, for nearly eight months, for a complete overhaul. Curiously, it is after the ship has been refitted with a brand-new copper hull, and is finally ready to sail again, that the rats decide to abandon it. Marlow, the narrator of the story, recalls the incident as follows:

> Then, on a fine moonlight night, all the rats left the ship.
>
> We had been infested with them. They had destroyed our sails, consumed more stores than the crew, affably shared our beds and our dangers, and now, when the ship was made seaworthy, concluded to clear out. I called Mahon to enjoy the spectacle. Rat after rat appeared on our rail, took a last look over his shoulder, and leaped with a hollow thud into the empty hulk. We tried to count them, but soon lost the tale. Mahon said: "Well, well! Don't talk to me about the intelligence of rats. They

> ought to have left before, when we had that narrow squeak from foundering. There you have the proof how silly is the superstition about them …"
>
> And after some more talk we agreed that the wisdom of rats had been grossly overrated, being in fact no greater than that of men.[1]

So, the *Judea* set off without the rats, and of course, the superstition about them—namely, that rats are intelligent and that they abandon a sinking ship—proves to be true. In the middle of the Indian Ocean, the ship's cargo starts combusting spontaneously, and eventually it burns up. The crew have to abandon the ship themselves.

This story is autobiographical, and the *Judea*'s doomed trip closely follows that of the *Palestine*, on which Conrad served as a young sailor. As the *Glasgow Herald* reported on March 19, 1883: "The Palestine, from Newcastle to Bangkok, has been burnt at sea in Banca Straits. Crew saved."[2] As for the authenticity of the rat episode, it has been vouched for by Conrad's friend G. F. W. Hope, who himself was a sailor. According to Hope, "the description of the novel is true in every respect": "Amongst other things [Conrad] told me, was how the rats had left the vessel after she had been recaulked. He thought them, at the time, very foolish rats. But after-events proved the rats were quite right to desert ship for she was burnt out on her way to Bangkok."[3] The episode in *Youth*, then, can be taken as an eyewitness account of rats at sea in the 1880s.

Recently, critical attention has been paid to the historical importance of the ocean as a site of global interactions, where networks of humans and nonhumans are formed culturally, economically, politically, and ecologically. This chapter sheds fresh light on the sea as an inherently cosmopolitan and interconnected space by focusing on the figure of rats as sea-travelers in the nineteenth century. It was common for ships to have some rats on board, and, as we can tell from Conrad's story, some ships were totally infested with them. Rats kept humans company, living, multiplying, gnawing, and causing havoc on the ship, and yet taking full advantage of the human communication networks that they endangered.

In thinking of rats as seafarers, it is important to bear in mind that the link between rats and the plague was yet to be formed. Even though people were aware of ships' role in transmitting plague and other diseases, a plague of rats was not associated with plague in general; as

Christos Lynteris puts it, "Whereas rats had long been considered to be damaging to human livelihood, due to consuming and spoiling food resources, their only redeeming characteristic was, erroneously, widely believed to be their supposed disease-free nature."[4] Rats were thus tolerated as part of the life of the ship, and it was also common for the quarantine stations at ports of entry to be infested with vermin, "swarming with rats, bugs, and fleas."[5] The centuries-old tradition of ship rats abruptly came to an end at the turn of the century, when, following the discovery of the bacteria *Yersinia pestis* in 1894, rats were identified as a vector of bubonic plague. It became a requirement for ships to be rat-free, which also led to the radical rewriting of the history of rats' travel from the medical standpoint, as that of disease spreaders or "epidemic villains."[6]

The figure of rats as fellow travelers, then, invites us to unlearn our modern bacteriological training and to imagine the form of companionship with, and knowledge about, rats that was once possible. The proverbial phrase "rats abandon a sinking ship" (and its variants) is now chiefly used metaphorically to indicate "desertion or abandonment of something when failure or difficulty seems inevitable."[7] However, the phrase attests to the faith sailors had in the rats' knowledge of a ship's condition, and also that rats were once accepted as an integral part of any ship's journey. Merriam-Webster traces the idiom back to the sixteenth century, when "the original setting for the fleeing rats was a decrepit house, one that was on the verge of falling down." It was not until the late seventeenth century that "the expression took on a new mode of egress: decamping from a foundering ship."[8] The phrase, modified to include the agency of sea rats, flourished throughout the eighteenth and nineteenth centuries, which coincides with Britain's expansion and ascendancy as a maritime nation. It is therefore a record of what I would call "Rattus-Homo-Machine," the partnership between humans and rats formed on ships. This chapter will explore the nature and workings of this multispecies assemblage, shaped and powered by the ship and its global trajectory.

The Colonizer's Shadow

Lucinda Cole, in her brilliant book on vermin, *Imperfect Creatures* (2016), draws attention to the curious absence of rats in Daniel Defoe's

Robinson Crusoe (1719). Crusoe's ship had some rats; this can be guessed by the references made to bags of grain eaten and spoiled by them. But when the storm struck, the rats seem to have sunk with the ship, allowing Crusoe to prosper on a rat-free island. This makes a striking contrast with the case of Alexander Selkirk, the Scottish sailor who became marooned on an uninhabited island in the South Seas in 1704. According to Captain Woodes Rogers, who rescued Selkirk in 1709:

> [Selkirk] was at first much pestered with cats and rats that bred in great numbers from some of each species which had got ashore from ships that put in there for wood and water. The rats gnawed his feet and clothes whilst asleep, which obliged him to cherish the cats with his goats' flesh, by which so many of them became so tame, that they would lie about in hundreds, and soon delivered him from the rats.[9]

Defoe, in writing his novel, drew his inspiration from Selkirk's life story, and yet chose not to include the rat episode. The joy of mastery and control, over his island and his native servant Friday, and the accumulation of wealth through his hard work—these colonial fantasies that Defoe's novel explores would not have been possible if Crusoe had had to cope with rats constantly threatening his safety, as Selkirk had to do. In particular, Crusoe's successful agricultural project depends on "the *absence* of the rats that plagued Selkirk and the millions of others across the early modern world, all struggling to protect their grain supplies against rodent infestation."[10] Crusoe's island is devoid of rats, which Cole, "given the 200 year history of rat infestations in European colonies," finds "noteworthy, if not cognitively jarring."[11]

Cole's discussion of *Robinson Crusoe* provides a useful reference point for our stories of seafaring rats: Defoe, who dreamt of a rat-free agricultural economy in the form of a desert island, did not keep Crusoe's ship totally free of rats. Unlike Crusoe's island, imagined as a "closed" and controlled world, the ship that carried him was "an open, dynamic ecosystem,"[12] of which we can think of Selkirk's rat-ridden island as being a part. And it is on the latter island that we see the flowering of the figure of rats as seafarers. For instance, Rogers in the above quote notes that the rats that terrorized Selkirk were the descendants of those that "had got ashore from ships that put in there for wood and water." They were not simply vermin to get rid of, but also fellow castaways and travelers; as Samuel G. Goodrich, a nineteenth-century American author of children's books who retold Alexander Selkirk's story, puts it, "[the rats] were not natives and children of the soil. At least, their ancestors were foreigners, as well as Alexander."[13] Rats may be absent from colonial grand narratives such as *Robinson Crusoe*, but it is remarkable that there are many references to their sea travels once we look for descriptions of them in newspapers, articles, and eyewitness accounts. For instance, as an 1857 article in the *Quarterly Review* put it:

> Scarcely a ship leaves a port for a distant voyage but it takes in its complement of rats as regularly as the passengers, and in this manner the destructive little animal has not only distributed himself over the entire globe, but, like an enterprising traveller, continually passes from one country to another. The colony of four-footed depredators, which ships itself free of expense, makes, for instance, a voyage to Calcutta, whence many of the body will again go to sea, and land perhaps at some uninhabited island where the vessel may have touched for water. In this manner many a hoary old wanderer has circumnavigated the globe oftener than Captain Cook, and set his paws on twenty different shores.[14]

Though Defoe removes rats from his colonial narrative, they are here characterized as master colonizers, far more enterprising than the Europeans on whose ships they traveled. In reality, Crusoe's uninhabited island would have had rats' paw-prints all over it, long before he spotted a man's footprint on the sand along the shore.

In the European history of navigation, two species of rats made their name as seafarers: the black rat and the brown rat. Black rats—with the Latin name *rattus rattus*—were said to have arrived in Europe in the Middle Ages, though archaeological evidence suggests that they were already around in Europe before the Roman period.[15] They are the rats who had till recently been held responsible for causing the Black Death in the fourteenth century.[16] Ship rat references, made prior to the eighteenth century, would be to black rats. According to the Peruvian-born Spanish chronicler Inca Garcilaso de la Vega, black rats arrived in South America during the time of Blasco Núñez Vela, the first viceroy to Peru (1544–46). After that, cities on the coast of Peru were devastated by "such an infinite number of Rats" that "no Cat dares to contend or deal with them."[17] It is interesting to observe that *A Waggoner of the South Sea* (1685), a book of nautical charts and sailing directions of the South American Pacific Coast made by the London mapmaker William Hack, includes three maps containing warnings about rats, with precise instructions on where to anchor. For instance, to anchor in the port of Carquin in northern Peru, "you must ride where the Anchor is drawn in 7 fathom water; if you should ride to windward, you would sustain damage by the Rats to your cables"[18] (see figure 6.1, the instruction on the top left of the map). Hack's work, beautifully colored and decorated, is based on a Spanish book of sea charts, captured by an English privateer, Bartholomew Sharp, from a Spanish vessel in 1680. These charts were strategically important, and it has been speculated that they helped Sharp to procure a full pardon for his pirating activities from Charles II when he presented the book to the king.[19] The charts were well-guarded state secrets, which importantly included the whereabouts of rats; without them, a ship might stray into a rat-infested port without any preparation, with devastating consequences.

Brown rats, the bigger and chubbier cousins of black rats, arrived in Europe at the beginning of the eighteenth century, presumably from high central Asia.[20] In Britain, they were so successful that they quickly drove out the smaller black rats and established themselves as the "common" rat.[21] This led the British to identify themselves with black rats: Englishness under threat from the invasion of foreigners—but that is another story.[22] Two of the names given to brown rats brand them as alien seafarers. First, their scientific name *Rattus norvegicus*, or the "Norway rat," comes from the belief that they were "brought to England originally from Norway in ships trading from that country."[23] Another is the "Hanover rat": they were said to have come from Germany on board the ship that brought the "foreign" king, George I of the House of Hanover (reign: 1714–27), to England.[24] The name evokes a mental picture of the fateful day on which the brown rats were "seen swimming in a shoal from the ship to the shore."[25]

During the latter part of the eighteenth and first half of the nineteenth century, brown rats overshadowed and supplanted black rats as the dominant species of ship rat, to the point that many believed that black rats were being driven to near extinction in Europe and the many

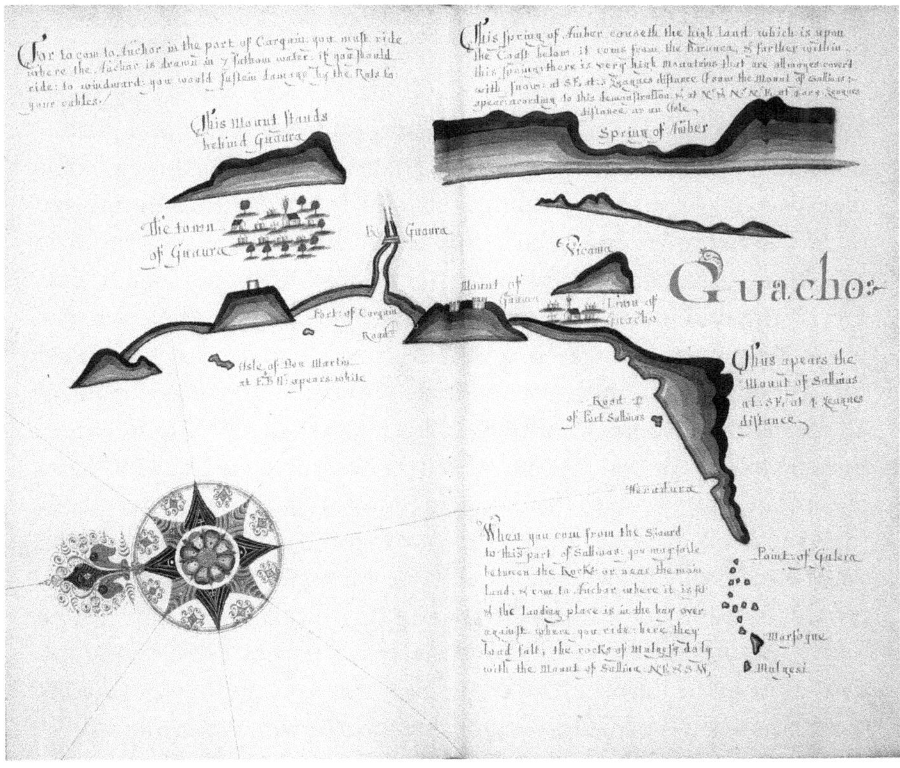

Figure 6.1 The map of Guacho in *A Waggoner of the South Sea describing the sea coast from Acapulco to Albermarle Isle, made by William Hack at the signe of great Britaine and Ireland in Wapping. Anno 1685*. P/33 (94). © National Maritime Museum, Greenwich, London.

other parts of the world visited by brown rats.[26] This makes the brown rat a totem animal of the British colonizers, as its arrival and maritime hegemony coincided with that of the British Empire. Having said that, black rats seem to have made a comeback at some point during the latter half of the nineteenth century. For instance, Henry Moseley on HMS *Challenger* was surprised to see that the rats who boarded the ship while it was moored at Bermuda were all black rats, contrary to the widespread belief that they had disappeared (see the introduction to this volume).[27] According to I. A. E. Atkinson, this change was "in some way associated with the change from sailing ships to steamships, helped perhaps by the warm micro-climate of the steamer's engine room giving an advantage to ship rats which are less tolerant of cold than Norway rats."[28] Furthermore, when both species coexisted in the same ship, they would occupy different quarters to avoid competition,[29] and the larger size of steamships must have made it easier for black rats to find their space.

Black or brown, rats followed colonizers everywhere they went. They did not merely cause havoc in European settlements and plantations; they also presented a significant hazard to the wildlife of the colonial space. Closer to home, Puffin Island, off the coast of Wales, became the home of brown rats "who swam ashore after a shipwreck in 1816," and whose descendants drove away a large breeding population of puffins by the mid-nineteenth century.[30] The same happened all over the world: where rats swam ashore, they destroyed birds' nests, threatened the lives of native competitors and other vulnerable animals, and ate up all the natural resources available. In his 1864 article in *Natural History Review*, Joseph Dalton Hooker, a British botanist and Darwin's close friend, drew attention to the damaging impact that the plants and animals introduced by Europeans were having in colonies and elsewhere, and he mentions brown rats as a prime example. He does so by citing this striking quote from a letter by a New Zealand naturalist: "The native (Maori) saying is, 'as the white man's rat has driven away the native rat, so the European fly drives away our own, and the clover kills our fern, so will the Maoris disappear before the white man himself.'"[31] This native saying, which can be easily read as the Maori's attack on the European invasion of, and settlement in, his native land, was instead used to substantiate the evolutionary theory of the survival of the fittest. According to Herbert Spencer, the disappearance of Maoris and native races at the hands of European newcomers neatly demonstrated the "universal tendency of the superior to overrun the habitats of the inferior."[32] Darwin similarly discusses the inevitability of the extinction of the weaker "Races of Man," such as Maoris: "The New Zealander seems conscious of this parallelism, for he compares his future fate with that of the native rat now almost exterminated by the European rat."[33] Both scientists, then, accept the parallelism between brown rats and Europeans. In ship rats, the Europeans came to see their own shadow as the deadliest invasive species.

Water Economy

J. M. Coetzee's novel *The Childhood of Jesus* (2013) features dockyard warehouses swarming with rats. When Simon, a newly employed stevedore, complains about the situation, the foreman says to him: "Wherever you have ships you have rats. Wherever you have warehouses you have rats. Where our species flourishes rats flourish too."[34] This makes a striking contrast with the way in which the prosperity of Crusoe's island depends on the absence of rats. Here, the bags of grains spoiled by rats do not signify the collapse of a human-managed agricultural economy, but are a sign of homo-rattus multispecies flourishing. The foreman goes on to say:

> Yes, they consume some of the grain we offload. Yes, there is spoilage in the warehouse. But there is spoilage all along the way: in the fields, in the trains, in the ships, in the warehouses, in the bakers' storerooms. There is no point in getting upset about spoilage. Spoilage is part of life.[35]

The foreman's philosophical view on the nature of grain spoilage provides an excellent reference point for considering the human-rat relationship formed on board ship. It is true that the ship, like Crusoe's island, is a "closed" system, in which human survival depends on the management of limited food and other resources. Measures thus needed to be taken to keep the number of vermin down, with the help of ratcatchers, human and nonhuman (e.g., cats, dogs, and mongooses). However, rats, though highly destructive, were hardly the only cause of wastage in the ship's stores. The provisions were spoiled by a wide range of other factors, such as the heat and dampness in the ship's hold, the accidental incursion of salt water, mold, and other vermin.[36] Traditionally, the purser (who was in charge of the ship's stores) was allowed to keep an eighth of the ship's provisions to balance his accounts, "in full indemnity for Waste and for destruction by vermin."[37] That is to say, the ship's economy made allowance for rats and their agency. The famed destructiveness of rats also represented the collective force of vermin on board ship, which accelerated the perishability of the ship's provisions.[38]

In a ship, rats and humans coexisted and flourished together by sharing the danger of the sea. Of course, rats were a potential danger to the safety of the crew and of the ship itself. They would nibble passengers' toes and other body parts if given a chance, and this provided a basis for many a shipborne gothic tale, such as that of a stowaway devoured by rats while hiding in the wellhole of a ship.[39] Rats' actions also triggered many types of surprising accidents: for instance, rats could set fire to a ship by stealing a lighted candle (they ate tallows) or nibbling at friction matches, and such incidents were by no means uncommon.[40] And if a ship mysteriously sprung a leak, the rats were the first ones to be suspected of having caused it by "gnawing a hole in the vessel's side."[41] And yet, the awareness of the destructive and mischievous propensities of seafaring rats curiously coexisted with the belief that the presence of rats was a sign of a ship's seaworthiness, as encapsulated in the phrase "rats abandon a sinking ship." James Rodwell, in his book *The Rat: Its History & Destructive Character* (1858), points out a surprising and yet "well-known fact" that "[ship rats] do not sink the vessels by boring holes so as to admit the water"; although rats "may gnaw their way through the interior of the ship, they never pass through the sides." This fact, according to Rodwell, has "led to strong discussions as to the reasoning powers of the rat."[42] Rats, being intelligent, were trusted not to do any damage to the ship that would compromise their own safety at sea.

Indeed, the confined space of a ship was a good place for humans to witness the famed sagacity of rats. In particular, water casks provided the best opportunities to observe this, as rats require daily access to water, and will do anything to get to it. G. F. W. Hope recalls witnessing a trick used by rats to extract water out of a cask:

> In the tropics, on a fine bright night, I have seen rats on the water-butts which stood on the deck, putting their tails into the bung-holes, then drawing them out and sucking them. . . . In a wooden vessel it is impossible for the rats to get any fresh water, unless they resort to such devilish tricks: in an iron vessel it is easier for them to get water, as the vessel sweats and they can lick the sweat off with their tongues.[43]

Rats' need of water is so great that in rainy weather they would boldly come on deck to drink, and "even ascend the rigging to sip the moisture which lies in the folds of the sails."[44] When there was no other source of water available, they would attack water casks, which made them dangerous animals to have on board. To quote one writer, "Mice, although they are disgusting, troublesome, mischievous, and noisy, are not so much to be dreaded at sea as rats; for they require so little drink, that no apprehension is entertained for the safety of the water casks."[45]

In 1879, the science journal *Nature* published a series of articles and correspondences on the topic of "Intellect in Brutes." In this thread, rats' tricks to drink water from the ship's water casks became a point of discussion. Arthur Nicols, the author of popular zoology books, reported a story he had heard from a ship's carpenter: "In the old days before the use of iron tanks on board ship became general, the rats used to attack the water casks, cutting the stave so thin that they could suck the water through the wood, without actually making a hole in it." Nicols urged the reader to submit information to "substantiate" this, as "it would have an important bearing on the question under consideration."[46] If proven true, the episode would demonstrate that rats have a "reasoning faculty"—that is, the ability to drink water in such a way as to prevent leakage and prevent detection, to conserve water, and to secure regular access to fresh water.

To Nicols's call for further evidence, E. J. A'Court Smith, the geologist, responded with his own experience of a rat incident dating back to 1840. He was on a ship traveling from Sydney to London via Madras. Three weeks after leaving Madras, it was discovered that "as many as ten or twelve butts had been perforated by rats" and were leaking. While two or three of these casks were completely empty from leakage, "the remainder contained ullages from about half to a few gallons," suggesting the rats' careful usage of water. The fresh damage showed that the rats had perforated the water cask "so as to cause a slight weeping," and Smith suggests that they were very systematic about where to gnaw. The rats, who must have come on board in Madras, had been secretly sucking water from the casks for three weeks, without draining away the water at once, though this activity led to significant leakage and thus discovery.

This is a remarkable episode, but what makes it even more so is the ways in which the ship's crew dealt with this rat incident. Instead of going on the rampage to kill off all the rats on board, they decided to provide tins and tubs full of water for rats to drink, throughout the rest of the journey.[47] Charles Darwin was another reader who responded to Nicols's article, and he reports a similar account of the sailors on a ship providing rats with water:

> Capt. Wickham, when First Lieutenant on board H.M.S. *Beagle*, told me that when he was a midshipman it was his duty, on

> one of the king's ships to see that certain vessels on deck were always kept full of water, in order to prevent the rats gnawing holes through the water casks, and that through such holes nearly all the water in a cask would leak away.[48]

John Clements Wickham (1798–1864), explorer and naval officer, entered the navy as a midshipman in 1812, so this episode refers to a practice of the early nineteenth century. Indeed, it is important to note that Hope's and Nicols's rat episodes are both set in "the old days" before the advent of iron vessels and iron tanks, which became widely used only after 1840.[49] "The Rats and Water Casks" is thus a fable about the good old days and old shipborne customs: once upon a time, taking care of a ship included taking care of the rats on board, and there was a crew member who was put in charge of this. The new age of iron tanks and vessels meant that there was less need for humans to guard their supply of water, and this is not just because iron tanks were more durable than wooden casks. As Hope noted in the quote above, an iron vessel made it easier for rats to get water, as "the vessel sweats and they can lick the sweat off with their tongues." The water cask ceased to be a place where humans and rats met to negotiate the use of shared resources.

However, even in the era of iron vessels, rats' access to water was not necessarily guaranteed; therefore, there was bound to be rat-related damage, wherever water was stored. Robert White Stevens's *On the Stowage of Ships and their Cargoes,* which was originally published in 1858 and soon became the standard authority on the topic, acknowledges this: rats, when driven by their "unconquerable thirst," will attack the waterways, injuring the cargo and putting "the lives of all on board . . . in jeopardy." Therefore, Stevens recommends that "where [rats] are so numerous it seems better to give them a daily supply of water rather than risk such perils."[50] Likewise, the *Nautical Magazine* in 1875 reports:

> We have seen a leaden pipe belonging to Mr. Inman completely gnawed through by rats in their endeavours to get at the water—nothing seems to stop them. On board a ship on one occasion, some rat-holes were found, when the ship got into dry dock, eaten right through to the copper, and to prevent a recurrence of the same thing, a daily allowance of water was served out to them on the hatches on the 'tween decks, and they used

> to come as regularly to drink it as if they had signed articles, and considered it their right.[51]

Rats and sailors were bonded by a secret contract, signed with water, a language that rats understood and abided by. Sailors accepted the impossibility of getting rid of all the rats from the ship, and instead learned to live and share resources with them.

Jules Skotnes-Brown, in an article on ship rats, gives an interesting example of a late eighteenth-century rat encounter: "Rear-Admiral Beaufort of the HMS *Woolwich* . . . was one morning awoken by the disturbing sensation of the cold nose of a rat licking his lips."[52] This unfortunate episode for the admiral is yet another example in which rats tried to get water or even some moisture on board the ship. Human bodies were an obvious source of water for rats—and in the cases of shipwrecks and other maritime disasters, rats conversely proved to be a lifesaver: the survivors, who were "fortunate" to find a rat or two, ate them to ease the pangs of hunger and thirst.[53] In many more ways than one, the lives and deaths of seafaring rats were entwined with those of their human counterparts. Rats recognised that ships contained a water supply system, and thus were suitable for their habitation. Or, to put it another way, rats trusted sailors to be part of such a system, and were happy to follow them across the salty waters.

Rattus-Homo-Machine

Rats were not merely the colonizer's shadow, or vermin to be dealt with in the course of a ship's journey. They were fellow travelers, whose maritime existence humans shared and identified with. The precarious life of a ship rat inevitably overlapped with that of a sailor. For instance, William Richardson, who served in the Royal Navy in the early nineteenth century, recalls how infested with rats his ship HMS *Tromp* was, and how the crew, with the help of a professional ratcatcher, killed all of them except one.[54] The only remaining one—"a large rat"—was eventually spotted in the dirt-tub and shot by a carpenter called Oades. In narrating this episode, Richardson evokes a graphic image of the killing—"he almost touched [the rat] with the muzzle of the piece before he fired"—and goes on to add that "little did poor Lewis Oades think at this time it would be his fate to be shot, and which actually happened three years after, on board the *Téméraire* at the Battle of Trafalgar."[55] The end of the rat foreshadows that of the carpenter, whom Richardson describes as "a chubby little fellow."[56] Conversely, the rat, in Richardson's narrative, was transformed into an English mariner, who was unceremoniously shot during a historic battle.

Ship rats, who accompanied human travels, were also an important part of the fast-growing global networks. I started this chapter with the image of rats abandoning a ship on a moonlit night. An 1863 editorial in *The Times* similarly reports an account of rats abandoning a ship for another ship, but the reason for this desertion was very different. The ship which the rats decided to move into was a fruit ship from the Mediterranean: "The captain, who was still on board, was waked at midnight by his mate, and asked to step on deck as quietly as he could. . . . 'Look there!' whispered the mate, pointing to the rope, which in darkness seemed to be slowly moving towards the fruit ship. It was alive with rats, which in a continuous stream were migrating from the empty ship to the stranger, whose fragrance told the tale of its delicious freight." This rope, "alive with rats," was then used by the editorial to discuss global migration: "That is the very spectacle we are now witnessing on a world-wide scale. The hawser is across the Atlantic, and in one incessant, endless train, hundreds of thousands of our fellow-citizens are passing to a richer continent."[57] Unlike Conrad's ship, which was abandoned by rats and sank, the ship here becomes connected with other ships by ropes, representing the worldwide networks of ships, communications, and commerce, across which rats freely moved at will. In their search for richer food sources, rats wished to be part of the global circulation of goods and people. Just like millions of humans at that time, who traveled across the ocean, driven by the promise of a better life, rats were willing participants in the British Empire and other international networks, and embodied their energy and movement.

The title of my chapter is "Rattus-Homo-Machine," which I think captures well the centuries-long human-rat relationship. On the one hand, it refers to rats' ability to take advantage of the ship as the Homo-Machine, to attach themselves parasitically to it, and to become part of its apparatus. As such, it was a deadly colonizing machine. On the other hand, it also represents humans' capacity to embrace rats as important members of this ship's company, without whose cooperation humans could not operate the machine properly. Thus the rats, clever enough to escape cats and traps, had to be reasoned with, in order to safeguard the seaworthiness of the ship that they shared. The following quote from the entry on rats in the *British Cyclopedia of Natural History* (1837) shows the difference in attitude towards rats in the nineteenth century:

> Every animal, indeed, which follows man in all his migrations, and multiplies in proportion as his numbers multiply, is always useful to him. Most of these animals are, no doubt, annoying, and many of them are positively offensive; but, in all cases where they are so, man will find that he himself is generally to blame.[58]

They were accepted as fellow travelers, and the troubles they caused were part of the package that humans gracefully had to endure and deal with in exchange for having their company. The disappearance of rats as seafarers thus cannot be solely attributed to the new understanding of rats as vectors of rat fleas and disease. The Homo-Machine kept evolving, in such a way that rats could no longer be part of the machine. Armed with solid metals, humans became less worried about the rats' damage to the ship, and the human-rat relationship, sustained by the need to cater for rats' needs, became unnecessary and soon forgotten.

This abandonment of the duty to care for rats as passengers arguably occurred when it was most needed. Transoceanic steamers came into wide use in the latter half of the nineteenth century, and played a significant role in spreading the plague; to quote Myron Echenberg, "modern steamship navigation allowed *Yersinia pestis* free and especially rapid passage around the world in the bodies of infected rat and flea stowaways."[59] The shift from sailing ships to steamships also facilitated the resurgence of black rats on board ship. These factors, combined with the increasing size of steamships, must have aided the explosion of the ship rat population. The rats, however, would not have been able to aggravate the pandemic without their association with the Homo-Machine. If ship rats were then found "positively offensive," it was humans who were to blame.

In the twentieth century, a maritime community that I have called Homo-Rattus-Machine collapsed. Michel Serres, in his book *Biogea* (2010), dramatizes the rivalry and deadly fight to death between rats and sailors on a ship. This seems to me to be a perfect illustration of the human-rat relationship after the nineteenth century. It is a battle between the two most deadly invasive species, "dynamic, expansive, [whose] populations readily flood the world." [60] In Serres's episode, the rats triumph over the sailors, evoking the image of a ghost ship, in which they exhaust all the resources and turn against each other: rats "no longer had anything for their teeth to gnaw on—hawser, barrel, dried cod, biscuits, or sailors—they would end up, starving, dying with open mouths, rabid, or by killing each other so as to eat one another, like cursed shipwrecked people."[61] The rats' fate is of course our own: that of the invasive species that is voraciously consuming the earth's resources till there will be nothing left for us to consume. Serres thus asks:

> Which species, finally, uniquely victorious, will reign on this ship . . . on this island I call the Biogea? What will happen if one species, ours for instance, prevails? Who will it eat then, if not its fellow men? . . . How then do we control the propagations of these living things, small, swarming, often caused by our own transportation?[62]

In this context, we may regard the nineteenth-century rat-human maritime community as having contained an alternative vision of the Biogea, in which humans traveled with rats, in which killing them and living with them did not necessarily contradict each other. What has been lost is a better working order between species, invasive or otherwise, for each other's survival, and to protect the ship's resources. Indeed, would we really want to be on board a ship totally abandoned by rats? Such a ship would be unsuitable for any living thing to trust its life to.

Notes

1. Conrad, *Youth*, 19–20.
2. "Shipping Intelligence," *Glasgow Herald*, March 19, 1883: 8.
3. Hope, "Friend of Conrad," 36.
4. Lynteris, "Introduction," 3.
5. "Lloyd Vapore Austriaco—Egyptian Quarantine and Steam Navigation in the Red Sea," *Times*, December 15, 1838: 3.
6. Lynteris, *Framing Animals*. Also see Zinsser, *Rats, Lice and History*.
7. *OED Online*, s.v. "rat, n.1.," accessed July 19, 2020, www.oed.com/view/Entry/158382.
8. "'Like Rats Fleeing.'"
9. Rogers, "Cruising Voyage," 432.
10. Cole, *Imperfect Creatures*, 146–47; emphasis in the text. See also Cole, "Plagues, Poisons, and Dead Rats," for further discussions about the role of rats in *Robinson Crusoe*.
11. Ibid., 146.

12. Ibid., 147.
13. Goodrich, *Story of Alexander Selkirk*, 89.
14. "Rats," *Quarterly Review*, 125.
15. Rackham, "Rattus Rattus."
16. A recent scientific study found that it was not black rats but more likely "human ectoparasites, like body lice and human fleas," that were the cause of the Black Death. Dean et al., "Human Ectoparasites," 1304.
17. Vega, *Royal Commentaries of Peru*, 384.
18. The map of Guacho, in "A Waggoner of the South Sea," National Maritime Museum, P/33 (94). Two other ports with rat references are Pacasmayo (P/33[80]) and Truxilo (P/33[83]); all ports are in northern Peru.
19. Howse and Thrower, *Buccaneer's Atlas*, 2.
20. Burt, *Rat*, 30.
21. Rodwell, *Rat*, 11.
22. See Waterton, "Notes," 212, in which the author argues that the brown rat, since its arrival, "has nearly worried every individual of the original rat of Great Britain," driving them to extinction. Rudyard Kipling's political fable "Below the Mill Dam" (1902) also features "a genuine old English black rat, a breed which, report says, is rapidly diminishing before the incursions of the brown variety." Kipling, *Traffics and Discoveries*, 287.
23. Swaine, *Universal Directory*, 14.
24. Waterton, "Notes," 211–12.
25. Rodwell, *Rat*, 13.
26. Audubon and Bachman, *Quadrupeds of North America*, 27.
27. Moseley, *Notes by a Naturalist*, 515.
28. Atkinson, "Spread of the Ship Rat," 460.
29. "Rats," *Shields Daily Gazette*, April 26, 1880: 3.
30. Brian Moynahan, "The Isle of Rats," *Sunday Times*, April 11, 1971: 8.
31. J. Haast, quoted in Hooker, "Note on the replacement of species," 126.
32. Spencer, *Principles of Biology*, 1: 389.
33. Darwin, *Descent of Man*, 1: 239–40.
34. Coetzee, *Childhood of Jesus*, 133.
35. Ibid., 134.
36. Nagai, "Vermin Writing," 64–65.
37. Great Britain, Admiralty, *Regulations and Instructions*, 5. Also see Macdonald, *Feeding Nelson's Navy*, 13–14.
38. Nagai, "Vermin Writing," 65.
39. "A Man Devoured by Rats," *Times*, April 24, 1861: 9.
40. "Mischief Wrought by Rats on Board Ship," *Edinburgh Evening News*, October 29, 1875: 3; "Rats Set a Steamship on Fire," *Newark Advocate*, August 3, 1877: 4.
41. From the entry for the *Hero*, foundered off the Isle of Wight on March 28, 1880, in *Shipwrecks*, 185. Also see Nagai, "Vermin Writing," 63–64.
42. Rodwell, *Rat*, 162–63
43. Hope, "Friend of Conrad," 25.
44. "Rats," *Quarterly Review*, 126. Also Stevens, *On the Stowage*, 158.
45. Griffith, *Our Neighbourhood*, 296.
46. Nicols, "Intellect in Brutes," 433.
47. A'Court Smith, "Rats and Water Casks," 529.
48. Darwin, "Rats and Water-Casks," 481.
49. Plumbly, "Royal Navy's Difficulties," 434.
50. Stevens, *Stowage of Ships*, 158.
51. "Rats on Board Ship," 982.
52. Skotnes-Brown, "Scurrying Seafarers," 7.
53. "Living on Rats at Sea," *Edinburgh Evening News*, December 29 ,1887, 4.
54. Richardson, *Mariner of England*, 197.
55. Ibid., 198.
56. Ibid., 197.
57. *Times*, December 4, 1863: 8
58. "Rats," in Partington, *British Cyclopedia of Natural History*, 527.
59. Echenberg, "Pestis Redux," 436.
60. Serres, *Biogea*, 106.
61. Ibid., 98.
62. Ibid., 106.

Bibliography

Audubon, John James, and John Bachman. *The Quadrupeds of North America.* Vol. 2. New York: V. G. Audubon, 1851.

A'Court Smith, E. J. "Rats and Water Casks." *Nature* 19 (1879): 529.

Atkinson, I. A. E. "Spread of the Ship Rat (*Rattus r. rattus* L.) in New Zealand." *Journal of the Royal Society of New Zealand* 3, no. 3 (1973): 457–72.

"A Waggoner of the South Sea describing the sea coast from Acapulco to Albermarle Isle, made by William Hack at the signe of great Britaine and Ireland in Wapping. Anno 1685." National Maritime Museum, London (NMM), P/33.

Burt, Jonathan. *Rat.* London: Reaktion, 2006.

Coetzee, J. M. *The Childhood of Jesus.* London: Vintage Books, 2014.

Cole, Lucinda. *Imperfect Creatures: Vermin, Literature, and the Sciences of Life, 1600–1740.* Ann Arbor: University of Michigan Press, 2016.

———. "Plagues, Poisons, and Dead Rats: A Multispecies History." In *The Palgrave Handbook of Animals and Literature*, edited by Susan McHugh, Robert McKay, and John Miller, 589–603. Cham: Palgrave Macmillan, 2018.

Conrad, Joseph. *Youth; The End of the Tether.* Harmondsworth, UK: Penguin, 1975.

Darwin, Charles. *The Descent of Man, and Selection in Relation to Sex.* 2 vols. London: John Murray, 1871.

———. "Rats and Water-Casks." *Nature* 19 (March 27, 1879): 481.

Dean, Katharine R., Fabienne Krauer, Lars Walløe, Ole Christian Lingjaerde, Barbara Bramanti, Nils Chr. Stenseth, and Boris V. Schmid. "Human Ectoparasites and the Spread of Plague in Europe During the Second Pandemic." *Proceedings of the National Academy of Sciences of the United States* 115, no. 6 (2018): 1304–9.

Echenberg, Myron. "Pestis Redux: The Initial Years of the Third Bubonic Plague Pandemic, 1894–1901." *Journal of World History* 13, no. 2 (Fall 2002): 429–49.

Goodrich, Samuel G. *The Story of Alexander Selkirk.* Philadelphia: H. F. Anners, 1841.

Great Britain, Admiralty. *Regulations and instructions for the pursers of His Majesty's ships and vessels.* 2nd ed. London: Winchester & Co., 1825.

Griffith, Mary. *Our Neighbourhood: Or, Letters on Horticulture and Natural Phenomena, Interspersed with Opinions on Domestic and Moral Economy.* New York: E. Bliss, 1831.

Hooker, J. D. "Note on the replacement of species in the colonies and elsewhere." *Natural History Review* (January 1864): 123–27.

Hope, G. F. W. "Friend of Conrad." In *Conrad Between the Lines: Documents in a Life*, edited by Gene M. Moore, Allan H. Simmons, and J. H. Stape, 1–56. Amsterdam: Rodopi, 2000.

Howse, Derek, and Norman J. W. Thrower, eds. *A Buccaneer's Atlas: Basil Ringrose's South Sea Waggoner.* Berkeley: University of California Press, 1992.

Kipling, Rudyard. *Traffics and Discoveries.* Edited with an introduction and notes by Hermione Lee. Harmondsworth, UK: Penguin Books, 1987.

"'Like Rats Fleeing a Sinking Ship': A History." *Word History* (blog). Accessed July 19, 2020. https://www.merriam-webster.com/words-at-play/like-rats-fleeing-a-sinking-ship-history.

Lynteris, Christos, ed. *Framing Animals as Epidemic Villains: Histories of Non-Human Disease Vectors.* Cham: Palgrave Macmillan, 2019.

———. "Introduction: Infectious Animals and Epidemic Blame." In *Framing Animals as Epidemic Villains*, edited by Christos Lynteris, 1–26.

Macdonald, Janet. *Feeding Nelson's Navy: The True Story of Food at Sea in the Georgian Era*. London: Chatham Publishing, 2004.

Moseley, Henry Nottidge. *Notes by a Naturalist: An Account of Observations made during the Voyage of H.M.S. "Challenger" round the world in the years 1872–1876*. A New and Revised Edition. London: John Murray, 1892.

Nagai, Kaori. "Vermin Writing." *Journal for Maritime Research* 22, nos. 1–2 (2020): 59–74.

Nicols, Arthur. "Intellect in Brutes." *Nature* 19 (1879): 433.

Partington, Charles F., ed. *The British Cyclopedia of Natural History*. 3 vols. London: W. S. Orr & Co., 1837.

Plumbly, Andy. "The Royal Navy's Difficulties with Implementing Iron Water Tanks, About 1815 to 1840." *Mariner's Mirror* 106, no. 4 (2020): 422–35.

Rackham, James. "*Rattus rattus*: The Introduction of the Black Rat into Britain," *Antiquity* 53, no. 208 (1979): 112–20.

"Rats." *Quarterly Review* 101, no. 201 (January and April 1857): 123–41.

"Rats on Board Ship." *Nautical Magazine* 44, no. 12 (December 1875): 982–89.

Richardson, William. *A Mariner of England: An Account of the Career of William Richardson from Cabin Boy in the Merchant Service to Warrant Officer in the Royal Navy [1780 to 1819] as Told by Himself*. Edited by Colonel Spencer Childers. London: John Murray, 1908.

Rodwell, James. *The Rat: Its History & Destructive Character*. London: G. Routledge & Co., 1858.

Rogers, Woodes. "A Cruising Voyage Round the World." In *Travel Writing 1700–1830: An Anthology*, edited by Elizabeth A. Bohls and Ian Duncan, 430–33. Oxford: Oxford World's Classics, 2005.

Serres, Michel. *Biogea*. Minneapolis: Univocal, 2010.

Shipwrecks. Merchant Ships—Foundered and Missing. 1st January 1873 to 16th May 1880. London: George Edward Eyre and William Spottiswoode, 1880. Proquest U. K. Parliamentary Papers, House of Commons Parliamentary Papers Online. Accessed October 16, 2021. https://parlipapers.proquest.com/parlipapers/docview/t70.d75.1880-056644.

Skotnes-Brown, Jules. "Scurrying Seafarers: Shipboard Rats, Plague, and the Land/Sea Border." *Journal of Global History* (2022): 1–23. doi:10.1017/S1740022822000158.

Spencer, Herbert. *The Principles of Biology*. 2 vols. London: Williams and Norgate, 1864.

Stevens, Robert White. *On the Stowage of Ships and their Cargoes*. London: Longmans, 1858.

Swaine, Thomas. *The Universal Directory for Taking Alive, or Destroying, Rats and Mice*. London: J. Bew, 1783.

Vega, Garcilaso de la. *The Royal Commentaries of Peru in Two Parts. Rendered into English by Sir. Paul Rycaut*. London: M. Flesher, 1688.

Waterton, Charles. "Notes on the History and Habits of the Brown, or Grey, Rat." In *Essays on Natural History, Chiefly Ornithology*, 210–18. London: Longman, Orme, Brown, Green, & Longsman, 1838.

Zinsser, Hans. *Rats, Lice and History*. London: George Routledge & Sons, 1935.

CHAPTER 7

"BELOVED MEMBER OF OUR TEAM"

The Sled Dogs of the St. Roch

Lea Edgar

How did sled dogs—bred on land and often by Inuit—fare when taken into such a foreign environment as a ship? Donna Haraway, writing on the transporting of Puerto Rican "Satos" dogs to the United States, describes the airplane as "an instrument in a series of subject-transforming technologies. The dogs who come out of the belly of the plane are subject to a different social contract from the one they were born into."[1] This could also be said of the sled dogs of the *St. Roch*, a floating police detachment of the Royal Canadian Mounted Police (RCMP) that operated in the Canadian Arctic during the early twentieth century. Likely having never experienced a ship before, the dogs were stepping into a new relationship with different humans, one with unique rules far different from the ones with which they were raised. On board the *St. Roch*, they underwent a series of subject-transformations, crossing the boundary between land and sea, settler and Indigenous, and human and dog.

This chapter explores the life and career of the *St. Roch*'s sled dogs and the unique relationship they formed with the human crew. The *St. Roch* was built in British Columbia in 1928, captained by a Norwegian immigrant, crewed by farm boys from across Canada, and guided by Inuit. The ship was the first vessel to sail the Northwest Passage from west to east, the first to complete the passage in one season, and the first to circumnavigate North America. Those were the *St. Roch*'s claims to fame, but its primary role in the Arctic was to carry out police and government duties among the settlers and Inuit. This included such tasks as taking the census, delivering mail, and investigating crimes, as well as transporting the sick, prisoners, and Inuit children to and from residential schools. To access the remote Arctic communities, the RCMP required purpose-built patrol vessels such as the *St. Roch*. The ship and its crew were actively working in the Arctic between 1928 and 1954.

The vessel is now permanently preserved and accessible to the public at the Vancouver Maritime Museum in Vancouver, British Columbia. The *St. Roch* is a not only a museum ship but also a National Historic Site visited by thousands of people every year. Nonetheless, the ship's sled dogs represent the overlooked nonhuman crew and their connection to the long-term effects of the police presence in the Canadian Arctic. The purpose of the dogs, how they lived, how they were treated, and their relationships with human partners deserve investigation and reveal an interesting cultural entanglement. By examining both published and unpublished records created by the crew—including reports, diaries, memoirs, and photographs—this chapter seeks to fill in those gaps in historical interpretation.

In our exploration into the human-canine relationships on the *St. Roch*, it is important to bear in mind that the sled dogs were part of a broader process of Arctic colonization. The *St. Roch*'s dogs are examples of the *Qallunaat* (non-Inuit) cultural appropriation of Inuit dogsledding and animal husbandry. In addition, the animals are symbolic of the civilizing mission of the RCMP on behalf of the Canadian state. At the time the *St. Roch* patrolled the Arctic waters, the government of Canada was gradually pushing Inuit into settlements, thereby endangering the future of the indigenous sled dogs. That is to say, they were much more than a simple mode of transportation for the ship's crew; theirs was a time of transition towards the "social conformity to the new political economy" in the Arctic.[2] When one examines the *St. Roch*'s dogs, one must recognize that they come from a long line of historical happenings. Their story unfurled a problematic future, for both human and nonhuman Arctic animals, that is truly apparent with the gift of hindsight.

The preservation of the *St. Roch* vessel as a National Historic Site of Canada shifts its purpose from a police patrol vessel to a place of remembering. As North American museums evolve past glorifying the accomplishments of colonists, so too must we broaden the *St. Roch*'s story to reflect its true complexities. As part of the vessel's interpretive evolution, the sled dogs must be included to inform the story not only of the RCMP, but of all Arctic residents.

Recently, more documents have come to light detailing unsettling stories of the alleged systematic killing of Inuit sled dogs by the RCMP and other government officials, which took place between the 1950s and 1970s. As Susan McHugh demonstrates in her powerful analyses of these stories, Inuit sled dogs were "a source of livelihood, protection, and even identity" for Inuit communities, and therefore the killing signified not only the loss of working animals but also the obliteration of Indigenous knowledge and ways of life.[3] Importantly, these killings started when the sled dogs lost their importance as the chief means of transport (largely due to the advent of snowmobiles) and the government phased out sled dogs from official duties. Before this development, to quote McHugh, "there were RCMP members who owned and cared for sled dogs and clearly recognised [their] value."[4] The *St. Roch*'s time mostly predates the period in which the killings of sled dogs by the RCMP were said to have taken place. Moreover, though not every crew of the *St. Roch* was enamored with the "savage" Inuit sled dogs, and European sled dogs were used alongside them, these dogs were nevertheless important members of the ship and key to survival in the Arctic. Thus, the stories of the *St. Roch* present a rather different picture of the RCMP's relationship with the sled dogs, both Inuit and European: that of interspecies and intercultural coexistence and collaboration, formed through a shared service and life together in the Arctic.

The History of the RCMP and Sled Dogs

During the Alaskan Gold Rush in the late 1800s, the precursor to the Royal Canadian Mounted Police—the North West Mounted Police—attempted to maintain order among the influx of prospectors and fur traders in the Klondike. This was when the police force first began using dog sleds. Because the force originated in the western sub-Arctic, many Alaskan and Indigenous influences can be seen in early police dog sledding techniques. Originally, all the dogs were purchased from outside of the Arctic regions, such as Labrador.[5] The North West Mounted Police eventually folded, and the RCMP was established in 1920. At this stage, the police started pushing into the Arctic regions to establish detachments further north.

In 1934, the RCMP set up a Siberian husky breeding station in Fort Norman, which was later transferred to Herschel Island. The officers tried to donate Siberian huskies to Inuit, but, for the most part, they did not want them.[6] Most detachments used sled dogs from the breeding station. The RCMP likely mixed some dog breeds. For example, there is a type called the Mackenzie husky that was a mix of sled dog breeds with the aboriginal Inuit sled dog.[7] The *St. Roch*'s captain, Henry Larsen, mentioned in his autobiography the Mackenzie breed being used in the 1930s:

> I had another pair of brothers, Mate and Coon. They were completely black Mackenzie dogs from further south and weighed about a hundred pounds each. The cold weather and the wind were hard on these two dogs, who were less endowed with fur than the Huskies.[8]

At the individual detachments, the police sometimes had their own breeding programs, where they, like the breeding station, likely mixed various dog breeds with the local aboriginal dogs. The dogs used by Inuit—the Inuit sled dogs—are classified as a landrace rather than a breed.[9] Inuit special constables were hired as guides and brought their own teams with them, most likely of "pure" Inuit sled dogs. Sometimes after a severe outbreak of disease, the RCMP brought in dogs from other provinces. These were likely the Newfoundland breed that can be seen in many of the *St. Roch* photographs.

Upon examination of the photographs from the many *St. Roch* voyages, one can notice the vast differences among and influences of various breeds on the RCMP sled dogs. All the dogs with folded or dropped ears are likely the Newfoundland breed.[10] We can also see Siberian husky influences. It is difficult to determine simply by analyzing photographs, but there are a large number of what appear to be "pure" Inuit sled dogs, such as the one Henry Larsen is holding in a photo from that time (figure 7.1).[11]

Perhaps the use of European sled dog breeds by the RCMP can be explained by comparing the disdain some of the police officers felt towards the indigenous dogs to their ideas about Inuit themselves. As

Figure 7.1 Henry Larsen poses with an example of an Inuit sled dog. Larsen and Olga, ca. 1928. HCWD-20-05, Vancouver Maritime Museum.

McHugh points out, the canine breed system "emerged as part of the process by which the world's people were for the first time scientifically catalogued according to race, sex and gender," and "this taxonomic process was inseparable from the imperialist politics it served."[12] That is to say, European dog breeds acted as a symbol of the power of the police over Inuit, while the perceived "wildness" of Inuit sled dogs was representative of the "wildness" of Inuit. The RCMP dogs (largely mixed sled dog breeds) were supposed to be friendlier and more manageable than the indigenous dogs. The dogs and their management became a distinguishing factor between the White Canadian police officers and the Indigenous peoples they were, in many respects, there to subjugate.

On the other hand, the Inuit sled dog, or *qimmiq* in Inuktitut, had its metaphorical paws placed on either side of the wild and domestic boundary. Although these dogs can be technically classified as domesticated, their relationship with their human partners was such that "wild" characteristics of the animal remained and were even *maintained* for reasons of survival in one of the world's most inhospitable places. In this sense, it is important that the *St. Roch* employed "pure" Inuit sled dogs with Inuit guides as part of the crew; many of the other RCMP dogs also had an Inuit sled dog lineage. Furthermore, these Arctic animals represented the innate "wildness" of all the sled dog breeds—that is, the toughness and resourcefulness necessary to survive in the Arctic.

Sled Dogs on Board and on Land

Sled dogs were brought on board the *St. Roch* primarily as a means of off-ship transportation in the Arctic. The *St. Roch* crew relied on them to deliver mail to the various inland communities and RCMP detachments in the North, and also to carry out police patrols, the many duties of which included: observing ice conditions, investigating complaints and crimes, observing living conditions in the area, and registering firearms. At this time, air travel, although it was used, was still unreliable, and there were no effective mechanized snow vehicles.

Hunting was another purpose for the dogs. Traditionally, Inuit used the dogs to find seals' breathing holes. The crew of the *St. Roch* followed this example. According to Larsen, only dogs and bears can find seal holes, and thus "[the dogs] are kept on a long leash and when they start to smell a hole they are pulled back and tied down so that they will not scare the seal away."[13] At the first sign of a polar bear, they were set loose and chased the animal down until the hunter could catch up and kill it.[14] Both hunting methods were Inuit in origin.

Dogs were also used for protection. They were always the first to warn if polar bears or wolves were nearby. Myles F. "Jack" Foster, in his audio memoir, telling a story about visiting a cache of food, recalls:

> We knew something was wrong before we arrived there by the way the dogs were acting. They appeared uneasy, looking from side to side, sniffing the air and whining. We stopped the team and checked our rifles. Andy said, the way the dogs are acting can mean only one thing. There's wolves about.[15]

In the presence of wolves, the dogs would put the crew on their guard to prevent an ambush. They were valuable to the crew for more reasons than just as a mode of transportation.

For many of the voyages of the *St. Roch*, none of the crew had any experience with sled dogs. The exception was Larsen, who had traveled in the Arctic on board such ships as the *Maid of New Orleans* with

Christian Klengenberg, the Danish whaler-turned-trader who was famous for opening trade routes to Copper Inuit territory. Indeed, it was with Klengenberg, while cutting ice for fresh water, that he had driven a sled dog team for the first time.[16] Klengenberg borrowed dogs from several people to create his team; therefore, the dogs were not broken in and Larsen had to learn quickly. On the *St. Roch*, Larsen drew on these previous experiences to train his canine and human crew.

The *St. Roch*'s dogs were generally picked up from one of the last stops on the voyage before freeze-up in the winter months. While on board the *St. Roch*, the dogs were often chained to the forecastle head, and they were kept far apart so they could not reach each other and fight. On the deck with the dogs were Inuit families who were either being transported by, or guiding, the *St. Roch*. Frequently, they would bring their own dog teams, which could bring the total number of dogs on the deck to twenty.

First impressions among the crew were largely that the dogs were vicious. Often, they were referred to as "huskies" and only occasionally did a crew member differentiate between the RCMP-bred dogs and the Inuit sled dogs by referring to the latter as "Eskimo dogs." It is impossible to know the dogs' first impressions of the human crew, but being on board ships was apparently an unsettling experience for them. As Patrick Hunt observed in 1940, "The dogs who have been chained on deck since leaving Coppermine on the 19th are anxious to get on land again and now are letting everyone know about this desire in no uncertain manner."[17] Cpl. Farrar, who wrote about his experience of *St. Roch* in 1940–42, also noted that the dogs, when first coming aboard, "did not look too impressed with their new surroundings."[18] Evidently, they did not like the sea and could even get seasick.[19] In rough weather, Farrar found that "[the] howls of the seasick dogs . . . were trying."[20] Likewise, Larsen recalled when "*St. Roch* twisted and turned and heaved for six hours . . . our poor dogs ran from one side of the deck to the other in wild panic."[21] William Hall (crewman in 1945) described the dogs' opinion of the wet weather when he wrote: "We are still at anchor, with a strong south west wind blowing with rain and snow. The dogs do not [like] the wet and howl their objections continuously."[22]

Once, when they were passing through Lancaster Sound, the weather turned so foul that freezing spray stiffened the dogs' fur, which was aggravating for them. Larsen ordered their release from the chains and had them sheltered inside the ship's cargo scow. The crew then drew a tarp over them until the weather improved.[23]

At one point during one of the voyages, the ship seemed like she might be going down. Larsen again ordered the dogs to be let loose: "Let the dogs loose, boys. If the *St. Roch* is smashed to pieces, we can't have our dogs dragged to their deaths at the end of a chain. They must be given the same chance as the rest of us."[24] Luckily, the ship survived this ordeal, but this story teaches us that the dogs were not seen as disposable. This incident was perhaps influenced by Larsen's experience with the sinking of the *Fort James* in 1937. When the ship was going down, all thirteen dogs and three pups were shot to prevent their drowning.[25] It seems a quick and painless death was preferable to an icy drowning. In both instances, the dogs' lives appear to have had value and there was no need for unnecessary suffering.

However, the shipborne life was not all about bad weather and rough seas. In calm weather, the dogs seemed content on board. As Farrar wrote, "The crouching sled dogs, tied up to the railing on the forecastle head, began to stir. Big Red, the leader, put his front paws on the deck rail and looked down over the side as if enjoying the scenery. . . . The rest of the dogs stretched themselves and began prancing on the deck."[26] It appeared that the dogs asserted themselves, and even protested, when they were met with what they saw as unfair treatment; this incident, reported by Forster, took place when they were chained near, and therefore tempted by, the stores of fish:

> In short order they had the tarp off the fish, but being tied up short they just couldn't reach the baled fish. So, to show their contempt they swung around and sprayed everything within reach.[27]

The crew spent most of the time with the sled dogs on patrols rather than on the ship. Those who remained on the ship during the winter months had few interactions with the dogs. Rather, those who used them for patrols had the most involvement with them, and therefore documented more frequently their experiences with and feelings towards the animals.

At the first sign of freeze-up, the crew were busy winterizing the vessel. Most of the supplies were unloaded to lighten the ship, but the first to go ashore were the dogs. As Hunt suggested above, no doubt they were excited to disembark from the ship, perhaps more than the crew. Once on land, they were tied up on a dog line at eight-foot intervals so they could not reach each other to fight. Meanwhile, the crew covered the deck of the *St. Roch* with canvas so they would have a work area for the winter and a place to cook dog food.

Once they were off the ship, the next task for the crew was obtaining fresh water. They used the dog sleds to pull large blocks of freshwater ice from local lakes back to the ship. Retrieving ice was a good way to introduce the crew to driving dogs. As mentioned previously, that was how Larsen first started working with dogs. The crew also needed a schedule of training the dogs. To pull long distances, the dogs needed to be kept in top physical form, and the crew joked about it being a good opportunity to keep themselves fit as well:

> As soon as there is sufficient snow to make travel by canine a reasonable proposition, the dogs are exercised by the simple expedient of hauling ice. You need the ice, the dogs need the exercise, the men need the exercise too, but don't kid yourself into thinking that many men are enthusiastic supporters of the idea.[28]

On the first voyage of the *St. Roch* in 1928, the crew knew nothing about dog sledding. As Foster put it, "To start with we had plenty of dogs, but not the least idea as to where they worked in the team—wheel dogs, or swing dogs, didn't mean a thing to us, as we had never worked them before."[29] Thus the crew and the dogs had to learn quickly to work together. After some training, they were ready for conducting patrols.

Feeding Dogs

Sled dogs, and particularly Inuit sled dogs, have a reputation for having a voracious appetite. One thing the crew had to look out for on patrol was the dogs going after them when they were defecating. Typically, if the patrol was staying anywhere for any length of time, the men would build an igloo as a toilet. Larsen told a humorous story of having to be on his guard when nature called:

> While visiting Father Henri, he built a snow house for his bathroom and had a stick to use while visiting it. I picked it up and started to wander over towards the igloo, and soon was surrounded by dogs who felt that something was up. Familiar as I was with the nature and behaviour of Eskimo dogs I was glad to have the stick and backed up to the wall of the igloo, as fast as I could get. Squatting down, I waved the stick at the dogs now sitting in a semicircle in front of me. A little bitch, bolder than the rest, seemed to think that I took my time with what I was doing and suddenly let out an impatient bark, with the result that I quickly pulled up my pants and stepped aside. With the bitch in the lead, the dogs forged ahead to the attack, but not on me. Life in the Arctic truly could have its problems.[30]

Their appetite was such that anything organic had to be kept away from them. Sled dogs were known to even eat the leather on their harnesses. The crew, therefore, had to take extra steps to control the dogs and their appetites. Insatiable hunger appears to have been behind some of their perceived vicious behavior.

Providing the dogs with food was often a vital reason for journeys on the dogsleds. Hunting and fishing were a continual complaint for the crew. In their journals there are countless entries of "fishing for dog food" as the only activity they did that day and for many days. The fish would also feed the crew, but much of the catch went to the dogs. This food was only used if hunting failed for that season. It was considered much healthier, and more traditional, for the dogs to be kept on a local diet of marine mammals.[31] However, the RCMP seemed to favor feeding them fish. This appears to be connected to the Arctic game laws and attempts to conserve the number of seals.[32] Dean Hadley wrote in his memoir, "if I remember correctly, the official ration of fresh fish was 6 pounds of fish per dog per day, so it meant that on average we had to catch a little over 100 pounds of fish per day."[33]

The crew complained much more about cooking dog food. Apparently, it was very unpleasant, as it was smelly and gave the dogs gas.[34] The cooking was done in a ten-gallon drum on the deck, where it was placed on two primus stoves. When fish were few, they mixed a huge mass of rice, cornmeal, and rolled oats with tallow and seal blubber. Some seasons they would cook thousands of pounds of oatmeal and rice for the dogs.[35] The RCMP experimented with many kinds of dog food; however, Larsen was known to favor this recipe.[36] If there was a skinny dog, he would cook this "porridge" for them to add some extra weight.[37]

The job of feeding the dogs largely fell to the crew who went on patrols. This was often Larsen, Chartrand, Duke, Hunt, and a few others. Hunt claimed, "I never found the dogs dangerous, except when feeding them, at which time they were very excitable & became savage. You would not try to make a pet out of them."[38] When the ship was in winter quarters and the dogs were kept on the shore, sometimes the crew would use oars to feed the dogs and keep out of reach.[39] A notable exception was Albert "Frenchy" Chartrand, a longtime resident of the Arctic and *St. Roch* crewman, who enjoyed cooking for and feeding the dogs.[40] He was well known as an animal lover, and, while there are no surviving documents by him that speak to his connection with the dogs, several crewmen noted his special bond with them. He was quoted as saying that "I love dogs and my dogteam."[41] If there were sick or injured dogs, he would nurse them. In January 1941, a dog was injured from falling in a crack in the ice. Chartrand simply gave the dog rest, and it recovered and was returned to the harness in two days.[42] Chartrand was a frequent visitor to the mission house at the Inuit hamlet of Coppermine (now Kugluktuk), when Gontran de Poncins, the French writer and adventurer, stayed there during his exploration of the Canadian Arctic in 1938–39. Poncins recalls, "there was nobody like Frenchy to look after a sick dog."[43] Chartrand is pictured here with his lead dog Tommy (figure 7.2). This image perhaps demonstrates Chartrand's love for the dogs as he holds Tommy close to his face. Another photograph shows that when Tommy died, a grave marker was created for him (figure 7.3).

Other than Tommy's, no further evidence of dog graves has been discovered from the *St. Roch* voyages. That said, the crew's feelings surrounding the dogs indicated that those who worked with them had a certain level of love and respect for them. They were hard work to control, but a relationship with them was worth the effort. However, not everyone on the crew felt that way: those who did not go on patrols, where their very lives relied upon the dogs, often had only a grudging respect or an explicit disdain for them. They hated cleaning up after them while they were on board and cooking the horrible-smelling food. Having witnessed many dogfights, they had likely decided the sled dogs were "vicious" and simply avoided them.

Figure 7.2 "Frenchy" looks into the face of his lead dog. D. E. Parkes, ca. 1938–1941. HCRE-30-07, Vancouver Maritime Museum.

Figure 7.3 Grave of Tommy, "Frenchy" Chartrand's lead dog. Ca. 1938–1941. HNSO-30-09, Vancouver Maritime Museum.

Caring for Dogs

The *St. Roch* dog teams experienced injuries, illnesses, and deaths. Perhaps the biggest threat to their health was disease. Mentions of a distemper-like illness in the records are prevalent. There are three primary possibilities for the type of illness experienced by the sled dogs: canine distemper, rabies, or encephalitis.[44] What was labelled as "distemper" in the records may have been any of these three, or something else entirely. Without contemporary laboratory testing it is impossible to know for certain. There is no known cause for the outbreaks, but the contemporary consensus was that it was spread by contact between sled dogs.[45]

The outbreaks of this illness seemed to have been particularly severe during the 1940–42 voyage of the *St. Roch*. Hunt reported on such an instance of disease in his personal diary:

> The Eskimo . . . had a sick dog so we did not wait for him. We later heard that his dog died. There is a strange sickness something like the horse disease on the prairies which is killing off the dogs in a terrible rate up here this winter. Some of the Eskimo have lost all their dogs and are in a very bad fix. A dog in this country is worth from $40.00 to $70.00 and most natives cannot do without seven.[46]

In this extract, Hunt acknowledges the devasting effect such outbreaks had upon Inuit, who relied on their dogs as an integral part of their way of life. The losses from the various outbreaks in the 1940s were documented at anywhere between 30 and 75 percent.[47] Joseph Panipakuttuk, an Inuit guide for the *St. Roch*, noted that in 1944 while on a trip to Aklavik he had sixteen dogs on the way there, but only returned with eight.[48] The reason for their deaths was not given, but most likely it was the same disease that was spreading across the Arctic at this time.

The *St. Roch* crew appear to have made little effort to keep dog teams separate to stop the disease from spreading. However, they did recognize the contagious nature of the disease; as Hunt recorded in 1941, "this dog sickness is very infectious or contagious, but we have been lucky so far and have lost none of our animals."[49] Perhaps efforts at separation were not made simply because it was too complicated while in the field.

Later in the voyage the disease did in fact spread to the *St. Roch* dogs. In June of 1941, Hunt wrote, "one of our dogs died last week and now two more are showing signs of the sickness. Thank goodness most of our patrols are done or we would be in a bad way."[50] A later entry described having to shoot two dogs due to them becoming sick and going "crazy."[51] A month later, Hunt documented losing one of their leaders: "We lost one more dog 'Buck' our leader followed his pal and went insane too and now his worries are over. Will not be long before we loose [*sic*] our entire team if they keep on dying at this rate."[52] It is possible that this was a case of rabies, as it was documented as being spread by foxes in the Arctic at this time.[53]

The deaths from disease directly affected the activities of the *St. Roch* as a floating police detachment. Crewman William Hall reported that in 1945, most of the dogs left by the *St. Roch* at Herschel Island died from disease. He states, "so, being handicapped for winter patrolling, just enough crew will be kept to put the ship into winter quarters."[54] This indicates that adjustments to plans for police patrols had to be made as a direct result of losing so many dogs from disease.

Injuries were also a risk the sled dogs faced. In 1933, a dog called Gin was "badly injured by native dogs while tied on the dog lines, and died two days later November 13th."[55] Similarly, another dog, Sellie, was reported to have been "badly frozen whilst on charge to Herschel Island Detachment and cannot be used when the weather is severe."[56] The exact injury Sellie experienced was not reported, but it was possibly frostbite. Larsen explained that it was difficult to tell when a dog was frostbitten and that one had to observe the animal. The telltale sign was when the hind legs started to shiver.[57] Sellie was later reported to have died while on patrol at Bathurst Inlet.[58] Both Sellie and Gin were replaced by two pups raised by the detachment and taken on charge at four months old.

Minor injuries could also occur while the team was on patrol. A condition the crew was concerned about was damp snow in the spring. This snow would ball up in the fur of the dogs' feet and could cut them. In addition, candle ice[59] could slash the dogs' feet and legs. For protection, the crew would make booties for the dogs (figure 7.4).

However, the booties could wear out on the trail, and if so, the dogs would struggle to continue. Foster explained such a situation from 1929 in his taped memoirs:

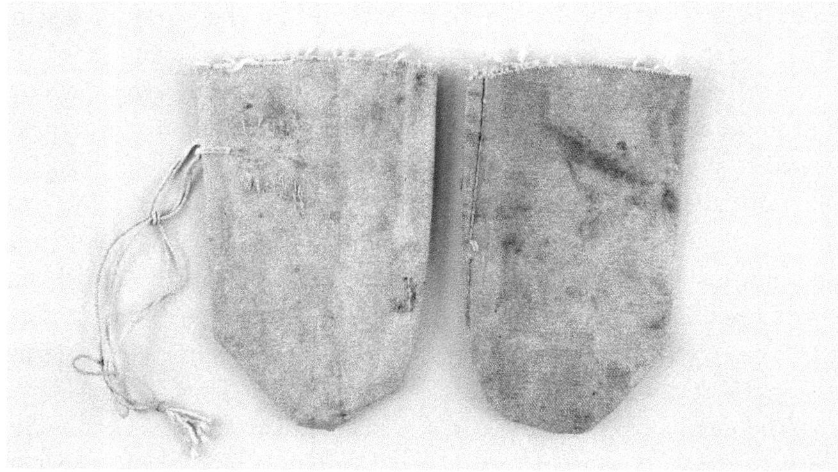

Figure 7.4 Pair of canvas dog booties. Artifact number 2010.012.014 a,b, Prince of Wales Northern Heritage Centre, Yellowknife, NT. Reproduced by permission of the Prince of Wales Northern Heritage Centre, Government of the Northwest Territories.

> If you are unfortunate enough to be late coming home from a patrol, your dogs sure take a beating as the candled ice not only cuts their pads but cuts their legs to ribbons. We always carried a number of dog moccasins made from moose-hide or canvas, but when these are worn out the dogs have a tough time of it.[60]

Though disease and injuries were a common risk during Arctic dog patrols, the evidence shows that the crew made efforts to protect the teams when circumstances allowed. When death was inevitable, the dogs were destroyed. For instance, Larsen recorded in his personal log on February 19, 1931: "One Doge [*sic*] froze up and had to be shot. Poor creature."[61] Such decisions around euthanasia were taken to lessen the dogs' suffering.

Working Together

Crewman William Carter in his later years visited the preserved ship at the St. Roch National Historical Site. While speaking to the staff about his experiences, he remarked that the dogs were very friendly and that the crew could walk among both the RCMP dogs and the Inuit dogs.[62] However, crewman Jim Diplock, who visited the ship in 1985, had a different opinion. He claimed that the only way to tell the difference between the RCMP dogs and the Inuit dogs was that the latter would bite you, while the former would merely growl at you.[63] Diplock reported that he was bitten on two or three occasions going in or out of the forecastle. This dichotomy of respect and admiration versus disdain and fear appears repeatedly in the surviving records. This seems largely to depend on whether the individual crewman worked with the dogs on patrols or not.

Only one record from a crew member mentioned beating the dogs as punishment. In fact, Larsen was against beating the dogs and endorsed the use of gentle encouragement instead.[64] He even sang to the dogs to encourage them in the harness.[65] What underlies his dealings with the dogs was a sense of respect. Larsen admitted how he learned to respect the dogs: "Eskimo dogs are good work animals if they are well treated with a reasonable mixture of love and discipline. Above all, they must have plenty of food."[66] And the dogs responded to the respect and good treatment from the human crew with a team spirit:

> Sgt. Anderton has his favourite dog along, a big strapping fellow named "Brandy." Later, in winter quarters, we would sometimes use a small hand sleigh to haul things not worth hitching up the whole team, and Brandy would set up an awful howl and jump around on the end of his chain as much as to say "That's my job, why don't you fellows let me at it!"[67]

It is here interesting to think how their role as "good work animals" falls outside the norm of human-dog companionships on board ship. As Sari Mäenpää argues, dogs and cats were usually brought aboard ships as pets or mascots, and as such performed the important function of unifying the shipborne community as "objects of collective affection."[68] In contrast, the sled dogs on the *St. Roch*—loathed by some, held in high regard by others—were hardly comparable to pets or mascots. As Sealey explains:

> They certainly were not "pets," they were working animals. The finest dogs the world has known. I've seen a team come in so

> tired that then a halt was called they just spreadeagled out on the snow. Half an hour later when called upon for another effort they jumped to their tired feet and were willing to go again.[69]

This unique dog-human companionship, formed through a shared life of working together in a most inhospitable land, was inevitably temporary. At the end of the voyages, usually during or near the end of the summer, the dogs would be dropped off at another detachment. As Larsen wrote in his autobiography: "Reluctantly we also left behind our remaining dogs, who set up a frightful howl when they saw the ship leave without them. We, too, felt the sadness of the parting; in the Arctic one becomes as attached to these four-legged friends as to one's fellow human beings."[70] This clearly demonstrates that by the end of a season, the crew and dogs had bonded.

Conclusion

Haraway reminds us that "every dog is immersed in practices and stories that can and should tie dog people into myriad histories of living labor, class formations, gender and sexual elaborations, racial categories, and other layers of locals and globals."[71] As mentioned at the beginning of this chapter, the dog stories of the *St. Roch* were part of the broader process of Arctic colonization, which the ship, now a National Historic Site, helps us to remember and reassess (see figure 7.5). Common perceptions of the sled dogs as "savage" were tied to perceptions of Inuit themselves. If the crew of the *St. Roch*, out of necessity, adopted many of the Inuit methods to survive in the Arctic, they still tended to use European sled dog breeds. The colonists took what they observed as useful from Inuit and discarded the rest. Even Larsen, who was sympathetic to Inuit and their dogs, was forced to contend with the changes wrought upon them; he was a prominent actor in the civilizing mission of the RCMP and went on to participate in destructive projects such as the eastern Arctic relocations. The view that the RCMP (including some of the *St. Roch* crew) had towards sled dogs contributed to the evolving cultural genocide Inuit experienced: if the dogs were wild and vicious, there was a seemingly good reason to destroy them and effectively cut their spiritual and cultural ties with Inuit.

Figure 7.5 The *St. Roch* in situ as a museum ship at the Vancouver Maritime Museum. Courtesy of the Vancouver Maritime Museum.

How the *St. Roch* crew felt about the dogs that they used and cared for is difficult to determine. Were they beloved members of the team? That very phrase is drawn from the caption of one of the photographs taken by crewman John Duke, who worked with the dogs. Using the term "beloved" implies, at the very least, a strong bond between the animals and their human partners. From the surviving diaries and published accounts of the crew, we can see that only those who worked with the dogs and understood their nature appreciated them. Those who did not get that opportunity focused on what they saw as flaws and perhaps judged them more along the lines of how one would judge an animal on the basis of its suitability as a pet rather than an essential working animal. As Haraway states, "respect and trust, not love, are the critical demands of a good working relationship," and this seems to prove true in the experiences of the *St. Roch* crew.[72] With working dogs, "some are loved and some are not, but their value does not depend on an economy of affection. In particular, the dogs' value—and life—does not depend on the humans' perception that the dogs love them. Rather, the dog has to do his or her job."[73] Although the terms "love" and "beloved" were used in relation to the *St. Roch*'s dogs, the true emphasis was indeed on their performance as a necessary tool in the Arctic.

John McGrath perhaps says it best when he states, "We cannot separate the dogs, the place and the people."[74] Without sled dogs, neither Inuit nor the RCMP officers would have survived in a place as perilous as the Arctic. Haraway declares that "companion species cannot afford . . . historical amnesia."[75] Therefore, we must acknowledge, remember, and appreciate the hard work and sacrifices the sled dogs endured for the *St. Roch* and its crew to accomplish their monumental feats. This will become a crucial task of the St. Roch National Historic Site as a place for remembering both human and animal crew, and for telling stories beyond the accomplishments of the RCMP's sailors. Bonds and relationships were built between human and dog crew, but the voyages of the *St. Roch* marked one of the last adventures for this iconic Arctic animal.

Acknowledgments

The Vancouver Maritime Museum (VMM), after taking over the management of the *St. Roch* from Parks Canada in the 1990s, actively collects records from the ship's various voyages. This chapter derives from the research I conducted on these unique materials as the Museum's Librarian and Archivist from 2013 to 2021. I am grateful to many colleagues and specialists who helped me in my research. In particular, I would like to thank Sue Hamilton, Geneviève Montcombroux, and Jeff Dinsdale for their assistance with learning about the Inuit sled dogs and Mackenzie huskies. I would also like to thank Dylan Burrows, Doreen Riedel-Larsen, and Shannon Bettles for their guidance and help with researching the *St. Roch* dogs.

Notes

1. Haraway, "Companion Species Manifesto," 184.
2. Bell and Schreiner, "International Relations of Police Power."
3. McHugh, "Arctic Nomadology," 123.
4. Ibid., 143.
5. Dinsdale, "Those Disney Dogs."
6. Montcombroux, *Inuit Dog*, 34.
7. Dinsdale, "What Is a Mackenzie Husky?"
8. Larsen, *Big Ship*, 73.
9. Johan and Edith Gallant define a landrace as "an aboriginal population of domestic dogs that emerged as an ecotype within a specific ecological niche." Gallant, "Breed, Landrace and Purity."

10. Geneviève Montcombroux, email message to the author, November 20, 2018.
11. Ibid.
12. McHugh, *Dog*, 66.
13. Larsen, *Big Ship*, 30.
14. Clarke, *Mounties Patrol the Sea*, 79.
15. Foster, *Maiden Voyage*, tape 1, side B, 10:56.
16. Larsen, *Big Ship*, 24.
17. Hunt, Personal journal, 78.
18. Farrar, *Arctic Assignment*, 9.
19. Ibid., 89.
20. Ibid., 90.
21. Larsen, *Big Ship*, 48.
22. Hall, *Trip to the Arctic*, 14.
23. Farrar, *Arctic Assignment*, 173.
24. Larsen, quoted in Farrar, 15–16.
25. Larsen, *Navigation Report*, 1937.
26. Farrar, *Arctic Assignment*, 9.
27. Foster, *Maiden Voyage*, tape 1, side A, 13:18.
28. Hadley, *Logbook*, 11–12.
29. Foster, *Maiden Voyage*, tape 1, side B, 3:24.
30. Larsen, *Big Ship*, 166.
31. Rokeby-Thomas, "Notes on Dogs and Sledges."
32. Larsen, *Patrolling the Arctic*, 3.
33. Hadley, *What a Life!*, 60.
34. White and White, *Mountie in Mukluks*, 63.
35. Larsen, *Big Ship*, 48.
36. Rokeby-Thomas, "Notes on Dogs and Sledges," 425.
37. Larsen, *Big Ship*, 74.
38. Hunt, Correspondence.
39. Duke, Diary, July 6 [1931?].
40. Larsen, *Big Ship*, 156.
41. Hunt, Personal journal, 3.
42. Chartrand, *Voyages*.
43. Poncins, *Kabloona*, 11.
44. Crandell, "Arctic Fox Rabies," 293.
45. Chitty and Nicholson, "Canadian Arctic Wild Life," 279.
46. Hunt, Personal journal, 122.
47. Chitty, "Canadian Arctic Wild Life," 185.
48. Panipakuttuk, "Historic Voyage," 160.
49. Hunt, Personal journal, 123.
50. Ibid., 128.
51. Ibid., 129.
52. Ibid., 130.
53. Chitty, "Canadian Arctic Wild Life," 185.
54. Hall, *Trip to the Arctic*, 15.
55. Makinson, *Semi-Annual Report* (1933), 2.
56. Ibid.
57. Larsen, *Big Ship*, 73.
58. Makinson, *Semi-Annual Report* (1934), 2.
59. Candle ice is disintegrating ice consisting of ice prisms formed perpendicular to the ice surface.
60. Foster, M. F. Foster's draft manuscript, 33.
61. Larsen, *Private log of St. Roch*.
62. Hudson, *Visit from Bill Carter*, 1.
63. Kowalski, "Drama in real life."
64. Larsen, *Big Ship*, 71.
65. Ibid.
66. Ibid., 24.
67. Sealey, "Arctic Ho," 7.
68. Mäenpää, "Sailors and Their Pets," 481.
69. Sealey, "Arctic Ho," 7.
70. Larsen, *Big Ship*, 175–76.
71. Haraway, Companion Species Manifesto," 188.
72. Ibid., 131.
73. Ibid., 129.
74. John McGrath, quoted in Brandson, "Carved from the Land."
75. Haraway, "Companion Species Manifesto," 173.

Bibliography

Manuscript Sources

VANCOUVER MARITIME MUSEUM, VANCOUVER, BC. (VMM)

Chartrand, Albert. *Voyages of the Cruiser "St. Roch."* File VMM03.02.2-3.9.19. Subseries 2.3: Parks Canada and Vancouver Maritime Museum crew files.

Duke, John. Diary. File VMM03.02.2-3.9.33. Subseries 2.3: Parks Canada and Vancouver Maritime Museum crew files.

Foster, Myles Frederick. *Conclusion of maiden voyage and start of voyage to Eastern Arctic* (read by author). June 14–15, 1966. Item LM2015.010.002. Reel-to-reel tape, MP3 copy, 71 min. Parks Canada St. Roch Research Collection.

———. *Maiden Voyage "St. Roch"* (read by author). 1966. Item LM2015.010.001. Reel-to-reel tape, MP3 copy, 72 min. Parks Canada St. Roch Research Collection.

———. M. F. Foster's draft manuscript about the St. Roch, 1928–42. Henry Larsen Collection. File VMM28.14

Hadley, Dean, Constable. *Logbook*. 1940–42. Vol. 2. LX.93.1.25.

Hall, William R. *A Trip to the Arctic, as told to H. D. Morton*. File 6, item 001.005.021. Photocopy. VMM03 Series 2.3.

Hudson, Lori. *Visit from Bill Carter*. June 12, 1983. Parks Canada St. Roch Research Collection.

Hunt, Patrick. *Copy of Pat Hunt Personal Journal*. 1940–42. LM2020.002.009. Pat Hunt Collection.

———. Correspondence from Hunt to Alice Gavin. January 15, 1991. File VMM03.02.2-3.10.10. Subseries 2.3: Parks Canada St. Roch Research Collection.

———. Personal journal. 1940–42. LM2020.002.010. Pat Hunt Collection.

Kowalski, Eric. "Drama in real life: 'I took James Diplock on a tour of the St. Roch.'" March 28, 1985. File VMM03.02.2-3.9.29. Subseries 2.3: Parks Canada and Vancouver Maritime Museum crew files.

Larsen, Henry A. *Navigation Report of the St. Roch*. 1937. File VMM03.03.3-2.13.38. Subseries 3.2: Semi-annual and other reports.

———. *Navigation Report—R.C.M.P. "St. Roch" Esquimalt, B.C. to Cambridge Bay N.W.T.* 1945. File VMM03.03.3-2.13.48. Subseries 3.2: Semi-annual and other reports.

———. *Patrolling the Arctic and the North-West Passage in the R.C.M.P. ship "St. Roch,"* 3. Self-published.

———. *Private log of St. Roch, Vancouver to Herschel Island 1928*. Diary. KX.85.107.1. Parks Canada St. Roch Research Collection.

Makinson, George T. *Semi-Annual Report of the St. Roch Detachment, Tree River N.W.T.* 1933. File VMM03.03.3-2.13.4. Subseries 3.2: Semi-annual and other reports.

———. *Semi-Annual Report of the St. Roch Detachment, Tree River, N.W.T.* 1934.

Sealey, Frederick William. "Arctic Ho with the St. Roch," File VMM03.02.2-3.12.6. Subseries 2.3: Parks Canada and Vancouver Maritime Museum crew files.

LIBRARY AND ARCHIVES CANADA, OTTAWA, ON

Alexander, Scott. *Correspondence from Alexander to his mother, Mrs. H. O. Alexander*, July 15, 1940. R1650-0-6-E. Scott Alexander fonds.

Printed Sources

Bell, Colleen, and Kendra Schreiner. "The International Relations of Police Power in Settler Colonialism: The 'Civilizing' Mission of Canada's Mounties." *International Journal: Canada's Journal of Global Policy Analysis* 73, no. 1 (March 2018): 111–28. https://doi.org/10.1177/0020702018768480.

Brandson, Lorraine E. "Carved from the Land: The Eskimo Museum Collection." *Fan Hitch* 5, no. 2 (March 2003). Accessed April 23, 2021. http://thefanhitch.org/V5N2/V5N2Book Review.html.

Chitty, Dennis, and Mary Nicholson. "Canadian Arctic Wild Life Enquiry,

1940–41." *Journal of Animal Ecology* 11, no. 2 (November 1942): 270. https://doi.org/10.2307/1361.

Chitty, Helen. "Canadian Arctic Wild Life Enquiry, 1943–49: With a Summary of Results Since 1933." *Journal of Animal Ecology* 19, no. 2 (November 1950): 180. https://doi.org/10.2307/1527.

Clarke, Tom E. *The Mounties Patrol the Sea*. Philadelphia: Westminster Press, 1969.

Crandell, Robert A. "Arctic Fox Rabies." In *The Natural History of Rabies*, 2nd ed., edited by George M. Baer, 291–306. Boca Raton: CRC Press, 1991.

Dinsdale, Jeff. "Those Disney Dogs and the R.C.M.P." *Mushing Past* (blog). December 23, 2014. http://mushingpast.blogspot.com/2014/12/hose-disney-dogs-and-rcmp.html.

———. "What Is a Mackenzie Husky?" *Mushing Past* (blog). November 17, 2014. http://mushingpast.blogspot.com/2014/11/what-is-mackenzie-husky.html.

Farrar, Frederick Sleigh. *Arctic Assignment: The Story of the St. Roch*. Toronto: Macmillan, 1955.

Gallant, Johan, and Edith Gallant. "Breed, Landrace and Purity: What Do They Mean?" *Fan Hitch* 13, no. 1 (December 2010). Accessed April 23, 2021. https://thefanhitch.org/V13N1/V13,N1Breed.html.

Hadley, Dean. *What a Life!* Philadelphia: Xlibris, 2008.

Haraway, Donna. "The Companion Species Manifesto: Dogs, People, and Significant Otherness." In *Manifestly Haraway*, 91–198. Minneapolis: University of Minnesota Press, 2016.

Larsen, Henry A. *The Big Ship: An Autobiography by Henry A. Larsen; in Co-operation with Frank R. Sheer and Edvard Omholt-Jensen*. Toronto: McClelland and Stewart, 1967.

Mäenpää, Sari. "Sailors and Their Pets: Men and Their Companion Animals Aboard Early Twentieth-Century Finnish Sailing Ships." *International Journal of Maritime History* 28 (2016): 480–95.

McHugh, Susan. "Arctic Nomadology: Inuit Stories of the Mountie Sled Dog Massacre." In *Love in a Time of Slaughters: Human-Animal Stories Against Genocide and Extinction*, 122–54. University Park: Pennsylvania University Press, 2019.

———. *Dog*. London: Reaktion Books, 2004.

Montcombroux, Geneviève. *The Inuit Dog of the Polar North*. Inwood, MB: Whippoorwill Press, 2015.

Panipakuttuk, Joseph. "The Historic Voyage of the *St. Roch*." In *Northern Voices: Inuit Writing in English*, edited by Penny Petrone, 155–62. Toronto: University of Toronto Press, 1997.

Poncins, Gontran de. *Kabloona*. New York: Reynal & Hitchcock, 1941.

Rokeby-Thomas, H. R. "Notes on Dogs and Sledges in the Queen Maud Sea and Coronation Gulf Areas." *Geographical Journal* 93, no. 5 (1939): 424–29. https://doi.org/10.2307/1788713.

White, Bill, and Patrick White. *Mountie in Mukluks: The Arctic Adventures of Bill White*. Madeira Park, BC: Harbour Publishing, 2004.

CHAPTER 8

THE DECONTEXTUALIZED DEEP

Fathoming the Whale

Jimmy Packham and Laurence Publicover

In summer 2017, London's Natural History Museum (NHM) transformed its Hintze Hall entrance, replacing its iconic Dippy the Diplodocus plaster cast with the skeleton of a creature far more modern, but perhaps no less alien: a blue whale, nicknamed Hope. The museum stated that the project aimed to help "shape a future that is sustainable" by "inspir[ing] a love of the natural world"—and to that end, the conservation team were "determined to show [the whale] in as lifelike position as possible."[1] They were, then, asking the skeleton to do two things: first, to evoke a full-bodied whale, and thereby enable an encounter between visitors and the "natural world"; and second, to point beyond itself—to serve as a spur towards environmental thinking.

Prompted by Hope and focusing predominantly on the nineteenth century—the period in which humans began more fully and systematically to fathom the ocean—this chapter explores the epistemological questions posed by raising creatures from watery depths. As our title suggests, we are especially concerned with the decontextualization involved in doing so. Across a range of nineteenth-century writing, we demonstrate, there is a nagging sense that what one sees on the surface is not quite the "thing itself"—that encountering the sea creature beyond its oceanic contexts, dredging it from the depths, enacts something like a botched apotheosis, robbing the prized object of its essence. While several sea-dwellers feature in this essay, at its heart is the whale, a creature whose cultural resonance has placed it in synecdochic and metonymic relation with the world below the surface. Carrying the deep within it, the whale both forms part of and stands in for our troubled fascination with the sea's lower reaches. Shuttling between the ocean's layers, it is a puzzling messenger from the deep, bringing knowledge difficult to decode; and while offering material value to humans through its blubber and other physical attributes, it appears, as we shall demonstrate, unwilling to remain straightforwardly material, instead continually prompting metaphysical reflections—not least on what the whole business of whaleness might involve.[2] Fundamentally, what are being raised here are issues of context, of contextualization and decontextualization, and of the qualitative differences of human-nonhuman encounters along horizontal and vertical axes.

We are not, generally speaking, accustomed to thinking along a vertical axis. As Stuart Elden has argued, we "all-too-often think of the spaces of geography as areas, not volumes. Territories are bordered, divided and demarcated, but not understood in terms of height and depth."[3] Along with Elden, geographers including Stephen Graham and Gavin Bridge have recently argued that the contemporary world is increasingly both high and deep—bringing together the two meanings of the Latin *altus*—and that it is so in a manner to which scholarship has not yet fully adjusted or responded. Geographers are surely correct to stress the increased relevance of the vertical axis in an era of drones, satellites, submarines, and deep-sea mining, and to link this stretched axis to the acquisition of geopolitical power. But it is not only in recent years that engagements with the sea's depths have been bound up in such matters.

In a manner that also remains relatively unexplored, colonial power generated by human encounters with the oceans, while predominantly playing out along a horizontal axis—depending, that is, on surface ships and the opening or closing of sea lanes—has also involved reaching below the surface. The art of fathoming—sending a plummet to the seafloor—has been vital to navigation since the classical period, and the fishing and salting of Atlantic cod went hand in hand with the long-distance voyaging on which European colonization in the early modern period was based. In the nineteenth century, encounters with the deep began even more fully to shape political and economic activity. For the United States in particular, whaling became both an economic driver and, due to the routes taken by whalers, an engine of imperial expansion. Around the same time, mapping the seafloor enabled the laying of cables that would vastly increase the speed of trans-oceanic communication. The *Challenger* expedition (1872–76), which involved the most thorough fathoming of the global ocean to that point, may have been scientific in intent, but it was undertaken by vessels of the world's greatest naval power.

In what follows, we are concerned more with the literary and philosophical questions prompted by nineteenth-century encounters with the deep and its inhabitants than with those encounters' political and economic implications. Moving across the cetacean writings of three voyagers—the naturalist Charles Darwin; the professional seafarer Edward Beck; and the author Herman Melville, who, among other forms of shipboard employment, served as a whaler—we demonstrate how the whales encountered and inscribed by these authors raise epistemological questions concerning the creatures themselves, the oceanic environments in which both observers and observed are situated, and, in the cases of Darwin and Melville, wider processes of knowledge-making.

We can begin to examine these issues by considering why a whale hangs in Hintze Hall.

Hope at the Natural History Museum

In his campaign for a new and, crucially, spacious national museum of natural history, Richard Owen stressed that only in such an institution could the gigantic creatures of the natural world be presented satisfactorily. The whale, and specifically the baleen whale, occupied a conspicuous place in Owen's thoughts on this matter. This was not simply because the museum should, in seeking to "gratify the curiosity of the people, and afford them subjects of rational contemplation," exhibit the "largest specimen of a whale that can be procured." Another imperative to obtain "the Mysticete or Great Whalebone whale" had to do with "the fact of the rapidly diminishing numbers of this species, and the probability of its utter extinction at no very remote period."[4] The whale's increasing *invisibility*, due largely to a newly mechanized whaling industry, demanded its heightened *visibility* in the public space of a natural history museum and for a public keen to know more about this elusive creature. But as Owen dwells on what makes the whale such a compelling figure to the naturalist, his expansive prose renders it not more but far less familiar:

> The diversity of structure shown in the different cetaceous genera, *Balaena*, *Balaenoptera*, *Physeter*, *Hyperoodon*, &c., are best exemplified in their skeletons; but, by reason of their size, such require for exhibition the resources of a National Museum. Here only can an intelligent public, or the special student of this least known and most difficult branch of mammalogy, expect the means of contemplating the characters and structures of the strangest as well as hugest of animals,—the most seldom seen by reason of their ocean haunts; air-breathers, yet living in water; hot-blooded, though ever surrounded by a rapidly cooling medium; the most closely allied to man's own class in all the essential parts of their organization; mammalian, but fishes in shape; a comparatively recent development in the series of life-forms that have succeeded one another on our planet, and the superseders of the great sea-lizards in their peculiar office in the ocean police.[5]

The whale is a creature of curious difficulties and contradictions: fish-like, yet a mammal; utterly strange, and yet strangely like us. And oddly, Owen suggests, our knowledge of whales involves their deconstruction, for their diversity is "best exemplified in their skeletons": the substance or body of the whale is, in this respect, an obstruction to our knowing the whale. In short, Owen's prose exhibits a feature common to a great deal of writing that engages with the deep sea and its creatures: an attempt at familiarization whose strain effects a radical *de*familiarization.

The skeleton now hanging in Hintze Hall was acquired by the NHM in 1891, the year before Owen's death, after a whale was beached and killed on the coast of Wexford in southeast Ireland. Linda Williams has recently argued that this exhibit is valuable for bringing into the heart of a city a species that has for so long remained invisible in distant seas and yet whose bodies were crucial to the manufacture of urban products—soap, oil, corsetry, piano keys, and so on. The display of Hope, argues Williams, "represent[s] a significant turn towards engaging the public in a more dynamic biotic imaginary than was once made available from the display of the diplodocus cast"; the public is "invited to imagine its ocean habitat in order to envisage its life, and thus potentially to make an imaginative leap from city to ocean, if not to deeper historical connections between them."[6] It is not difficult to agree with Williams that this is a move to be celebrated. Hope bodies forth the deep sea, bringing it into view in a hyper-public space; and she does so with a profoundly important ecological imperative that speaks urgently to our present moment.

Yet, even as we celebrate the blue whale, there are tensions to register, implicit in Williams's cautious appraisal of the whale's power over the public imagination. The public are "invited to imagine" the whale, "to envisage its life," and "potentially" to undertake an "imaginative" deep dive into the oceans: the effect of the whale remains contingent and, more importantly perhaps, the life of this whale, the life of the deep sea, remains at several literal and experiential removes from the museum's visitors. To reiterate: the whale is represented here by its skeleton—by the material evidence of its pastness—and it sits in a place most famous for hosting a creature that is a byword for both profound antiquity and irrevocable extinction: a dinosaur. This tension in the whale's imagined temporality is echoed in Owen's remarks quoted above: whales are "a comparatively recent" life-form and, at the same time, "the superseders of the great sea-lizards," the prehistoric marine reptiles. In this hall of bones, then, Hope needs somehow to represent life, endurance, survival, futurity. And as an audience, we need, through self-conscious observation of a skeleton—of death—to bear witness to a whale's life; we need to see through the whale's aerial suspension and fathom the oceanic deep. Hope gazes down on us all and remains significantly out of her depth.

The difficulty of situating and appreciating the whale and its significance recur in the writing of another famous figure associated with the NHM: Charles Darwin.

Charles Darwin: Bearing with the Whale

The whale is hardly the most significant creature in Darwin's oeuvre; this honor, surely, belongs either to the celebrated finches or to the tortoises of the Galápagos Islands. Nonetheless, considerations of the whale do serve in evocative—and embarrassing—ways in the published and unpublished works of the naturalist. In Darwin's writings, whales figure in efforts to grapple with the (dis)continuities between marine and terrestrial life, standing out as monstrous oddities in the modern geological era for their size, their peculiar evolutionary history, and their surprising diet. As we turn to Darwin, then, we continue to see the whale as a confounding puzzle from the depths. Indeed, in keeping with our reflections above on Hope and Richard Owen, the most visible, and consequently legible, whales in Darwin's accounts of his voyage are dead or skeletal; the living whale, and what its enormous presence in the oceans means, presents both literal and metaphysical difficulties.

On the shore of the Tres Montes Peninsula (located in the southwest of Chile's Taitao Peninsula), the *Beagle* passed the beached corpse of a whale, prompting Darwin to note: "A sight of a Whale always puts me in mind of the great fossil animals; he appears altogether too big for the present pigmy race of inhabitants. He ought to have coexisted with his equals, the great reptiles of the Lias epoch."[7] The monstrously antediluvian qualities of the whale are again alluded to in the first standalone edition of the *Journal of Researches* (1839).[8] Such responses reveal the awkward temporality into which the whale, in these nineteenth-century imaginaries, is repeatedly placed; where Owen claimed that whales are "the superseders of the great sea-lizards in their peculiar office in the ocean police," Darwin sees the whale as he "*ought* to have coexisted with his equals," the dinosaurs and marine reptiles of the early Jurassic (or Lias) period. Indeed, to return to the horizontal/vertical distinction outlined above, we might say that in Darwin's writings the most prominent encounters with whales occur along the horizontal axis—across the sea's surface and onto shorelines—and that these result in distorted forms of encounter.

Such an angle of encounter is, of course, to some extent inevitable for humans, who cannot survive for long in oceanic depths. But a more vertical perspective can be adopted if one attends not just to the whale itself, but to the minuscule sea creatures on which it feeds. More than once, Darwin's writing attests to the strangeness of the whale's diet. "Who would not think it monstrously improbable," he notes, in a brief thought experiment, "if he had never heard of a whale, that so gigantic an animal could subsist by sifting with its huge mouth the minutest animals from the waters of the sea!"[9] Somewhat counterintuitively, it is the "minutest animals" that help explain the ocean's most monstrous denizens. A keen dredger (like many amateur naturalists of his day[10]), Darwin made great use of a plankton net during his time on the *Beagle*, harvesting from the depths various small sea creatures. In his diary, he recorded:

> I am quite tired having worked all day at the produce of my net.—The number of animals that the net collects is very great & fully explains the manner so many animals of a large size live so far from land.—Many of these creatures so low in the scale of nature are most exquisite in their forms & rich colours.—It creates a feeling of wonder that so much beauty should be apparently created for such little purpose.[11]

Bereft of context, the zoophytes seem to have "little purpose," and these glimpses of the world beneath the waves reveal, as Darwin states in a letter to his cousin, things "disagreeably new": things difficult to fit into existing structures of relation.[12]

In similarly philosophical mood, Darwin elsewhere describes a polyp-like zoophyte that exists in vast colonies. "Well may one be allowed to ask," he writes in reflection, "what is an individual?"[13] Darwin's confrontation with the deep asks him to wrangle with questions of multiplicity perhaps most evocatively probed in Deleuze and Guattari's work on the rhizome.[14] Plunging into the deep has created epistemological and existential ripples, troubling the separation of the multiple and the individual and revealing to the dredger unfamiliar networks of relation between creatures (a nonhierarchical, multidirectional rhizomatic community) that may, in turn, inflect our understanding of the individual beyond the deep—the terrestrial, the human individual.

To take one final glance at Darwin's whales, we might note their presence in the farrago surrounding his most botched—or misunderstood—analogy in *On the Origin of Species* (1859): that of the whale-bear. In chapter 6 of the book (as it appeared in 1859), Darwin reports how the North American black bear has been seen "swimming for hours with widely open mouth, thus catching, like a whale, insects in the water." He goes on:

> Even in so extreme a case as this, if the supply of insects were constant, and if better adapted competitors did not already exist in the country, I can see no difficulty in a race of bears being rendered, by natural selection, more and more aquatic in their structure and habits, with larger and larger mouths, till a creature was produced as monstrous as a whale.[15]

The seemingly magical abruptness (or "dreamlike image," as Gillian Beer terms it[16]) of the bodily transformation of this whale-bear proved a handy crux on which Darwin's antagonists could hang their critiques. As Beer notes, "the mockery and confusion" directed towards this passage "serve to show one of the ways in which his theory opened out in popular imagination towards fairy-tale."[17] "The Bear case," as Darwin termed it in his correspondence, was "well laughed at, & disingenuously distorted by some into my saying that a bear could be converted into a whale."[18] Owen, whose relationship with Darwin might be considered fraught and frosty at best, seems to have taken particular delight in devoting special attention to this passage in his 1860 review of *Origin*.[19] Yet for all that these attacks might smack of opportunism, or that this might be an uncharacteristically poor piece of writing on Darwin's part, something meaningful about the whale nonetheless emerges here.

To imagine the bear's sea-change is to imagine something rich and strange: the whale is the expansive endpoint of this notional evolutionary trajectory—that into which (or "like" that into which) something may transform if it continues to grow "larger and larger." The difficulty of the simile, or obtuseness with which it was received, might stem in part from efforts to imagine the bear within the whale, or the whale within the bear. When might the one become the other? The resulting creature is the most monstrous hybrid in Darwin's book. In subsequent editions of *Origin*, Darwin toned down the force of this analogy, removing the longer second sentence and suggesting, more cautiously, that black bears had been seen "catching, *almost* like a whale, insects in the water."[20] This emendation serves to dislocate the "real" whale even further in this imaginative undertaking: what we end up with is "almost like" a simile twice-removed—a simile that will not commit. There is a glimpse of a whale here, but largely it has sunk from view.

Darwin's difficulty with the whale is productive of some quite ungainly rhetorical wrangling, and this is something we see echoed elsewhere—something, indeed, of which the whale itself seems productive.

Edward Beck's Animal Encounters

Our second author began dredging around the same time as Darwin, though in very different circumstances. Edward Beck signed up as an apprentice seaman in his late teens and undertook four oceanic voyages, personal accounts of which are held within the Caird Library archives at the National Maritime Museum, London.[21] Shipboard diaries composed by professional seafarers tend to have greater awareness of the ocean as a three-dimensional element than do those kept by passengers, in part because the running of the ship requires sailors to pay heed to the sea's vertical axis: as he reaches the Grand Banks on his first transatlantic voyage, for example, Beck's diary is peppered with depth-soundings. But it is not only navigational imperatives that make Beck interested in the deep. He is also keen on fishing, at one point implicitly differentiating his vertical perspective on the sea from the horizontal one assumed by his un-salty companions: "The passengers seem well pleased at the thoughts of land," he writes, "though for my part I wish it would fall calm, that we might catch some fish for a fish meal."[22]

Across his accounts, in fact, Beck displays a desire not simply to raid, but to *understand* the ocean's reaches; but this impulse is, as in the entry below, bound up in his desire to navigate its surface:

> I am getting forward in navigation as fast as I can expect, though my undivided attention to it has not let me pay much to Geography—but if I can get enough insight into the former to keep a journal of the passage home, I hope to acquire a pretty good knowledge of one quarter of the globe at least, if not of more. [. . .] There is a little black kind of fish that swims about the seas here, which hoists a beautiful sail like a bladder decorated with a fringe; it is called a Portuguese Man of War and I should conceive it to be something of the Nautilus kind, excepting the shell, [of] which I think it has none. We have endeavoured to catch some of them, but as yet have not succeeded;

> they are said to possess electric powers, but for the truth of the report I cannot speak, none of our people having experienced it. [. . .] On being struck, they furl their sail and descend into their briny abode.[23]

Given more time, Beck feels confident in gaining knowledge of the ocean's surface, which he regards as "Geography"; but he seems less sure of his capacity to fathom the voluminous depths emblematized by the "little black kind of fish." The creature is conceived as something like a ship—it is twice said to have a "sail"—but it operates along an axis perpendicular to Beck's, "descending" into a "briny abode" rather than giving up its secrets.

It is nonetheless intriguing that Beck finds analogy between the Portuguese man-of-war and the vessel on which he sails.[24] Jane Bennett defends the human urge to anthropomorphize, arguing that this process helps us "uncover a whole world of resemblances and resonances" that can, in turn, allow us to appreciate the agency of the nonhuman and our enmeshment within greater assemblages.[25] In Beck's diaries, there is certainly a sense that the author seeks resemblances between himself and the animals around him as a means better to understand his oceanic environment. Marine animals thus become strangely familiar, rather than (to recall Darwin's expression) "disagreeably new." In a passage composed off the coast of Scotland, and following several frustrating days without celestial observations, we find Beck implicitly connecting his own experience to that of a fin whale, a creature he "did not expect to find upon these coasts." "I think he must have missed his road," writes Beck sympathetically.[26] On other occasions Beck flips his gaze, imagining what his ship might look like to the sea creatures themselves. "[A] few porpoises playing about the ship," reads one entry; "I suppose they take her for a monster of the finny kind."[27] In such passages, two ways of seeing sit in tension. Resorting to the Augustan poeticism *finny*,[28] Beck reads his oceanic environment through the language of a landed culture; at the same time, his experience at sea appears to be prompting more creative modes of thought. He begins to ask not only what it might mean to be a "monster," but also how far context determines how one is seen (and understood) by others, including nonhuman others.

Throughout his diaries, Beck records attempts to grapple, firsthand, with the deep. The young seafarer fishes for sustenance, but also out of curiosity, dissecting the creatures he purloins in a manner that creates a *matryoshka* effect: hidden within the sea are large cod that, when opened up, themselves present "a complete cabinet containing curious mussel shells, small uncommon starfish, and a species of seaweed."[29] The sea is a *Wunderkammer* comprising further *Wunderkammers*. But "full" knowledge is perennially deferred.[30] "A large black whale was blowing about the ship this morning," Beck writes in mid-ocean, "but he did not show much of himself above the water."[31] Something of the deep remains elusive. Sometimes there are practical reasons for this: more than once, the captain's wife lays claim to specimens Beck feels should belong to him.[32] Other entries, like that on the Portuguese man-of-war, present Beck as a frustrated natural philosopher, painfully aware that the ocean does not constitute an environment in which he can conduct thorough investigations. "Another shark visited us this morning," he writes while rounding the Cape of Good Hope, "accompanied by 5 pilot fish [. . .] they attend the shark in all his motions, swimming above his large fins and back, and attending him with unwearied assiduity; I should very much like to know for what purpose."[33]

Beck's sense of an ocean keeping its secrets is perhaps most beautifully captured in a passage where he encounters bioluminescent plankton:

> Last night a number of porpoises were sporting about the ship and we could clearly distinguish all their movements in the water, on account of the path of light they left behind them; the water sparkles exceedingly hereabouts and sometimes one bright spot reflects light for a foot around it, but I have not been able to discover from what it arises. I have got the brilliant matter upon my hand but, upon bringing it into the light, I have not been able to discover it, though it again shone when brought into the dark.[34]

As Beck learns, there is something about this matter that cannot be decontextualized; take it out of its element—try to look at it in one's own realm—and it is no longer quite the same thing. It is while reflecting on belonging or non-belonging to an "element" that Beck has his most interesting encounter with a whale. "Abundance of whales have been about the ship this afternoon," he writes, remarking that "one in particular came very close to us & gave me a full view of him" and then, a few lines later, that the creatures are in "their native element." Beck thus *places* the whales and seems on the point of *fathoming* them—of gaining a "full view." At this very moment of understanding, however, the sea itself jeeringly intrudes: in the physical copy of the diary from which we have quoted here, the words immediately preceding "their native element" are illegible. Beck then explains why: "I had written this when the vessel shipped a bit of sea and the spray flying over my book obliges me to leave writing till it is again dry."[35] The sea itself obscures the linguistic process through which Beck thought he had captured its elusive denizen, "writing over" his attempts to come to terms with it.

Herman Melville: Boggy, Soggy, Squitchy Whales

The inscrutability of the whale (and of the deep) is considered more extensively, and more famously, in this chapter's final case study: Herman Melville's *Moby-Dick* (1851). If for Ahab, the tyrannous captain of the *Pequod*, the whale's inscrutable essence is a stimulus for prodigious horror and loathing, for the novel's narrator, Ishmael, it offers a wellspring of philosophical contemplation. Ishmael is consistently concerned with the difficulty of capturing the whale—not only with harpoons, but also through communicative forms. As a result, *Moby-Dick* serves as a productive final port-of-call for this chapter, helping us to begin resolving some of the questions raised earlier. Specifically, *Moby-Dick* speaks to the question of how and to what purpose we might fathom a deep from which we are seemingly always estranged. As we have already seen, the whale and the deep can operate not only as the ground for metaphor and allegory in their own right, but also prompt epistemological reflection, gesturing towards wider issues of comprehension and, more specifically, to the prospect that we may always be reading or understanding things out of context. *Moby-Dick*'s multitudinous meditations on the whale, we wish to suggest, proffer ways we might live productively with our own partial or inadequate perspectives.

Midway through the novel, Ishmael turns his attention to the abiding shortcomings of visual representations of the whale. He acknowledges that their failures are "not so very surprising," for

> most of the scientific drawings have been taken from the stranded fish; and these are about as correct as a drawing of a wrecked ship, with broken back, would correctly represent the noble

> animal itself in all its undashed pride of hull and spars. Though elephants have stood for their full-lengths, the living Leviathan has never yet fairly floated himself for his portrait. The living whale, in his full majesty and significance, is only to be seen at sea in unfathomable waters; and afloat the vast bulk of him is out of sight, like a launched line-of-battle ship; and out of that element it is a thing eternally impossible for mortal man to hoist him bodily into the air, so as to preserve all his mighty swells and undulations.[36]

The issues of context and decontextualization are absolutely at the forefront of Ishmael's thought. First, Ishmael makes a practical point that echoes Beck's remarks on the "large black whale": it is very difficult to lift whales entirely out of the water to get a good look at them; and, in a reflection that might resonate suggestively with the displaying of Hope, Ishmael implies that a beached whale is not really a "whale" in the sense that a standing elephant is an "elephant," because we are not looking at it in its proper environment. Consequently, says Ishmael, "there is no *earthly* way of finding out precisely what the whale really looks like."[37] In another episode, Ishmael, like today's visitor to the NHM, gazes on a whale skeleton; and despite his unusual access to the interiority of the whale, he is nonplussed. "The skeleton of the whale," he opines, "is by no means the mould of his invested form"; this mould can provide only "half of the true notion of the living magnitude" of the whale in its flesh.[38] Nor is it simply a matter of bulk. Ishmael repeats his earlier assertion that *context* is important. The whale can be "truly and livingly found out" only "in the heart of quickest perils; only when within the eddyings of his angry flukes; only on the profound unbounded sea."[39]

Melville's whales are continually being encountered and inspected only in bits and pieces, most frequently as they are hauled onto deck and dissected by whalers. Such encounters do not simply decontextualize the whale by wrenching it from its ocean, but also sever each part of the whale from its bodily context. Richard Owen, as we have seen, believed that whales were best known through their skeletons; for the literary critic Samuel Otter, by contrast, "the cetological axiom that the skeleton of the whale does not accurately reflect the shape of the whale's body [. . .] raises questions about the ethnologist's abilities to make dry bones speak."[40] Attempting to ask a skeleton—or a head, a fluke, a fin, or a tooth—to tell us about the whale is as epistemologically risky as whaling is physically dangerous. What *Moby-Dick* teaches us, K. L. Evans argues, is that "the whale is not a whale unless in the context of an ocean. It cannot be divorced from its world and thought to be understood."[41] Anyone claiming to know the whale is leaving themselves exposed to the kinds of questions with which God batters Job: "Hast thou entered into the springs of the sea?"[42] (The correct answer is: "No, I haven't. Please pardon my presumption.")

Ishmael certainly preaches this homily.[43] But he also goes further: the specific qualities of the whale-containing sea gestured towards above—its profundity and boundlessness—suggest a confounding of human categories. Fully to understand the whale is to acknowledge its involvement in an element that cannot be measured ("unfathomable waters") and cannot be communicated (as we learn from the experience of Pip, the *Pequod*'s shipkeeper, who falls into the ocean and thereafter seemingly speaks a kind of gibberish). These pronouncements explain the cautious language with which Ishmael elsewhere promises to offer the reader a representation of the whale: "I shall ere long paint to you as well as one can without canvas, something like the true form of the whale as he actually appears to the eye of the whaleman when in his own absolute body the whale is moored alongside the whale-ship so that he can be fairly stepped upon there."[44] The tolling repetition of the word *whale* in this sentence draws attention to the very thing that cannot be fully represented; we are put back in mind here of the hedged discourse that characterizes Linda Williams's reading of Hope. Ishmael will give us "*something like* the true form of the whale" as it appears to a very particular demographic, "the whaleman." (This latter term describes those employed in the whale fisheries, but as a compound noun it also suggests a form of hybridity—involving the nonhuman with the human, and the marine with the terrestrial—that is suggestively akin to Darwin's whale-bear.) Further, this picture will be a snapshot of a moment when the whale itself, while still in its "absolute body," is nonetheless lashed to a ship; in this respect, it is not merely accessible as something to be "fairly stepped upon," but verging on the terrestrial—a piece of *terra firma* in the midst of the fluid and unstable ocean. A serious question is being raised here: At what point in its translation from ocean to ship, and from being to nonbeing, and from referent to signifier, does this whale cease to be, or cease to have any meaningful overlap with, the "real" whale that Evans suggests remains fully immersed in its oceanic element?

The question, as we have already indicated, is impossible to resolve. It is perhaps appropriate, then, that the one picture of a whale of which Ishmael approves is not obviously of a whale at all. Yet it is this image—and Ishmael's efforts to comprehend it—that can help reconcile us to our estrangements and limited perspectives. The picture hangs in the entrance to the Spouter-Inn in the whaling port of New Bedford:

> On one side hung a very large oil-painting so thoroughly besmoked, and every way defaced, that in the unequal cross-lights by which you viewed it, it was only by diligent study and a series of systematic visits to it, and careful inquiry of the neighbors, that you could any way arrive at an understanding of its purpose. Such unaccountable masses of shades and shadows, that at first you almost thought some ambitious young artist, in the time of the New England hags, had endeavored to delineate chaos bewitched. But by dint of much and earnest contemplation, and oft repeated ponderings, and especially by throwing open the little window towards the back of the entry, you at last came to the conclusion that such an idea, however wild, might not be altogether unwarranted.
>
> But what most puzzled and confounded you was a long, limber, portentous, black mass of something hovering in the centre of the picture over three blue, dim, perpendicular lines floating in a nameless yeast. A boggy, soggy, squitchy picture truly, enough to drive a nervous man distracted. Yet was there a sort of indefinite, half-attained, unimaginable sublimity about it that fairly froze you to it, till you involuntarily took an oath with yourself to find out what that marvellous painting meant. Ever and anon a bright, but, alas, deceptive idea would dart you through.—It's the Black Sea in a midnight gale.—It's the unnatural combat of the four primal elements.—It's a blasted heath.—It's a Hyperborean winter scene.—It's the breaking-up of the ice-bound stream of Time. But at last all these fancies yielded to that one portentous something in the picture's midst. *That* once found out, and all the rest were plain. But stop; does it not bear a faint resemblance to a gigantic fish? even the great leviathan himself?[45]

Ishmael's confrontation with what ultimately seems to be—but, of course, may not be—a whale reads as a virtual allegory for the meaning-making process and of how, through this process, we might shore up the incertitude of our own knowledge; furthermore, it suggests how we might come better to comprehend our relationship with the object of this knowledge—in this case, the whale.

In the first instance, Ishmael's ekphrasis bears out the claims made in the passages already cited: that our fathoming of the whale's obscurity depends upon (re)situating the creatures of the deep within their context. The exegete begins almost literally in the dark, in the environs' "unequal cross-lights." Over time, the image in the painting gradually reveals itself to be a whale only after Ishmael has attended to the image, returned to it, adopted a new perspective, consulted the objects around it, cast extra light on it, and entered into discourse with other people who have undertaken the work of interpretation before him—the "many aged persons with whom I conversed upon the subject."[46] In short, we learn to read what might be a whale by means of the environment in which a whale might be found: the whale finds its meaning as part of an assemblage, rather than in isolation. Indeed, Ishmael is not so much hunting the animal itself here; rather, he seeks to find out "what that marvellous painting *meant*." He seeks not knowledge of the object but instead how that object becomes meaningful because of its interaction with, and influence on, the more-than-whale world in which it circulates.

Such a reading celebrates flux and fluidity; the whale gradually appears as if out of some magic-eye picture, as the viewer reads the image as one constituted by movement. It is a "gale," a "combat of the four primal elements," "the breaking-up of [. . .] Time," and so on. (This whale is only truly glimpsed "in the heart of quickest perils; only when within the eddyings of his angry flukes.") These movements or actions are in turn complemented by the ever-shifting reading the viewer is encouraged to undertake of the painting. As Steve Mentz has recently argued, it is just this kind of work that constitutes an oceanic turn in critical perspectives: we need to develop tools, a "saltwater" language, to think with "a dynamic environment, fluid, saline, moving, and moved." What happens, Mentz asks, if instead of thinking about expertise and knowledge as defined by critical fields, "we redescribe the adventures of thinking as currents [. . .]? Why not emphasize movements and connections between or through differences?"[47] Philip Steinberg similarly contends that proper comprehension of oceanic movement means rethinking how we think with it, namely, "through its movements, through our encounters with its movement, and through our efforts to interpret its movement."[48] As Ishmael works to embody this perspectival shift, he comprehends the "boggy, soggy, squitchy picture" not as a landlubber, nor even as a seafarer, but rather as something akin to an oceanic citizen.

There is a final caveat to register here, however. Ishmael ultimately sees the picture as an image of a ship and whale because he lives and moves within a world of ships and whales; his reading is inflected by his own inescapable subject position. As a result, his sense of what the whale might finally "mean" will be subtly different from that of, say, a seaborne naturalist (like Darwin) or a curious professional mariner on board a collier (like Beck). There are, as we have seen, significant overlaps in these seafarers' cetacean writings. In all three cases, the whale is a figure whose elusiveness has prompted reflection on (knowledge of) the deep ocean and its denizens and on the means of attaining such knowledge. But the results of these reflections remain determined by their situatedness; and whatever perspective is adopted, and however this perspective might be combined with further perspectives, such creatures continually surface only to sink from view again. The whale itself, the "real" whale, is the absence around which all such thinking orbits; there is no whale (singular), only whales (plural)—infinite approximations of "whale." Melville's work dramatizes what is implicit in our encounters with Beck, Darwin, Hope, and Owen: our vision of the whale emerges somewhere between oceanic object and observing subject; and what the whale is, and what it means, are matters always determined by the myriad contexts into which we bring it as we haul it into view.

From here, we can return for one last dart at Hope.

The Value of Hope

Ecocritics have, quite reasonably, questioned the ethics of the conceptual and textual maneuvers of allegory and analogy, suggesting that when the sea fades into metaphor we become blind to its material presence and, in turn, our capacity to affect it. Deploying the sea as an image of eternity is especially invidious, they argue, diluting as it does our direct encounter with the sea while also implying it has a quality that, in fact, it lacks—not least thanks to human agency.

Is the NHM's Hope, for all its environmental aims, guilty of a similar effacement of the thing itself? In April 2019, Extinction Rebellion (XR) demonstrators occupied Hintze Hall to stage what they and the media referred to as a "die-in" beneath the blue whale skeleton. What work, beyond that of being and representing (*meaning*) "whale," was Hope being asked to perform here? According to the NHM's publicity, as we have seen, Hope is being asked both to be herself (to be "lifelike") and to point towards a "future that is sustainable"—and in this sense XR's decision to place her at the heart of a protest around ecocide was apt. But can she really do both these things?

Following Ishmael, what we might say of the skeleton in Hintze Hall is that it is not, in any real way, a whale. What we encounter, instead, is the NHM's own approximation of a whale, inflected not least by the carefully curated context (and politics) of the museum, by the city beyond the museum's doors, and by the histories behind the bones themselves. Hope helps us to consider the power that de- and re-contextualization has over the life and meaning of such things as sentient marine creatures. And, more than this, it offers the opportunity to state exactly what we mean when we talk about "maritime" or "marine" animals. Our encounters with such animals are, of necessity, shaped by the technologies of the terrestrial, whether it is Hope in the museum, the sea creature glimpsed from the ship, or the translation of the deep sea into our living rooms by a series like *Blue Planet II* (2017). Indeed, the maritime itself exists partway between the marine world and the terrestrial world. At what point might we consider our encounter with the oceanic sufficiently divorced from the terrestrial to celebrate it as a truly oceanic experience? At what point might we see the maritime not from the vantage of the terrestrial, but instead the marine? The onus, we have argued, is on us, the terrestrial creatures, to undertake self-conscious and conscientious observation of the whale: to acknowledge (because we cannot negate) the decontextualization effected by the maritime.

Notes

1. Brown, "Museum Unveils 'Hope' the Blue Whale Skeleton."
2. Also beginning his analysis of whales' significations with a discussion of Hope, Graham Huggan calls the whale an "outsize standard-bearer for marine and other environmental issues" and notes: "There seems no end to the ways in which whales can be turned, whether literally or

metaphorically, into something *else* even as they are now increasingly acknowledged as enjoying special status among the earth's creatures, as being ecological subjects in their own right." Huggan, *Colonialism, Culture, Whales*, 2–3.

3. Elden, "Secure the Volume," 35. See also recent remarks by Kimberley Peters, Philip Steinberg, and Elaine Stratford that stress the growing geopolitical significance of sites such as "airspace, the underground, the ocean, the seabed [. . .]: spaces notable for their indeterminacy, dynamism, and fluidity." Peters et al., "Introduction," 3.
4. Owen, *Extent and Aims*, 14–16.
5. Ibid., 19–20.
6. Williams, "Deep Time," 171.
7. Keynes, *Charles Darwin's* Beagle *Diary*, 278.
8. See Darwin, *Journal of Researches*, 473.
9. Stauffer, *Charles Darwin's Natural Selection*, 346.
10. On the popularity of dredging in the mid-nineteenth century, see Rozwadowski, *Vast Expanses*, 113–22.
11. Keynes, *Charles Darwin's* Beagle *Diary*, 21–22.
12. Charles Darwin to William Darwin Fox (May 23, 1833), in Burkhardt et al., *Correspondence of Charles Darwin*, vol. 1, 316.
13. Darwin, *Journal of Researches*, 117.
14. Deleuze and Guattari, *Thousand Plateaus*, 3–25.
15. Darwin, *Origin of Species* ([1859] 2009), 169.
16. Beer, *Darwin's Plots*, 98.
17. Ibid.
18. Charles Darwin to William Henry Harvey (September 20–24, 1860), in Burkhardt et al., *Correspondence of Charles Darwin*, vol. 8, 371.
19. See Owen, "Darwin on the Origin of Species," especially 517–19.
20. Darwin, *Origin of Species* (1860), 184, emphasis added.
21. The accounts are gathered (and lightly edited) in Hay and Roberts, *Sea Voyages of Edward Beck in the 1820s*, from which we quote.
22. Hay and Roberts, *Sea Voyages of Edward Beck*, 58.
23. Ibid., 56–57.
24. Albeit unbeknownst to Beck, the Portuguese man-of-war is also analogous to a ship in that it is a "colonial organism": its different entities work in harmony and cannot exist alone. Similarly, shipboard communities operate through shared knowledge; as Beck's entry indicates, he would accept as "truth" something reported by his shipmates. In both cases one might ask, with Darwin, "What is an individual?"
25. Bennett, *Vibrant Matter*, 99.
26. Hay and Roberts, *Sea Voyages of Edward Beck*, 121.
27. Ibid., 75.
28. See also ibid., 131, and compare "briny abode."
29. Ibid., 106.
30. See also Beck's frustrated attempts to come to grips with cuttlefish (ibid., 168) and another shark (ibid., 201).
31. Ibid., 54.
32. Ibid., 106, 107.
33. Ibid., 142–43.
34. Ibid., 58.
35. *Journal of Edward Beck*, 52. For further thoughts on the sea's intrusion into Beck's diary, see Liebich and Publicover, "Introduction," 1–2.
36. Melville, *Moby-Dick*, 263.
37. Ibid., 264, emphasis added.
38. Ibid., 453.
39. Ibid., 453–54
40. Otter, *Melville's Anatomies*, 132.
41. Evans, *Whale!*, 112.
42. Job 38:15.
43. See Melville, *Moby-Dick*, 136.
44. Ibid., 260.

45. Ibid., 12–13.
46. Ibid., 13.
47. Mentz, *Ocean*, xv–xvi.
48. Steinberg, "Of Other Seas," 161.

Bibliography

Beck, Edward. *Journal of Edward Beck on the collier brig* Lady Francis. 1823. JOD/266/1. Caird Library, National Maritime Museum, London.

Beer, Gillian. *Darwin's Plots: Evolutionary Narrative in Darwin, George Eliot and Nineteenth-Century Fiction*. 3rd ed. Cambridge: Cambridge University Press, 2009.

Bennett, Jane. *Vibrant Matter: A Political Ecology of Things*. Durham: Duke University Press, 2010.

Brown, Natasha. "Museum Unveils 'Hope' the Blue Whale Skeleton." *Natural History Museum*. July 13, 2017. Accessed August 6, 2020. http://www.nhm.ac.uk/discover/news/2017/july/museum-unveils-hope-the-blue-whale-skeleton.html.

Burkhardt, Frederick, and James A. Secord, eds. *The Correspondence of Charles Darwin*. 28 vols. Cambridge: Cambridge University Press, 1985.

Darwin, Charles. *Journal of Researches into the Geology and Natural History of the Various Counties Visited by the H.M.S.* Beagle, *Under the Command of Captain Fitzroy, R.N. from 1832 to 1836*. London: Henry Colburn, 1839.

———. *On the Origin of Species by Means of Natural Selection, or the Preservation of Favoured Races in the Struggle for Life*. London: John Murray, 1859. Reprinted, edited and with introduction by William Bynum. London: Penguin, 2009.

———. *On the Origin of Species by Means of Natural Selection, or the Preservation of Favoured Races in the Struggle for Life*. 2nd ed. London: John Murray, 1860.

Deleuze, Gilles, and Félix Guattari. *A Thousand Plateaus: Capitalism and Schizophrenia*. Translated by Brian Massumi. London: Continuum, 2003.

Desmond, Adrian, and James R. Moore. *Darwin*. London: Penguin, 1992.

Elden, Stuart. "Secure the Volume: Vertical Geopolitics and the Depth of Power." *Political Geography* 34 (2013): 35–51.

Evans, K. L. *Whale!* Minneapolis: University of Minnesota Press, 2003.

Hay, Michael, and Joy Roberts, eds. *The Sea Voyages of Edward Beck in the 1820s*. Edinburgh: Pentland, 1996.

Huggan, Graham. *Colonialism, Culture, Whales: The Cetacean Quartet*. London: Bloomsbury Academic, 2018.

Keynes, Richard Darwin, ed. *Charles Darwin's* Beagle *Diary*. Cambridge: Cambridge University Press, 1988.

Liebich, Susann, and Laurence Publicover. "Introduction: Shipboard Literary Cultures and the Stain of the Sea." In *Shipboard Literary Cultures: Reading, Writing, and Performing at Sea*, edited by Susann Liebich and Laurence Publicover, 1–40. New York: Palgrave Macmillan, 2021.

Melville, Herman. *Moby-Dick; or, The Whale*. Edited by Harrison Hayford, Hershel Parker, and G. Thomas Tanselle. Evanston, IL: Northwestern University Press, 1988.

Mentz, Steve. *Ocean*. London: Bloomsbury, 2020.

Otter, Samuel. *Melville's Anatomies*. Berkeley: University of California Press, 1999.

Owen, Richard. "Darwin on the Origin of Species." *Edinburgh Review* 111 (1860): 487–532.

———. *On the Extent and Aims of a National Museum of Natural History*. London: Saunders, Otley, & Co., 1862.

Peters, Kimberley, Philip Steinberg, and Elaine Stratford. "Introduction." In

Territory Beyond Terra, edited by Kimberley Peters, Philip Steinberg, and Elaine Stratford, 1–13. London: Rowman and Littlefield, 2018.

Rozwadowski, Helen M. *Vast Expanses: A History of the Oceans*. London: Reaktion Books, 2018.

Stauffer, R. C., ed. *Charles Darwin's Natural Selection: Being the Second Part of His Big Species Book Written from 1856 to 1858*. Cambridge: Cambridge University Press, 1975.

Steinberg, Philip E. "Of Other Seas: Metaphors and Materialities in Maritime Regions." *Atlantic Studies* 10, no. 2 (2013): 156–69.

Williams, Linda. "Deep Time and Myriad Ecosystems: Urban Imaginaries and Unstable Planetary Aesthetics." In *The Aesthetics of the Undersea*, edited by Margaret Cohen and Killian Quigley, 167–79. Abingdon, UK: Routledge, 2019.

CHAPTER 9

THE ENCRUSTING OCEAN

Life-Forms of the Spongy Wreck

Killian Quigley

The first national marine sanctuary in the United States was established in the Atlantic Ocean in 1975. It safeguards the remains of the USS *Monitor*, a Civil War–era ironclad warship that sank off Cape Hatteras, among the barrier islands of North Carolina, in late 1862.[1] Despite its being washed by the warm, vivifying waters of the Gulf Stream, the site has historically been defined almost exclusively as a repository of "cultural," rather than "natural," resources. What limited inquiries *have* been made into the life encouraged by the "artificial reef" reveal a diverse and thriving neighborhood of resident and migratory species. Among the most successful of all are the "encrusting faunal organisms," including perhaps forty varieties of sponge. Along the *Monitor*'s best-preserved sections—its foreparts—iron has been cladded anew with a layer of "thick marine calcareous growth," an exceptionally hospitable habitat of and for poriferans and soft corals (figure 9.1).[2]

Despite their relative neglect of the wreck's other-than-human stories, the *Monitor*'s own administrators have obliquely confirmed the interdependence of its "cultural" and "natural" identities. An official report on the state of the sanctuary, published in 2008, points out that encrusting fauna can have an ameliorative impact on the rate and intensity of corrosion. Therefore, when such "material" is removed from the

Figure 9.1 Wreck of the USS *Monitor.* 2008, Monitor National Marine Sanctuaries (MNMS), National Oceanic and Atmospheric Administration. Flickr (CC BY 2.0).

vessel in the course of archaeological recovery, the result is often to accelerate disintegration of the site as a whole.[3] Brought to dry land, the ironclad's propeller, steam engine, turret, and cannons are cleaned of oceanic matter and made to perform as the "primary data" of material culture and its institutions.[4] Ironically, as such removals tidy lively encrustations away, they also diminish the likelihood that the ship's other parts will survive at all, let alone accede, some day, to the status of artifact.

Underwater, among the ruins of a ship, the borders that attempt to distinguish categories like artifact and ecofact rapidly corrode. Delimiting a wreck's ontology—as historical "time capsule,"[5] national war grave, ecological "stepping stone,"[6] or otherwise—entails selecting for temporality, object, subject, and story. Attending instead to a wreck's dynamism, its proclivities for ontological shiftiness and multiplicity, begins to account for the unique natural-cultural capacities of this planet's approximately three million drowned craft.[7] As the *Monitor* indicates, those craft are more than Romantic *memento mori*.[8] They are nexuses of matter, symbol, narrative, and life, transversally relating and continually changing. Moreover, they are other-than-human places, and by acknowledging their "sea ontologies,"[9] it may be possible more fully, and more ethically, to reckon the wreckage (figure 9.2).

Keeping in rhythm with this book's general scheme, the present chapter attends primarily to a single group of animals: the sponges, which animal taxonomy gathers under the phylum Porifera. It nearly goes without saying that, by distinguishing one sort of wreck-dweller from all the others, I risk carrying out a misleading kind of interpretive disarticulation. After all, individual sponges themselves frequently host symbiotic algae and bacteria (to say nothing of their wider networks of relation).[10] Nonetheless, I hope to make clear the value of a discrete, "ethico-aesthetic" choice to prioritize poriferans, invertebrate animals who do not simply inhabit a wreck but inflect, and even give rise to, wrecky meaning.[11] Ultimately, the figure I aim to trace and heed is

Figure 9.2 Wreck of the USS *Dixie Arrow*. 2010, photograph, Monitor National Marine Sanctuaries (MNMS), National Oceanic and Atmospheric Administration. Flickr.

neither the animal nor the ship alone but the spongy wreck, an assemblage whose emergent properties include unforeseen modes of liveliness.[12] What ecologies of memory, to borrow Caitlin DeSilvey's term, emerge in proximity to the spongy wreck—and what ecologies of futurity?[13] What stories emerge from the depths when some of their coauthors are spineless and mostly sessile?

By addressing such concerns, this essay responds to calls for more and better consideration of both invertebrate stories and marine stories.[14] Because they do not grow "true" tissue or organs, sponges occupy what Graham Edgar calls an "intermediate" space between most invertebrate animals and the protozoans (figure 9.3).[15] Sponges are morphologically promiscuous, too, sometimes taking encrusting forms and sometimes standing erect—and frequently varying their postures even among members of a single species. Poriferans range, moreover, from nearshore waters to abyssal depths. Phylogenetically and environmentally, therefore, human beings are mostly highly alien to sponge-hood. (The great exceptions to this are the sponge divers, of whom more later.) At actual depth, and in company with backboneless animals, "immersive" practices of multispecies storytelling become subject to intensified, if not simply insupportable, pressures.[16] While I am conscious of the risks inherent in an analytical approach that appears to valorize otherness, I am also convinced of the need for stories that operate in situations where human relating is strained, extreme, and even absent.[17] At the spongy wreck, anthropic matter, time, and memory are literally enveloped by poriferan substances and sensibilities. A poetics of encrustation sustains maritime story at the same moment that it renders it richly, strangely, and irredeemably other-than-human.

Toward theorizing an encrusted poetics, this chapter interprets the spongy wreck in terms of a distinctive formal relation among wrecky substrate and poriferan ornament. Unlike paradigms of soily rootedness, encrustation at the wreck frequently operates through the "superficial attachment" of a sponge's holdfast to a hard surface.[18] In Western thought, superficiality has so often been set up as a useful foil for the authentic, the substantive, and indeed the natural. The spongy wreck compels a reconsideration of these presuppositions, mobilizing meaning at and among superficies and through decoration and adornment. "The deep," writes Alphonso Lingis, "is all in surface effects."[19] The apparently paradoxical coincidence of the deep and ("in") the surficial signifies the possibilities of an encrusted poetics, a storying that does

Figure 9.3 Strawberry vase sponge (*Mycale laxissima*). Nick Hobgood, 2010, photograph. Wikimedia Commons (CC BY-SA 3.0).

not mistake immersion for penetrative illumination. Along its faces, the spongy wreck bears witness not only to drowned boats and invertebrate ecologies but to novel kinds of reading, storytelling, and even life.

Submerged Ruins, Drowned Becomings

Like all ruins, shipwrecks embody and exemplify distinctly strange material and temporal interactions of nature and culture, past and progressive, human and other-than-human. Unlike terrestrial remains, however, submerged wreckage has often been interpreted as a synecdoche of undersea ontology: Judeo-Christian cosmogonies have frequently posited submarine realms as wrecked repositories of wrecks. In the book of Ezekiel, for example, the prophet foretells the drowning of the Phoenician city of Tyre, a society "made very glorious" through maritime trade. As punishment for the Tyrians' alleged mistreatment of Jerusalem, their "market," "riches," "merchandise," and "companie" are condemned to "fall into the middest of the seas."[20] For the early modern theologian and natural philosopher Thomas Burnet, those seas were agents as well as repositories of wreck. In his influential *Telluris Theoria Sacra* (*The Sacred Theory of the Earth*, 1681), Burnet describes how the "old World" had "perish'd" in the course of the Noachian deluge, which formed the "image of the present Earth in the ruines of the first."[21] A "vast *morgue*" was Henry David Thoreau's not-unadmiring epithet for the jetsam he observed along the "endless beach" in *Cape Cod* (1865), fragments appearing to offer the equivocal knowledge that "we, too, are the product of sea-slime."[22]

The trope of the ruined and ruining ocean also figures prominently in certain contemporary, secular accounts of marine precarity. Terrigenous pollution has devastated coastal biodiversity, sometimes so terribly as to generate marine "dead zones."[23] As seas absorb more of the atmosphere's increasing quantities of carbon dioxide, they in turn become increasingly acidic, spoiling the carbonate structures of coral reefs.[24] The great Pacific Ocean gyres churn with anthropogenic plastic so abundant as to make it, in Patricia Yaeger's words, "impossible to find a seabird without a little product inside or a square foot of ocean without debris."[25] Great machines indiscriminately drag the deep-water plains of the hadal zone for "polymetallic nodules" that contain the precious ingredients for battery-making.[26] Barring widespread improvements in ecosystem governance and a rapid and radical reduction in human use of fossil fuels, the near future may furnish nothing short of a "marine holocaust."[27]

The status of actual shipwrecks in these stories is ambiguous. Thanks in large part to petroleous disasters, from the *Exxon Valdez*, which ran aground off the southern coast of Alaska in 1989, to the sinking of the *Sanchi* in the East China Sea in 2018, ruined vessels represent deadly threats not only for their human crews but for the incalculable lives touched by their seepage. Simultaneously, sunken ships have been accumulating unusual virtue for serving as so-called artificial reefs, thereby contributing to resilient futures.[28] This paradox signifies wrecks' ontological dynamism, as well as the sea floor's reception and cultivation of entities that challenge natural-cultural divisions with special force. It is worth noting that knowledge of the heterodoxy of the undersea is not a new phenomenon. The "natural and casual treasuries of the seas" was the seventeenth-century natural philosopher John Beale's phrase for submerged stuff—"casual," in this instance, meaning undesigned,

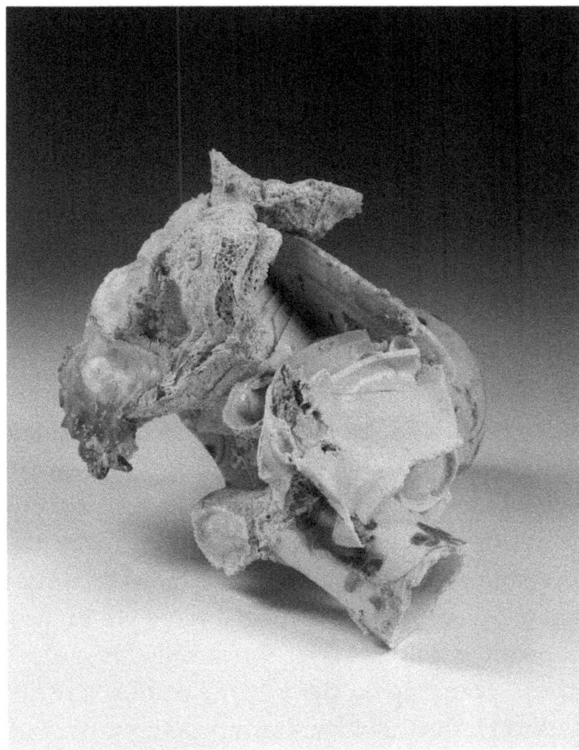

Figure 9.4 "Sea sculpture." Ca. 1725, underglaze of cobalt-blue decorated porcelain pieces fused together by fire and encrusted with shell and coral growths. © Victoria and Albert Museum, London.

accidental, fortuitous.[29] Fished from the water and arranged among the cabinets of curiosity of seventeenth- and eighteenth-century virtuosi, natural-casual "hybrids" confronted their observers with what James Delbourgo suggestively calls an "encrusted natural history."[30]

In William Shakespeare's *The Tempest* (1611), Ariel urges Prince Ferdinand to understand that his father has not survived their shipwreck and does now "suffer a sea-change / Into something rich and strange." So doing, the tricksome spirit conjures Alonso metamorphosed by pearly and coralline ornament. The prospect's bewitching power issues from Ariel's insistence that the king's drowned body does not entirely deteriorate, or "fade." Instead, it transmogrifies, as "bones" and "eyes" are sheathed by marine matter that not only covers but refigures them into parts of some unnamable thing.[31] One term for that thing might be "sea-sculpture," the title given by London's Victoria and Albert Museum to a porcelaneous-coralline-conchological object salvaged from the 1725 wreck of a Chinese junk off Ca Mau, in present-day Vietnam, in 1998 (figure 9.4). The hybrid, explains an official description, "was created through accident and nature" in a performance of natural-casual fusion enacted over the course of more than two and a half centuries.[32] "Sea-sculpture" is an appealing (and sibilant) metaphor, but a better word is concretion, from the Latin *concrēscĕre*, meaning to grow together: this encrusted something is not so much the product of art as a coalescence interrupted, like the image of Alonso in Ariel's song, in the flow of its becoming.

Hans Blumenberg's influential treatment of shipwreck "metaphorics" tracks a pivotal dialectic of "progress and sinkings" in European thought.[33] For Blumenberg, the figure of the spectator who, from the safety of dry land, looks over the waters at a vessel in peril exemplifies the formatively ironic aesthetics of an observer who bears witness to the moment of catastrophe while not participating in it themselves. The concretions of submerged wreckage suggest another, hardly less ambivalent logic whereby what Steve Mentz calls the "historical drama" of shipwreck is comprehended—and complicated—as constitutively other-than-human.[34] Drowned somethings become estranged from historicity as ornamenting animals layer synchronic (or coalescent) atop diachronic times. Standing on the viewing platform at the National War Grave at Pearl Harbor, looking down past the surface of the sea to the remains of the USS *Arizona* and *Utah*, James Hamilton-Paterson reflected that the sailors' "skeletons, the events of 1941 and the fish now inhabited the same world."[35] What sorts of stories does—can—a world like this tell?

Poriferan Practice and Eccentric Knowledge

For as long as shipwrecks have been sought and stumbled upon, knowledge of their whereabouts has been mediated by sponge divers. Like all hunters, divers negotiate among human and other-than-human worlds.[36] Unlike terrestrial prey, however, commercially valuable sponges induce their pursuers to enter an element they cannot survive. In this instance, as in others, the undersea encourages apparently preternatural acts of immersion, as well as prosthetic expansions in human capability. Skilled divers are transversal figures whose ability has been monumentalized in art and story—and encouraged and exploited by the agents of science, trade, slavery, and empire.[37] Sometimes they ascend to the sea-surface with reports of drowned things, like the remains of a now-famous Roman shipwreck found in 1900 off the island of Antikythera, at the western edge of the Aegean Sea. The artifacts sponge divers found there included numerous notable works of classical statuary, "decomposed bodies" in bronze, and marble partly "carved," as Amalie Smith has it, by excavating sponges, like the empurpling *Cliona schmidtii*, over the course of nearly two millennia.[38]

All poriferans are aquatic, and most of them are marine. Their ranges extend from coastal shallows to extreme depths; at many sites along the sea bottom, they are the most abundant animals around.[39] Their apparent longevity and habits of growth are as varied as their habitats: Antarctic glass sponges, whose life span has been estimated at 15,000 years, may be the longest-living animals on earth.[40] The possibility is startling, but it also refuses resolution, because poriferan morphology is inconsistent even among "different parts of the [same] organism," to say nothing of different individuals of the same species. Moreover, sponges do not offer legible markers of year-on-year development in the manner of, say, reef-building corals. In the Caribbean Sea, scientists making photogrammetric images of spongy wrecks use the received temporal coordinates of sinkings to make inferences about the histories of encrusting animals, in a kind of inversion of conventional analytic logic.[41] Reading spongy stories is, in many instances, simply impossible without such narrative assistance: when an organism's "pivotal" taxonomic "characters" are so often lost or radically altered in the course of its life, the classifier has no choice but to become more flexible in their method.[42]

No other choice, that is, except ignoring the phylum altogether. Despite evidence that their numbers are increasing in the Caribbean, marine surveys frequently leave sponges unremarked because their "demographic data" is so uncertain.[43] A "piece of debateable land" was the Victorian naturalist George Johnston's metaphor for the ontological territory inhabited by the subjects of his *A History of the British Zoophytes* (1838) and its supplement, *A History of British Sponges and Lithophytes* (1842). As Pandora Syperek has observed, "zoophyte" was a common nineteenth-century designation for those seeming "plant-animals," like jellyfish, coral, and sponges, that troubled the boundaries between taxonomic kingdoms.[44] Johnston understood that, like sketchy demography, questionable classification could prove as ready an inducement to scientific neglect as to fascination. He speculates, in a preface to *A History of British Sponges and Lithophytes*, that "no other naturalist was likely to devote his time" to continued work on the zoophytes, "a comparatively limited and isolated class of organized beings, obscure in character, and possessed of less interest than attaches to almost every other." Investigations into spongy and lithophytous lives were, therefore, work for such an "eccentric borderer" as might "find his pleasure in cultivating an intimacy" with the "rude tenantry" of this apparently unsettled domain of nature.[45] Liminal subjects, in other words, invite attention from observers who incline toward the strange satisfactions of intermediate states of being.

Johnston's sense suggests an intriguing kind of fellow-feeling, not to say a spongy transference. To an extreme (if not actually singular) extent, sponges are scrupulous imagists of the environments they inhabit.[46] In Johnston's view, most "are very irregular and variable, their shape depending, in a great measure, on the peculiarities of their site, to which they easily accommodate themselves." They "incrust" their substrates with what Johnston figured as a kind of solicitude, "following" in their growth "every protuberance and sinuosity."[47] This meticulousness is really enabled by sponges' modularity, their consisting of not a "unitary" structure but "a set of repetitive main structural components," the number whereof shifts over the course of a sponge's life and the character and configuration whereof is thoroughly environmentally contingent.[48] Sponges are mutable concatenations, their parts iteratively reading, telling, and retelling the forms and characters of the "hard substrates," such as wrecks, where they prefer to live.[49]

Encrusting poriferans are something like chorographers, describing in exquisite detail the districts they inhabit. Saying as much must amount to more than simply assigning eccentric agents to the standard calculus of subject and object, delineator and delineated. In the performance of their "discursive practices," to channel Karen Barad's treatment of the invertebrate oceanity of the brittlestar, sponges "intra-act" with their environments through material entanglements that are always in process and mutually constitutive.[50] For Johnston, spongy practices ultimately tended to undermine the signifying behavior of their substrates, to "render the original shape of the thing they grow upon irrecognizable." Poriferan habits of concretion and coalescence perforce occasioned minor but real crises for language and "the nomenclator": "we labour, perhaps in vain," he wrote, "to devise phrases which shall aptly pourtray to others the characteristics of objects that have no fixed shape, and whose distinctive peculiarities almost cheat the eye."[51] In contact with wrecks and their abundant meanings, the difficulties of spongy observing, recognizing, naming, and phrasing—and the idiosyncratic, expressive potential of spongy discourse—acquire special consequence.

Encrusted Poetics, Parergonal Aesthetics

Because ships are locations of human habitation, explains the archaeologist Chryssanthi Papadopoulou, they are "places" as well as "artefacts." Wreck sites are haunted by the "phantoms" of the "bygone present" fragmentarily signified by each of the artifacts they gather, including (but by no means limited to) the vessels themselves. The interventions of underwater archaeologists, therefore, happen amidst "a proliferating con-fusion of past and present places."[52] This would seem to make wrecks the more or less direct, saltwater analogues of terrestrial sites, were it not for the incommensurable modalities of ocean time, which are not only unlike land time but at extraordinary variance across the water column.[53] What makes drowned graves different from earthy ones, reflects Hamilton-Paterson, is that when it has "swallowed something, the sea washes it over less with water than with time." The eight hundred or so sailors whose remains are still aboard the USS *Arizona* thus occupy a space that is no great physical distance from the sea's surface but is nonetheless totally estranged from topside temporality—and forms a weird, metachronous community among the American seamen, "the *Titanic*'s victims and those of the *Mary Rose* or any Phoenician galley."[54]

The ethical and political ramifications of such confusion and coevality are left unsaid in these evocative studies, and so are the roles of other-than-human players in wrecky situations. Diving on the SS *Thistlegorm*, an English re-supply ship sunk by German bombs in 1941 at Sha'ab Ali in the Red Sea, Stephanie Merchant observed the signs of "transgression from the human world" (figure 9.5). The wreck, she writes, is "semi-natural," "semi-manmade," discoverable in a state of "partial destruction and disarray": its ontology, in other words, is neither securely anthropic nor utterly inhuman but defined by intermediacy.

Figure 9.5 Aft view of the wreck of the SS *Thistlegorm*. Woodym555, 2007, photograph. Wikimedia Commons (CC BY-SA 3.0).

Invoking Jacques-Yves Cousteau, who shot film of the *Thistlegorm* for *Le monde du silence* (*The Silent World*, 1956), Merchant describes the "ambiguous" matter she encounters there, the inversions of insides and outsides, the covering and camouflaging of propellers and tanks by marine flora and fauna.[55] Merchant aptly cites Caitlin DeSilvey, whose sense of a ruin as "a dynamic entity that is entangled in both cultural and natural processes" operates in a uniquely submarine fashion at a wreck.[56]

DeSilvey's subject, a forsaken homestead in Montana, is essentially terrestrial, but her consideration of invertebrate articulations, and of the poetic and aesthetic characters of other-than-human ruins, bear describing. A "forest map" with an "insect-eaten fringe"; a surprisingly lovely "montage of indeterminate effect," crafted by mold and a magazine; a poem fashioned from "shards of text" recovered from a basket, coauthored with mice; an "accidental collage of seeds and text . . . on the wall of a dismantled cabin": these natural-casual assemblages are seen to testify to the "mutable character of material presence, the transformative powers of decay and revitalization."[57] The litany reads like evidence of the kind of practice Jane Bennett calls "aesthetic-affective openness to material vitality."[58] Through DeSilvey's method of attending, and specifically through her deployment of language and image, these things also testify to the subtle but crucial ways that an aesthetics of concretion and coalescence, as well as decay, generates impressions—and perhaps even presences—of an intermediate poetics.

Wreckage is a lively situation that variously invites, sustains, and frustrates human story and memory. It offers the prospect of an encounter with—to interpolate Adrienne Rich's "Diving into the Wreck" (1973)—"the thing itself and not the myth." Rich's poem is both a vivid account of the physiological and phenomenal experience of submergence and an allegory of seeking, seeing, feeling, and naming beyond the strictures of the normative, that is to say, the strictures of dualism, authoritarianism, and sexism. This undersea is subtly but suggestively invertebrate: clad in dive gear, the poet enters the water inhumanly, "like an insect." Depth delivers the knowledge that topside motility will not apply, that "I have to learn alone / to turn my body without force," as if in emulation of those "who have always / lived here / swaying their crenellated fans." Swimming as though sessile, the poet identifies with some "half-destroyed instruments" and other intermediate objects. This is a poetics that inhabits the center of contrary energies, of "damage" and "threadbare beauty," of "rot" and "treasures." Rich's poem orients itself with and toward a "fouled compass" and other ornamented artifacts, natural-cultural treasuries that hold fast the evidentiary remains of wrecked worlds while progressively reshaping their contours.[59]

The fouled compass and the spongy wreck are works of encrustation. They challenge the mainstream Western tradition of understanding ornament as literally external to, or even antipathetic toward, substance and self.[60] The story of the spongy wreck does not lie below its exterior layer, among the "non-sponge objects" that might appear there.[61] Nor does it confine itself only to poriferans and their numerous other faunal and floral cohabitants. It consists, rather, through a more dynamic and indeterminate formal relationship between encrustation and substrate. Interpolating from Jacques Derrida's account of Kantian aesthetics, Gunalan Nadarajan amplifies the capacities of the "parergonal"—from the Latin *parergon*, for supplement or ornament—to signify a relationship that confuses the hierarchy of embellisher and embellished. A parergonal aesthetic, ventures Nadarajan, is one that establishes contact between things while frustrating attempts to distinguish between "the fundamental and the secondary, the natural and the created," and so forth.[62] The sponge is literally secondary to the wreck in the chronological sense of arriving subsequently. As parergon, however, it covers, camouflages, and refigures—while sometimes, as at the *Monitor* and upon the fouled compass, sustaining its counterparts with what looks a great deal like care.

Conclusion: Telling Encrusted Stories at Sea

Shipwrecks are, and have long been, sites of marine natural-cultural hybridity, good places to imagine and live with. The stories of spongy wrecks are unfolding, and hearing and reading them attentively entails understanding that they form, as DeSilvey says of ruins, through "chance" arrangements of matter, life, and meaning.[63] Naturally and casually, vessels and their encrustations concresce unanticipated, animate-inanimate ecologies of remembrance, forgetting, and futurity. As Johnston intuited, encrusting organisms do more than spur received epistemology to expand and refine its categories. They imitate their substrates so closely and completely—so lovingly, we could say—as to generate new things: lively, unfixed, and sportive things that defy the eye, and defy language. And as Rich insinuated, a poetics commensurate with the spongy wreck is one that knowingly and assiduously relinquishes terrestrial stories, motions, and rhythms, declines the fantasy that the depths offer any ultimate escape from the facts of disaster, and recognizes the metamorphic potential of sessile sensibility and fouled arrangements. As parergon, spongy life not only conserves the wrecks it adorns but resituates wrecky stories—uncertain and ongoing as they are—among oceanic times and submarine relations.

Of course, the story of the spongy wreck is fundamentally a sea story, and there is still much to know about the wider ornamental habits of saltwater bodies. The ocean, wrote the eighteenth-century zoologist John Ellis, "wherever it is possible to observe, abounds so much with Animal Life, that no inanimate Body can long remain unoccupied by some Species."[64] Ellis, whose researches helped establish that sponges were indeed animals, summons the sea as an animate-inanimate element and agent of natural-casual adornment.[65] Much more recently, the geographers Kimberley Peters and Philip Steinberg have theorized how the stuff of shipwrecks, hybrid growth, and encrustation is not only contained *by* marine realms but inheres within marine ontology. The sea's "detritus," they write, can be reimagined as "an ocean articulated differently," a "more-than-planetary, artificial materiality."[66] This is a parergonal sort of program, and it is one that the spongy wreck exemplifies with unusual charisma. Along and through its eccentric borders, unforeseen concretions are becoming legible.

Notes

1. Broadwater, "Digging Deeper," 653.
2. Monitor *National Marine Sanctuary Condition Report 2008*, 13.
3. Ibid., 17.
4. Prown, "Mind in Matter," 1.
5. Adams, "Ships and Boats as Archaeological Source Material," 296.
6. Schulze et al., "Artificial Reefs in the Northern Gulf of Mexico," 1.
7. I draw this number from *The UNESCO Convention on the Protection of the Underwater Cultural Heritage*, 3.
8. See, for example, Cusack, introduction to *Framing the Ocean*, 10.
9. DeLoughrey, "Submarine Futures of the Anthropocene," 33.
10. Bakus and Campbell, "Sponges."
11. I am invoking Félix Guattari's call for an approach that attends, above all, to how paradigms in knowledge participate in "modelising subjectivity." See Guattari, *Chaosmosis*, 10–11. I am also thinking of Thom van Dooren and Deborah Bird Rose's discussion of the ways ethographic writing might recognize and mobilize the liveliness of the apparently nonliving. See van Dooren and Rose, "Lively Ethography," 87.
12. I am working alongside Jane Bennett's interpolation of Gilles Deleuze and Guattari's concept of assemblage. See Bennett, *Vibrant Matter*, 24. I am also attuned to Margaret Cohen's observation that a shipwreck is an unusually hospitable site for forms of "cross-species assemblage." See Cohen, "The Shipwreck as Undersea Gothic," 157.
13. DeSilvey, "Observed Decay," 336.
14. On marine neglect in the ethological literature, see Leane and Nicol, "Charismatic Krill?," 142. On a "vertebrate bias in human-animal studies scholarship," see Moore and Wilkie, "Introduction to *The Silent Majority*," 654.
15. Edgar, "Sponges," 77. The durability of the trope of intermediacy through time is striking. For another notable invocation of sponges' "intermediate" status written nearly two millennia before Edgar, see Pliny, quoted in Hooper and Van Soest, "Systema Porifera," 2.
16. Van Dooren, Kirksey, and Münster, "Multispecies Studies," 4.
17. For a resonant critique of the frame of the "exotic," see Eduardo Kohn, quoted in Kirksey and Helmreich, "The Emergence of Multispecies Ethnography," 562. On accounting for "forms of non-relating," see Yusoff, "Aesthetics of Loss," 586.
18. I borrow the quoted phrase from the entry for "holdfast" in the *Oxford English Dictionary*. For a scientific account, see Ehrlich et al., "First Report," 1–2. For a concise treatment of rootedness as a fundamental, and vexed, value in ecocritical thought,

see Garrard, "What Powers Have Words?," 48.

19. Lingis, "The Rapture of the Deep," 7.
20. Ezek. 27:25–27 (King James Version).
21. Burnet, *The Theory of the Earth*, 47–48.
22. Thoreau, *Cape Cod*, 127.
23. Earle, "The Sweet Spot in Time," 66.
24. Hoegh-Guldberg et al., "Coral Reefs Under Rapid Climate Change," 1737.
25. Yaeger, "Sea Trash, Dark Pools, and the Tragedy of the Commons," 527–28.
26. Hylton, "History's Largest Mining Operation Is About to Begin."
27. Zalasiewicz and Williams, *Ocean Worlds*, 264.
28. The literature on artificial reefs is substantial. For a study with particular pertinence for this chapter's concerns, see Walker et al., "Spatial Heterogeneity of Epibenthos on Artificial Reefs," 435–45.
29. John Beale to Robert Boyle, June 26, 1682, in Boyle, *The Works of the Honourable Robert Boyle*, 6:446.
30. Delbourgo, "Divers Things," 158.
31. Shakespeare, *Shakespeare's Tempest*, 19.
32. *Sea Sculpture*, 1725, sculpture (porcelain with shell and coral), 17 × 22 cm, Victoria and Albert Museum, London, accessed August 13, 2020, http://m.vam.ac.uk/collections/item/O172836/sea-sculpture-unknown/.
33. Blumenberg, *Shipwreck with Spectator*, 67, 59.
34. Mentz, *Shipwreck Modernity*, 2.
35. Hamilton-Paterson, *The Great Deep*, 127.
36. For a pertinent discussion of hunting, see Kohn, "Soul Blindness," 103–28.
37. Notable accounts of intersections of submarine skill, science, empire, and enslavement include Dawson, "Enslaved Swimmers and the Atlantic World"; Warsh, *American Baroque*; and von Mallinckrodt, "Exploring Underwater Worlds."
38. Smith, "The Sponge Diver," 329. For a taxonomic description of poriferan impacts on statues recovered from the Antikythera wreck, see Calcinai et al., "Endolithic and Epilithic Sponges of Archaeological Marble Statues," 1–18.
39. Hooper, "*Sponguide*," 3.
40. Marine Chesterton, "The Oldest Living Thing on Earth," BBC News, June 12, 2017, accessed August 14, 2020, https://www.bbc.com/news/science-environment-40224991.
41. Olinger et al., "Growth Estimates," 1–2.
42. Hooper and Van Soest, "Systema Porifera," 3.
43. Olinger et al., "Growth Estimates," 2.
44. Syperek, "'No Fancy So Wild'," 240.
45. Johnston, *A History of British Sponges and Lithophytes*, v.
46. Ehrlich et al., "First Report," 1; Olinger et al., "Growth Estimates," 1.
47. Johnston, *A History of British Sponges*, 10.
48. Ereskovskii, "Problems of Coloniality, Modularity, and Individuality in Sponges," S48.
49. Ehrlich et al., "First Report," 1.
50. Barad, "Invertebrate Visions," 227, 232, 234.
51. Johnston, *A History of British Sponges*, v, 10–11.
52. Papadopoulou, "The Phenomenon of Phantom Place," 370–71, 373, 379.
53. See, for example, Steinberg and Peters, "Wet Ontologies, Fluid Spaces," 255.
54. Hamilton-Paterson, *The Great Deep*, 130.
55. Merchant, "Deep Ethnography," 123–25. For an important reading of the *Thistlegorm*'s appearance in *Le monde du silence*, see Cohen, "The Shipwreck as Undersea Gothic," 159–65.
56. DeSilvey, "Observed Decay," 324.
57. Ibid., 323, 328–30, 333–34.
58. Bennett, *Vibrant Matter*, x.
59. Rich, "Diving into the Wreck," 22–24.

60. For a useful account of this tradition, see Davis, *Ornamental Aesthetics*, 5.
61. I adapt this phrase from Olinger et al., "Growth Estimates," 9.
62. Nadarajan, "Ornamental Biotechnology and Parergonal Aesthetics," 54.
63. DeSilvey, "Observed Decay," 328.
64. Ellis, *An Essay Towards a Natural History of the Corallines*, 102.
65. For a description of Ellis's scientific achievements, see Hamilton-Paterson, *The Great Deep*, 94.
66. Peters and Steinberg, "The Ocean in Excess," 302–3.

Bibliography

Adams, Jonathan. "Ships and Boats as Archaeological Source Material." *World Archaeology* 32, no. 3 (2001): 292–310.

Bakus, Gerald J., and Andrew Campbell. "Sponges." In *The Encyclopedia of Underwater Life*, edited by Andrew Campbell and John Dawes. Oxford Reference. Oxford: Oxford University Press, 2005.

Barad, Karen. "Invertebrate Visions: Diffractions of the Brittlestar." In *The Multispecies Salon*, edited by Eben Kirksey, 221–41. Durham: Duke University Press, 2014.

Bennett, Jane. *Vibrant Matter: A Political Ecology of Things*. Durham: Duke University Press, 2010.

Blumenberg, Hans. *Shipwreck with Spectator: Paradigm of a Metaphor for Existence*. Translated by Steven Rendall. Cambridge: MIT Press, 1997.

Boyle, Robert. *The Works of the Honourable Robert Boyle*. 6 vols. London: W. Johnston et al., 1772.

Broadwater, John D. "Digging Deeper: Deepwater Archaeology and the *Monitor* National Marine Sanctuary." In *International Handbook of Underwater Archaeology*, edited by Carol V. Ruppé and Janet F. Barstad, 639–66. New York: Kluwer Academic / Plenum, 2002.

Burnet, Thomas. *The Theory of the Earth*. 3rd ed. London: Walter Kettilby, 1697.

Calcinai, Barbara, Carlotta Sacco Perasso, Barbara Davidde Petriaggi, and Sandra Ricci. "Endolithic and Epilithic Sponges of Archaeological Marble Statues Recovered in the Blue Grotto, Capri (Italy) and in the Antikythera Shipwreck (Greece)." *Facies* 65, no. 21 (2019): 1–18.

Cohen, Margaret. "The Shipwreck as Undersea Gothic." In *The Aesthetics of the Undersea*, edited by Margaret Cohen and Killian Quigley, 155–66. London: Routledge.

Cusack, Tricia. Introduction to *Framing the Ocean, 1700 to the Present: Envisaging the Sea as Social Space*, edited by Tricia Cusack, 1–20. Farnham, UK: Ashgate, 2014.

Davis, Theo. *Ornamental Aesthetics: The Poetry of Attending in Thoreau, Dickinson, and Whitman*. New York: Oxford University Press, 2016.

Dawson, Kevin. "Enslaved Swimmers and the Atlantic World." *The Journal of American History* 92, no. 4 (2006): 1327–55.

Delbourgo, James. "Divers Things: Collecting the World Under Water." *History of Science* 49, no. 2 (2011): 149–85.

DeLoughrey, Elizabeth. "Submarine Futures of the Anthropocene." *Comparative Literature* 69, no. 1 (2017): 32–44.

DeSilvey, Caitlin. "Observed Decay: Telling Stories with Mutable Things." *Journal of Material Culture* 11, no. 3 (2006): 318–38.

Earle, Sylvia A. "The Sweet Spot in Time: Why the Ocean Matters to Everyone, Everywhere." *Virginia Quarterly Review* 88, no. 4 (2012): 54–77.

Edgar, Graham. "Sponges." In *Tropical Marine Life of Australia: Plants and Animals of the Central Indo-Pacific*, 77–79. London: New Holland, 2019.

Ehrlich, Hermann, Oksana V. Kaluzhnaya, Mikhail V. Tsurkan, Alexander Ereskovsky, Konstantin R. Tabachnick, Micha Ilan, Allison Stelling, et al. "First Report on Chitinous Holdfast in Sponges (Porifera)." *Proceedings of the Royal Society B* 280, no. 1762 (2013): 1–8.

Ellis, John. *An Essay Towards a Natural History of the Corallines*. London: John Ellis, 1755.

Ereskovskii, A. V. "Problems of Coloniality, Modularity, and Individuality in Sponges and Special Features of Their Morphogeneses During Growth and Asexual Reproduction." *Russian Journal of Marine Biology* 29 (2003): S46–S56.

Garrard, Greg. "What Powers Have Words?" Review of *Can Poetry Save the Earth? A Field Guide to Nature Poems*, by John Felstiner. *Science* 326, no. 5949 (2009): 48.

Guattari, Félix. *Chaosmosis: An Ethico-Aesthetic Paradigm*. Translated by Paul Bains and Julian Pefanis. Bloomington: Indiana University Press, 1995.

Hamilton-Paterson, James. *The Great Deep: The Sea and Its Thresholds*. New York: Random House, 1992.

Hoegh-Guldberg, O., P. J. Mumby, A. J. Hooten, R. S. Steneck, P. Greenfield, E. Gomez, C. D. Harvell, et al. "Coral Reefs Under Rapid Climate Change and Ocean Acidification." *Science* 318, no. 5857 (2007): 1737–42.

Hooper, John N. A. *"Sponguide": Guide to Sponge Collection and Identification (Version 2003)*. South Brisbane: Queensland Museum, 2003.

Hooper, John N. A., and Rob W. M. Van Soest. "Systema Porifera. A Guide to the Classification of Sponges." In *Systema Porifera: A Guide to the Classification of Sponges*, edited by John N. A. Hooper and Rob W. M. Van Soest, 1–3. New York: Kluwer Academic / Plenum, 2002.

Hylton, Wil S. "History's Largest Mining Operation Is About to Begin." *The Atlantic*, January/February 2020. Accessed August 10, 2020. https://www.theatlantic.com/magazine/archive/2020/01/20000-feet-under-the-sea/603040/.

Johnston, George. *A History of British Sponges and Lithophytes*. Edinburgh: W. H. Lizars; London: S. Highley, 1842.

Kirksey, S. Eben, and Stefan Helmreich. "The Emergence of Multispecies Ethnography." *Cultural Anthropology* 25, no. 4 (2010): 545–76.

Kohn, Eduardo. "Soul Blindness." In *How Forests Think: Toward an Anthropology Beyond the Human*, 103–28. Oakland: University of California Press, 2013.

Leane, Elizabeth, and Steve Nicol. "Charismatic Krill? Size and Conservation in the Ocean." *Anthrozoös* 24, no. 2 (2011): 135–46.

Lingis, Alphonso. "The Rapture of the Deep." In *Excesses: Eros and Culture*, 1–16. Albany: State University of New York Press, 1983.

Mentz, Steve. *Shipwreck Modernity: Ecologies of Globalization, 1550–1719*. Minneapolis: University of Minnesota Press, 2015.

Merchant, Stephanie. "Deep Ethnography: Witnessing the Ghosts of SS *Thistlegorm*." In *Water Worlds: Human Geographies of the Ocean*, edited by Jon Anderson and Kimberley Peters, 119-32. Farnham, UK: Ashgate, 2014.

Monitor *National Marine Sanctuary Condition Report 2008*. Silver Spring: Office of National Marine Sanctuaries, 2008.

Moore, Lisa Jean, and Rhoda M. Wilkie. "Introduction to *The Silent Majority:*

Invertebrates in Human-Animal Studies." *Society & Animals* 27, no. 7 (2019): 653–55.

Nadarajan, Gunalan. "Ornamental Biotechnology and Parergonal Aesthetics." In *Signs of Life: Bio Art and Beyond*, edited by Eduardo Kac, 43–55. Cambridge: MIT Press, 2007.

Olinger, Lauren K., Alexander R. Scott, Steven E. McMurray, and Joseph R. Pawlik. "Growth Estimates of Caribbean Reef Sponges on a Shipwreck Using 3D Photogrammetry." *Scientific Reports* 9, no. 18398 (2019): 1–12.

Papadopoulou, Chryssanthi. "The Phenomenon of Phantom Place: Archaeology and Ships." *Journal of Material Culture* 21, no. 3 (2016): 367–82.

Peters, Kimberley and Philip Steinberg. "The Ocean in Excess: Towards a More-than-Wet Ontology." *Dialogues in Human Geography* 9, no. 3 (2019): 293–307.

Prown, Jules David. "Mind in Matter: An Introduction to Material Culture Theory and Method." *Winterthur Portfolio* 17, no. 1 (1982): 1–19.

Rich, Adrienne. "Diving into the Wreck." In *Diving into the Wreck: Poems 1971–1972*, 22–24. New York: W. W. Norton & Company, 2013.

Schulze, Anja, Deana L. Erdner, Candace J. Grimes, Daniel M. Holstein, and Maria Pia Miglietta. "Artificial Reefs in the Northern Gulf of Mexico: Community Ecology amid the 'Ocean Sprawl.'" *Frontiers in Marine Science* 7, no. 447 (2020): 1–15.

Shakespeare, William. *Shakespeare's Tempest*, edited by J. M. Jephson. London: Macmillan and Co., 1864.

Smith, Amalie. "The Sponge Diver, or, Bodies on the Seabed." In *Narrating Life—Experiments with Human and Animal Bodies in Literature, Science and Art*, edited by Stefan Herbrechter and Elisabeth Friis, 327–30. Leiden: Brill, 2016.

Steinberg, Philip and Kimberley Peters. "Wet Ontologies, Fluid Spaces: Giving Depth to Volume Through Oceanic Thinking." *Environment and Planning D: Society and Space* 33, no. 2 (2015): 247–64.

Syperek, Pandora. "'No Fancy So Wild': Slippery Gender Models in the Coral Gallery." In *Framing the Ocean, 1700 to the Present: Envisaging the Sea as Social Space*, edited by Tricia Cusack, 239–56. Farnham, UK: Ashgate, 2014.

Thoreau, Henry David. *Cape Cod*. New York: Penguin, 1987.

UNESCO Convention on the Protection of the Underwater Cultural Heritage. Paris: UNESCO, 2007. https://unesdoc.unesco.org/ark:/48223/pf0000181217).

van Dooren, Thom, and Deborah Bird Rose. "Lively Ethography: Storying Animist Worlds." *Environmental Humanities* 8, no. 1 (2016): 77–94.

van Dooren, Thom, Eben Kirksey, and Ursula Münster. "Multispecies Studies: Cultivating Arts of Attentiveness." *Environmental Humanities* 8, no. 1 (2016): 1–23.

von Mallinckrodt, Rebekka. "Exploring Underwater Worlds: Diving in the Late Seventeenth- / Early Eighteenth-Century British Empire." In *Empire of the Senses: Sensory Practices of Colonialism in Early America*, edited by Daniela Hacke and Paul Musselwhite, 300–322. Leiden: Brill, 2018.

Walker, Simon J., Thomas A. Schlacher, and Monika A. Schlacher-Hoenlinger. "Spatial Heterogeneity of Epibenthos on Artificial Reefs: Fouling Communities in the Early Stages of Colonization on an East Australian Shipwreck." *Marine Ecology* 28, no. 4 (2007): 435–45.

Warsh, Molly. *American Baroque: Pearls and the Nature of Empire, 1492–1700*.

Williamsburg: The Omohundro Institute of Early American History and Culture and the University of North Carolina Press, 2018.

Yaeger, Patricia. "Sea Trash, Dark Pools, and the Tragedy of the Commons." *PMLA* 125, no. 3 (2010): 523–45.

Yusoff, Kathryn. "Aesthetics of Loss: Biodiversity, Banal Violence and Biotic Subjects." *Transactions of the Institute of British Geographers* 37, no. 4 (2012): 578–92.

Zalasiewicz, Jan, and Mark Williams. *Ocean Worlds: The Story of Seas on Earth and Other Planets*. New York: Oxford University Press, 2014.

CHAPTER 10

DRIFTING WITH SNAILS

Stories from Hawai'i

Thom van Dooren

Far out to sea, in the midst of the seemingly endless expanse of the North Pacific Ocean, an uprooted tree bobs around in the water. Washed out in a storm, the tree harbors within its branches some unlikely oceanic travelers: snails. These are not marine snails, or even freshwater snails; rather they are the snails of the forest who make their lives among the leaves. Their arboreal home has become a canoe of sorts—a canoe that just maybe, with enough time and the right conditions, will take its passengers to new shores, new lands and possibilities. This is the image that animates this chapter: an entirely hypothetical, speculative, and yet eminently probable, oceanic voyage. The maritime animal movements that interest me here are primarily, but not entirely, ones that involve no humans at all; movements that were taking place for millions of years before there were humans, but movements (and indeed lives and species) that today find themselves imperiled.

The story told in this chapter centers on the islands of Hawai'i. There are very few ships in this story. Instead, the oceanic voyaging is primarily undertaken by snails travelling on, in, and with various other-than-human vectors. But it is equally a story that takes place on land, exploring what happened after snails arrived in these islands, how their lives have become entangled with this landscape, and later with its peoples.

Hawaiʻi is home to one of the most diverse assemblages of terrestrial snails found anywhere on earth. How did all these snails end up out in the middle of the Pacific Ocean, in one of the most remote oceanic archipelagos in the world? Snails, after all, are not commonly known for their propensity to undertake long journeys—not by land, and certainly not by sea, where their low tolerance for saltwater must surely cause significant problems. So, how did they all get here?

Sadly, today the majority of the snails that once inhabited these islands are extinct. Most of the remaining species are thought to be heading swiftly in the same direction. There are many stories that might be told about these snails. In this time of extinctions, we need multiple stories, diverse efforts to experiment and explore, to thicken and enliven, the forms of life that are slipping away. This chapter is a reflection on extinction, one grounded in the captivating question of where all these disappeared and disappearing snail species came from, focused on the long history of their arrival and evolution in these islands. What might we learn by telling stories of unlikely gastropod voyaging, of the crossing of oceans, both literal and temporal? And equally as importantly at our present time, how might the ongoing extinctions of snails be understood *differently* if we pay attention to these processes? What might this context help us to see, appreciate, and perhaps hold on to?

A Land of Snails

It is not well known that, amongst its many biological riches, Hawaiʻi is a land of snails. While snails can be found all over the world—indeed, they inhabit every continent and island archipelago outside the Arctic—very few other places have supported anything like the variety found in this particular island chain. To date, over 750 species of Hawaiian land snails have been recognized. The actual number, though, is thought to be considerably higher, perhaps somewhere in the region of 1,000. But even at 750, the tiny patches of land that form these islands were once home to roughly two-thirds the number of snail species that can be found in the whole of continental North America, a landmass about 1,700 times the size. What's more, almost all of these species—roughly 99 percent—were endemic to these islands, found nowhere else.[1] By any reckoning, Hawaiʻi is a remarkable place when it comes to snails.

All of these species can, somewhat crudely, be divided into two groups: the tree snails and the ground snails, distinguished by their primary habitat and diet. These snails vary greatly in size, color, and shape, but none of them lead the kind of leaf-munching lives that most people associate with their kind. In fact, amongst all of Hawai'i's incredible snail diversity there are no species known to eat living vegetation. Instead, Hawai'i's tree snails consume the thin layer of fungi and other microorganisms that line the surface of leaves, utilizing their sandpaper-like radula (effectively a snail tongue lined with hundreds of tiny teeth) to scrape harvested materials into their mouths. Amongst their number are the incredible *Achatinella* tree snails of O'ahu, with shells about 2 cm in length when fully grown, found in a variety of striking colors including greens, yellows, and reds, many with spirals, stripes, swirls, or other intricate patterns. Meanwhile, Hawai'i's ground snails utilize their own specialized radula to eat dead and decaying leaf matter, recycling it back into the soil. While many of these snails are tiny, non-descript, brown creatures, there are others like *Laminella sanguinea* that have a beautiful red conical shell about 1.5 cm in length with a distinctive lightning-bolt stripe.

Today, however, close to two-thirds of these species are thought to be extinct. In addition, the majority of those species that do still remain are threatened with extinction.[2] The causes of this incredible decline are complex and multifaceted. The most significant threat faced by Hawai'i's snails today comes in the form of the predators—principally chameleons, rats, and carnivorous snails—that have been introduced to the islands with their human inhabitants. The carnivorous snails (*Euglandina rosea*), are thought to be of particular concern, able to detect and follow the slime trails of the local species to consume them with devastating efficiency.

But these impacts come in the wake of a longer history of snail decline. Key to this story is the widespread loss of the islands' forest. To a certain extent, this process began with the arrival of Polynesian peoples about 1,000 years ago. As they cleared lowland forests to make room for kalo (also known as taro), and the other agricultural plants that would allow these islands to sustain human life, they removed and transformed snail habitat. At the same time, the rats that they brought with them, voracious consumers of seed and fruit, are thought to have begun a process of significantly altering the composition of the islands' forests.[3]

But these impacts were drastically scaled up after the arrival of European, American, Japanese, and other settlers. With particular intensity from the early nineteenth century on, vast areas of forested land were taken over by ranching and plantations, as well as tourist, urban, and military developments. Many of those forests that did remain had already been heavily degraded by the arrival and widespread establishment of more conventional "maritime animals" brought by European explorers (such as cows, goats, and pigs) that severely damaged or removed the understories of Hawai'i's forests.

The arrival of Westerners in the islands also kicked off an intense period of shell collecting. For roughly 130 years beginning in the 1820s, some people gathered up these shells on a staggering scale. Millions of live snails were reduced to specimens in huge private collections, many of which were well in excess of ten thousand shells. This collecting craze was further fueled by the insatiable demand of museums and naturalists the world over.

Today, the impacts of climate change are being added to this difficult situation, transforming rainfall and temperature patterns across the islands in ways that can't yet be fully understood. Modeling, however, indicates that we can expect generally hotter and drier conditions in these islands, which does not bode well for moisture-dependent snails.

Getting a precise handle on the snail situation in Hawai'i is a truly difficult task. The simple fact is that we just don't know how bad things are—at least not in ways that can be readily quantified. We don't know how many snail species there are (or were) in the islands, let alone the current conservation status of all those species. The situation is significantly different to dealing with endangered birds or mammals, where species tend to be thought about and managed individually or in small groups. In the world of Hawai'i's snails, endangered species conservation must take place in bulk. It must deal with hundreds of species of tiny animals, generally identifiable only to specialists and possessing only a Latin name, and most of them relatively understudied until recently.

Current conservation efforts center on protecting the remaining species, either within a captive rearing facility—where they live out their lives in refrigerator-like environmental chambers—or within purpose-built fenced exclosure areas in the forest that seek to exclude predators through a series of barriers. As Dave Sischo, the head of Hawai'i's Snail

Extinction Prevention Program (SEPP), explained to me, restoration of these species is just not possible at the moment; "extinction prevention" is the best that we can hope for. All over the islands, the SEPP team are engaged in what Dave thinks about as an "evacuation": trying desperately to locate the last remnants of snail species. In the rugged terrain of many of the high islands in this chain, this work frequently involves long hikes and, when hiking isn't possible, the use of a helicopter to access remote areas. Just a few years ago Dave and his team would try to take only a small number of snails from these populations as a backup, leaving the rest in the forest. In the intervening years, however, he has seen numerous formerly robust populations, each comprised of hundreds of snails, completely disappear. As a result, Dave and his team are now often pulling out every snail they can find, carefully packing them into containers and bringing them into one of their captive facilities.

At Sea with Snails

In 2006, the biologist Brenden Holland placed a piece of tree bark with twelve live Hawaiian land snails of the species *Succinea caduca* into a saltwater aquarium. This is one of Hawai'i's non-endangered snail species, which is important because the purpose of this experiment was to see whether they would survive. The snails that Brenden enlisted into this experiment were from populations living as little as ten meters from the beach, snails that might readily get caught in the runoff of a heavy storm and washed out to sea. His purpose, of course, was not simply to understand their prospects for survival were this to happen, but rather to determine whether it might be possible for these kinds of events to play a role in the dispersal of snail species to new lands. The answer, it seems, is yes. Brenden and his colleague Rob Cowie later reported that "after 12 h of immersion, all specimens were alive, indicating that sea water is not immediately lethal and suggesting the potential for rafting between islands on logs and vegetation."[4] This is the only experiment to date that has explored these questions in relation to Hawai'i's snails.

Well beyond Hawai'i's shores, however, land snails have long been something of a puzzle in the effort to understand the evolution and distribution of species. Terrestrial snails are generally a pretty sedentary bunch, spending their lives close to the spot where they happened to be hatched or born (some snails come in eggs, others are live born). When we add to this situation their very low tolerance for sea water—as they have no control over their salt absorption and thus dehydrate readily—the diverse range of snail species found on remote oceanic islands like Hawai'i becomes even more confounding. And yet, terrestrial snails are to be found on pretty much every tropical and subtropical island around the world. We are faced, then, with a kind of snail paradox, as Brenden put it to me in an interview: How do organisms that are so sedentary end up being so incredibly widely dispersed?

Charles Darwin, along with many others before and since, pondered this question. In a letter to Alfred Russel Wallace in 1857, Darwin summed the situation up succinctly: "One of the subjects on which I have been experimentising and which cost me much trouble, is the means of distribution of all organic beings found on oceanic islands and any facts on this subject would be most gratefully received: Land-Molluscs are a great perplexity to me."[5] In an effort to address this perplexity, Darwin submerged snails in saltwater to explore whether and how long they might survive. Amongst his other findings was the fact that snails of the *Helix pomatia* species recovered after twenty days in sea water.

These snails survived by virtue of their being in a dormant state. When resting, many species of snail form an epiphragm, essentially a temporary cover of mucus used to seal their aperture to prevent them from drying out. This is the reason why it is sometimes hard to pull a garden snail off an object. As long as they are dormant, sealed up inside their shells, many snails can survive submerged in saltwater for weeks at a time.[6] Inspired by Darwin, a French study in the 1860s placed one hundred land snails of ten different species in a box with holes and immersed it in sea water. Roughly a quarter of the snails, from six different species, survived for fourteen days—which was calculated to be about half the time it would take for an object like a log to float across the Atlantic.[7]

All of these years of submerging snails—of gastropods drowned and survived—have produced one primary, albeit tentative, finding: it is at least possible that land snails are floating around the world to establish themselves in far-flung places. We just don't know enough about Hawai'i's snails in this regard to know how likely a vector this is for their movements: there is only a single, short-term study on one of the roughly 750 known species. Of course, the conditions for this kind of research no longer exist in Hawai'i, at least with regard to the vast majority of species.

But floating is by no means the only mode of transportation open to snails. In fact, most of the biologists I have interviewed on the topic are of the view that it probably isn't even the primary way in which they have moved across large distances. While snails have likely floated around *within* the Hawaiian archipelago, between islands, it is unlikely that the first snails to arrive did so in this way; the distances of open ocean are just too vast. Here, things get even stranger, and even less amendable to experimentation. Most scientists, it seems, think the most likely explanation is that the first snails traveled to Hawai'i by bird.

This is a suggestion that is pretty hard to swallow when we look at many of Hawai'i's snails in their current forms. Many of the better-known species, like the ones mentioned above, are 1–2 cm in shell length. The idea of one or more of them traveling for thousands of kilometers on a migratory bird is somewhat absurd. But these snails haven't always been this way. Many species change after arriving on islands; some, for example, undergo processes of "gigantism" or "dwarfism" in which their new environmental conditions lead to a significantly increased or decreased body size. In the case of Hawai'i's larger snails, many of their ancestor species were thought to have been tiny creatures. Some close relatives of these larger snails still endure in the islands, and amongst them are snails that grow to a maximum length of 1–2 mm, about the size of a grain of rice.

These tiny ancestor snails might have climbed on board a migratory bird as it perched or nested overnight; snails, after all, are nocturnal. The snail might then have hunkered down, deep in the bird's feathers, only climbing off once they had safely arrived at their destination. While it still seems horribly unlikely that this sequence of events would ever take place, in the fullness of evolutionary time, those are actually pretty reasonable odds.

Alongside these two possible vectors of travel, there are yet others, especially for shorter, inter-island trips. Some snails may well have traveled *inside* birds: recent studies have shown that a variety of species of snails around the world survive passage through avian digestive tracts at a relatively high frequency.[8] Others might have flown on leaves or other debris, high in the airstream.

These are, undoubtedly, all rather unreliable ways to travel. For every snail that successfully arrived in a strange new land on a bird, or a floating branch or log, countless millions must have been washed, blown, or flown out to sea without such luck. The odds must be slightly better traveling by bird than log: at least in theory, if you hop onto or into a migratory bird in a forest, you are quite likely to be taken to another forest. Of course, for those snails unfortunate enough to be traveling *inside* the bird, they would have to survive the journey through the digestive system too.

Snails are largely at the whim of external forces in these movements, subject to what biologists call "passive dispersal." As Brenden Holland helpfully summed it up for me in one of our conversations, "biogeographically, snails are plants": both groups share many of the same vectors for movement, the latter usually by seed or spore. This is clearly a system of island dispersal that can only hope to achieve results with immense periods of time at its disposal.

Over millions of years, a few lucky snails made these journeys successfully. We really can't know for certain how many times this happened in the Hawaiian Islands. Genetic studies indicate that some family groups may have arrived and established themselves on more than one occasion. At an absolute minimum, however, in order to have ended up with the diverse range of known terrestrial snails, things must have worked out for around twenty, and likely fewer than thirty, intrepid travelers over, roughly, the past five million years (when Kaua'i, the oldest of the current high islands with suitable snail habitat, was formed). This means, of course, that the vast majority of Hawai'i's snail species evolved on the islands from a relatively small number of common ancestors.

While snails certainly have many things working against them in their travels, the simple fact that they are found on islands almost everywhere tells us that, despite appearances, they are actually excellent at dispersing across oceans. While they might not fly or enjoy saltwater, they are small and robust enough to seal up and take advantage of other modes of movement. But these snails have another dispersal advantage—a reproductive advantage—over many other animals that only really becomes apparent after arrival. Hawai'i's land snails, like most others around the world, are hermaphrodites. This means that in order to successfully establish themselves in a new environment, any two individuals will do. In fact, in some cases one might be enough:

some snails are capable of "selfing" (or self-fertilization), and others are able to store sperm from copulation for long periods of time to utilize at a later date. It isn't entirely clear which of these reproductive feats Hawai'i's many snails are up to, but there is at least some evidence of both of these possibilities amongst them.[9]

While there is undoubtedly something very "passive" about this dispersal of snails—always at the whim of others, be they birds, storms, or tides, traveling under their power and direction—this isn't the whole of the story. Deep evolutionary histories have produced these possibilities. Snails' modes of passive movement only "work" because they have evolved some pretty remarkable traits that enable dispersal, survival, and reproduction, across and into isolated new lands: from epiphragms to hermaphroditism, sperm storage, and self-fertilization. Millions of years and countless generations of more or less successful journeying have selected for those individuals that survived and established themselves best.

There is a profound kind of evolutionary agency at work here, a creative, experimental, and adaptive working out of living forms with particular capacities and propensities.[10] For the most part, individual snails are indeed relatively passive in all this. The agency of snails, however, is not irrelevant. The particular actions of those little beings that crawled onto a bird, that opted to seal up their apertures, that safely stored away sperm for future use, mattered profoundly. But, snails also are not involved in the more active, sometimes even deliberate, dispersal undertaken by many other animals. Instead, if we pay attention, snails amaze us with their capacity to move so far, to spread so widely, while doing so little. This, it seems to me, is one of the real marvels of snail biogeography. Individuals do not need to exert great effort because natural selection has acted for them, acted on them, acted with them, to produce these beings that are so unexpectedly but uniquely suited to a particular form of deep time travel: drifting. From such a perspective, rather than being any kind of deficiency, the highly successful "passivity" of snails might be seen as a remarkable evolutionary achievement.

Patterns of Speciation

While oceanic journeys are a vital part of the story of Hawai'i's snails, in an important sense they are also only the first step. As we are seeing, the vast majority of the islands' snail species likely evolved on the islands. Single arrival events gave rise to one new species, and then another, and then another, as populations separated and diverged. As such, most of these snail species were found living only in this island chain. In fact, almost all of the larger species were what biologists call "single island endemics," found only on one island, and in many cases only a single mountain range or, within that range, on a single volcano or in a single valley.

But why did so many different species evolve in these tiny areas of land? In no small way, it was the Hawaiian Islands themselves that produced the conditions for this incredible diversity. They did so through the relatively ideal environment that they provided: plenty of moist, entirely or largely predator-free forests. As on islands elsewhere, snails in Hawaiʻi were also able to adapt to take up roles, or ecological niches, that are often filled by other species on continental landmasses. For example, in the absence of earthworms and other detritivores who specialize in breaking down leaf matter and other organic materials for the health of the forest, ground snails took up this work in Hawaiʻi. Meanwhile, others took to feeding on the thin layers of fungi and microbes that line the surface of leaves, cleaning as they eat.

We have no way of really knowing just how important these functions were in Hawaiʻi's forests prior to the decimation of the islands' snails. Certainly, soils benefited from this important work, but it is impossible to quantify the extent of that contribution. Similarly, some preliminary research has suggested that leaf-cleaning might have helped to ensure a high level of diversity of microbial communities on plants that may in turn limit the spread of pathogenic surface microbes.[11] Perhaps regular cleaning also enhanced plants' capacities for photosynthesis.

Alongside these adaptive possibilities, the Hawaiian Islands also offered plenty of opportunities for the kind of separation and isolation that allows snail populations to simply *drift* apart into different species. In some cases, a snail might be blown or float on a log to another part of an island, or to an entirely different island; in other cases, physical barriers opened up within existing populations, for example as deep valleys were eroded out of volcanic mountain chains, creating warmer and drier barrier zones that are less hospitable to snails. In many respects, the Hawaiian Islands offer an ideal environment for this kind of snail speciation, with their landscapes of incredible ecological diversity and patchiness providing defined borders across which snails cannot actively pass. Unlike animals like birds that are highly mobile and can spread across an island into all areas of similar, suitable habitat, snails rely on occasional dispersal across barriers by chance events. This means that snail populations, once separated, are unlikely to reconnect over intervals of hundreds of thousands of years.[12] This kind of isolation creates ideal conditions for populations to simply drift off in different evolutionary directions, giving rise to one or more new species in each locale.

Over the long duration of evolutionary time, there are numerous paths to this kind of separation of one or a few snails from a larger population. While the landscape of the Hawaiian Islands offered an ideal environment for this kind of speciation, snails, too, played their part. Snails are themselves ideally suited to this kind of speciation as a result of their largely sedentary form of life that is punctuated by occasional moments of long-distance dispersal. In this unique combination of landscape and organism, there is a perfect recipe for abundant speciation.

Voyaging with Snails

Since their first arrival in these islands, the lives of the Hawaiian people, the Kānaka Maoli, have also been tangled up with snails. Snail shells were used to adorn the bodies of hula dancers and their kuahu (altars). According to occasional references in the literature, some larger snails may have been eaten by people, both raw and cooked inside the leaves of the ti plant.[13] But perhaps more importantly than any of these kinds of uses, snails were potent hōʻailona (symbols or omens) in people's lives and stories, often indicating positive and righteous action and circumstance. At the heart of many of these stories is the notion that these snails sing in the forest. But the snails are not said to just sing at any old time; rather, their singing is deeply meaningful, often said to occur as a sign that after a series of adventures, changes, or turbulence, all is pono again—that is, righteous, correct, and good.[14]

As Kānaka Maoli learnt about and made themselves at home in these islands, they didn't only interact with the species of snails that were there prior to their arrival. They also brought snails of their own.

Since the wa'a (voyaging canoes) of the first Polynesian settlers ran ashore around one thousand years ago, people have acted as a conduit for snail movements to these islands. It is now well known that Polynesian peoples traveled with an assortment of animals and plants: from pigs, to kalo, to paper mulberry. These "canoe species" formed the basis of life for Kānaka Maoli: of food, medicine, cosmology, cultural, and religious practice. But what is less well known, or at least less often discussed, are all of the other species that traveled along with these plants and animals, some of them unseen and unintended. Amongst their numbers were a handful of snails.

Recent archaeological research suggests that a few Hawaiian species are likely candidates for Polynesian introduction. All of these species are small and inconspicuous, often found living on and around canoe plants, the kinds of snails that might easily have hitched a ride on these Polynesian wa'a voyages. In other parts of the Pacific, it seems likely that people intentionally moved larger, culturally significant snail species around, deliberately establishing them on their new island homes.[15] When I asked the biologist Carl Christensen about the logistics of this kind of movement, he replied: "It wouldn't be that difficult. A lot of snails can shut down physiologically. . . . For the few weeks that it's going to take you to sail from Tahiti to the Cooks, I don't think there'd be any problem at all. You'd just put the snails out of the sun so they're not going to overheat, and they'll be able to last." Here, we encounter yet another important adaptation for travel, another facet of the story of the prodigious transoceanic journeying of these seemingly most sedentary of animals.

Through their actions, intended and unintended, people here join birds, branches, and waves to become another vector in the unfolding biogeographical story of the snails of Hawai'i and the Pacific more broadly. Importantly, however, these particular people offered a distinctive kind of movement. Contrary to the stories long told about Polynesian travels—stories in which, as the missionary Hiram Bingham once put it, these people arrived "without much knowledge of navigation," just as "trees from foreign countries repeatedly land on their shores"[16]—it is now very clear that these journeys were made possible by the skill and knowledge of some of history's most successful oceanic voyagers. As Māori scholar Alice Te Punga Somerville has put it, discussing Polynesian and Pacific voyaging more generally, this was an "unparalleled and unparallelable feat of navigation and curiosity."[17] As a snail, to set off on a wa'a was most likely to be taken to another site of relatively suitable habitat, perhaps even to be cared for along the way and helped to establish in a new home.

Stories of Connection and Disconnection

Telling stories of oceanic snail journeys, both with and without human involvement, requires us to think carefully about how we understand and talk about island places and their relationships with a broader oceanic region. Decades of Indigenous scholarship from around Oceania has pushed back against the understanding of islands as tiny, remote patches of land in a vast ocean. Scholars like Epeli Hau'ofa have emphasized that these ideas about the region are grounded in a not-so-subtle continental thinking. As Hau'ofa noted:

> There is a gulf of difference between viewing the Pacific as "islands in a far sea" and as "a sea of islands." The first emphasises dry surfaces in a vast ocean far from the centres of power. When you focus this way you stress the smallness and remoteness of the islands. The second is a more holistic perspective in which things are seen in the totality of their relationships.[18]

Focusing on these relationships yields a vision of Oceania as an interconnected region, one in which islands and their peoples have long been in relationship, sharing histories, ideas, resources, and much more. Of course, many of those relationships were severed or degraded by processes of colonization in the region. As Tracey Banivanua Mar has argued, colonization "redrew the boundaries and borders that had previously joined and separated peoples from one another"—in some cases, connecting them in new ways through globalized networks, but frequently creating new modes of disconnection through various forms of "imposed isolation."[19] More than an abstract question of academic interest, many Pacific scholars have emphasized that this notion of the region as comprised of small, isolated, and poorly resourced patches of land, has been increasingly internalized by local people to, in Hau'ofa's words, "inflict lasting damage on people's image of themselves."[20]

Importantly, a related mode of thinking about this region and about islands more generally also dominates in the biological sciences. We see it in the way that island ecosystems are frequently described through comparison with an assumed continental norm. From this perspective, islands are presented as having "disharmonic" distributions that are disproportionately rich or poor in terms of the diversity of certain groups of plants and animals. One of the key differences frequently noted in this regard is a relative lack of predators for some species on many islands, leading to adaptations (like flightlessness among birds) that are less common on continental landmasses. These kinds of adaptations, combined with the relative isolation of islands, have grounded a general assumption that these places are "evolutionary dead ends": in short, that any species who arrive and establish themselves on remote islands are never going to make it back to a continent—or, at least, close enough to "never" for this kind of movement to be considered not worth looking for. In recent decades, however, this understanding has been increasingly unsettled, with a range of plants and animals found to have made such journeys from islands to continents.[21] Importantly, these modes of understanding islands—especially as isolated and self-contained systems ("island laboratories")—played a role in enabling the use of these places in the Pacific and elsewhere as sites for nuclear weapons testing, a process that was itself thoroughly bound up with the emergence of the ecosystem concept.[22]

These are some of the complex threads of understanding that snails ask us to consider. As we have seen, the particularities of this region, its oceans and its landmasses, have profoundly shaped the diversity of snail life that has emerged in Hawai'i. The size of these islands matters, as does their ecological patchiness, their mountainous terrain, and their capacity to support moist forests. Their distance from other snail-rich places also matters, influencing the (in)frequency of new arrivals and the vectors by which snails might make such journeys. But we have also seen that this is anything but a simple story of small, isolated places. Perhaps most importantly, these particulars of size and distance are not diminishing attributes; rather, in Hawai'i they have been an incredible engine for the diversification of snail life, and the evolution of one of the richest assemblages of gastropods found anywhere on the planet. At the same time, attending to snails reminds us of yet one more way in which this sea of islands has always already been profoundly connected. Places that may have seemed to some of us to be distant and isolated, have actually been shaped, right down to their snails, by ongoing patterns of movement and exchange that are utterly foundational to the environments we all inhabit.

A Conclusion to Drifting

The oceanic journeys of Hawai'i's snails are an epic, deep-time story that has been slowly unfolding over millions of years. It is hard to really make sense of this vast assemblage of life. I imagine it as something like a giant network with strands stretching out across the Pacific Ocean and beyond, back over evolutionary and geological timeframes. Each strand represents one of hundreds of unique species. Millions of years of unlikely journeys—nestled into a bird's feathers, or perhaps tucked away amongst a plant's leaves—heading to destinations unknown. Millions of years of intergenerational agency produced these intrepid, even if somewhat unlikely, island dispersers, along with the reproductive and other adaptations that made these movements possible. And then, after that most fortuitous of arrivals, countless generations more of chance movements gave rise to isolation and speciation: drifting snails, drifting valleys and hills, drifting genes. Each strand is a unique line of movement, of relationships, of branching transformations. These are at least some of the processes that have produced the intricate webs of lives and possibilities that are—that *were*—the worlds of Hawaiian snails.

Paying attention to drifting snails brings these realities into view, and in so doing it further expands the disruptive scope of maritime animal stories. By and large, accounts of animals traveling the world by ship are still about nonhumans getting caught up in human movements and processes, including empire, colonization, capitalism, and more. Sometimes these animals are vital to the achievement of human goals, other times they unsettle or redo them profoundly. Either way, however, at the end of the day, these are still largely stories of human dramas, played out across oceans. Certainly these kinds of stories exist also for Hawai'i's snails. As we have seen, humans are far from irrelevant here, including as facilitators of the arrival of new snails and many other species in Hawai'i, with a range of complex consequences. But drifting snails remind us that there are wholly other movements going on: journeys across oceans that predate the invention of ships, that predate the evolution of our species. From this perspective, shipbound travelers join the story late, after millions of years of other journeys, journeys that have played a significant role in shaping the environments into which these more recent travelers now enter—and journeys that continue now, albeit largely unnoticed, as snails and a host of other species move around the planet in their own ways.

Attending to these stories as well, alongside maritime adventures, might allow us to appreciate in new ways the environments, the species, and the possibilities for human and more-than-human life that have been created and fostered by long histories of nonhuman oceanic journeying, connecting up "distant places" in incredible—perhaps ultimately unfathomable—ways. Even more importantly in our current time, holding in mind the networks of drifting snails that I have described in this chapter might also help us to appreciate more fully the significance of what is today being lost. With the extinction of each species of Hawaiian snail, the world is stripped of yet another unique way of life, another part of its evolutionary heritage, another strand in this vast, improbable, breathtakingly diverse, and utterly unrepeatable, assemblage of snail life.

Notes

An earlier version of this chapter was given as a keynote speech at the conference "Maritime Animals: Telling Stories of Animals at Sea," at the National Maritime Museum, Greenwich, London (April 2019), which this edited collection originates from. Please note that there is substantial overlap of materials between this chapter and Thom van Dooren, *A World in a Shell: Snail Stories for a Time of Extinctions* (Cambridge, MA: MIT Press, 2022, introduction and chapter 2).

1. Yeung and Hayes, "Biodiversity and Extinction."
2. Here and throughout this chapter I have drawn on fieldwork and interviews conducted in Hawai'i (primarily on O'ahu) from 2018 to 2021, including ongoing interviews with a range of snail scientists.
3. Gon and Winter, "Hawaiian Renaissance."
4. Holland and Cowie, "Geographic Mosaic," 2432.
5. Charles Darwin, quoted in Holland, "Land Snails," 538.
6. Ożgo et al., "Dispersal of Land Snails," 341–42.
7. Ibid., 342.
8. Wada, Kawakami, and Chiba, "Snails Can Survive Passage."
9. Kobayashi and Hadfield, "Experimental Study."
10. See Plumwood, "Nature in the Active Voice," 125.
11. O'Rorke et al., "Dietary Preferences."
12. Thacker and Hadfield, "Mitochondrial Phylogeny"; Holland and Hadfield, "Islands Within an Island."
13. Stewart, "Addenda."

14. Sato, Price, and Vaughan, "Kāhuli."
15. Christensen and Weisler, "Land Snails from Archaeological Sites."
16. Vowell, *Unfamiliar Fishes.*
17. Somerville, *Once Were Pacific*, xvi.
18. Hau'ofa, "Our Sea of Islands," 7.
19. Banivanua Mar, *Decolonisation and the Pacific*, 17.
20. Hau'ofa, "Our Sea of Islands," 4. Thank you to Katerina Teaiwa and the other participants at "BLUE Openings: Approaches to More-than-Human Oceans" for a helpful discussion on the connections between these literatures and biogeography (November 16–17, 2021, Aarhus University, Denmark).
21. Heaney, "Is a New Paradigm Emerging?"
22. DeLoughrey, "Myth of Isolates."

Bibliography

Banivanua Mar, Tracey. 2016. *Decolonisation and the Pacific: Indigenous Globalization and the Ends of Empire.* Cambridge: Cambridge University Press.

Christensen, Carl C., and Marshall I. Weisler. "Land Snails from Archaeological Sites in the Marshall Islands, with Remarks on Prehistoric Translocations in Tropical Oceania." *Pacific Science* 67, no. 1 (2013): 81–104.

DeLoughrey, Elizabeth M. "The Myth of Isolates: Ecosystem Ecologies in the Nuclear Pacific." *Cultural Geographies* 20, no. 2 (2013): 167–84.

Gon, Sam 'Ohu, and Kawika Winter. "A Hawaiian Renaissance That Could Save the World." *American Scientist* 107, no. 4 (2019): 232.

Hau'ofa, Epeli. "Our Sea of Islands." In *A New Oceania: Rediscovering Our Sea of Islands*, edited by Eric Waddell, Vijay Naidu, and Epeli Hau'ofa, 2–16. Suva, Fiji: University of the South Pacific, 1993.

Heaney, Lawrence R. "Is a New Paradigm Emerging for Oceanic Island Biogeography?" *Journal of Biogeography* 34 (2007): 753–57.

Holland, Brenden S., and Michael G. Hadfield. "Islands Within an Island: Phylogeography and Conservation Genetics of the Endangered Hawaiian Tree Snail *Achatinella mustelina*." *Molecular Ecology* 11, no. 3 (2002): 365–75.

Holland, Brenden S. "Land Snails." In *Encyclopedia of Islands*, edited by Rosemary Gillespie and David Clague, 537–42. Oakland, CA: University of California Press, 2009.

Holland, Brenden S., and Robert H. Cowie. "A Geographic Mosaic of Passive Dispersal: Population Structure in the Endemic Hawaiian Amber Snail *Succinea caduca* (Mighels, 1845)." *Molecular Ecology* 16, no. 12 (2007): 2422–35.

Kobayashi, Sharon R., and Michael G. Hadfield. "An Experimental Study of Growth and Reproduction in the Hawaiian Tree Snails *Achatinella mustelina* and *Partulina redfieldii* (Achatinellinae)." *Pacific Science* 50, no. 4 (1996): 339–54.

O'Rorke, Richard, Brenden S. Holland, Gerry M. Cobian, Kapono Gaughen, and Anthony S. Amend. "Dietary Preferences of Hawaiian Tree Snails to Inform Culture for Conservation." *Biological Conservation* 198 (2016): 177–82.

Ożgo, Małgorzata, Aydin Örstan, Małgorzata Kirschenstein, and Robert Cameron. "Dispersal of Land Snails by Sea Storms." *Journal of Molluscan Studies* 82, no. 2 (2016): 341–43.

Plumwood, Val. "Nature in the Active Voice." *Australian Humanities Review* 46 (2009): 113–29.

Rundell, Rebecca J. "Snails on an Evolutionary Tree: Gulick, Speciation, and

Isolation." *American Malacological Bulletin* 29, nos. 1–2 (2011): 145–57.

Sato, Aimee You, Melissa Renae Price, and Mehana Blaich Vaughan. "Kāhuli: Uncovering Indigenous Ecological Knowledge to Conserve Endangered Hawaiian Land Snails." *Society & Natural Resources* 31, no. 3 (2018): 320–34.

Stewart, Charles Samuel. "Addenda: *Achatina stewartii* and *A. oahuensis* [1823]." *Manual of Conchology* 22 (1912): 404–7.

Te Punga Somerville, Alice. *Once Were Pacific: Māori Connections to Oceania.* Minneapolis: University of Minnesota Press, 2012.

Thacker, Robert W., and Michael G. Hadfield. "Mitochondrial Phylogeny of Extant Hawaiian Tree Snails (*Achatinellinae*)." *Molecular Phylogenetics and Evolution* 16, no. 2 (2000): 263–70.

Vowell, Sarah. *Unfamiliar Fishes.* London: Riverhead Books, 2012.

Wada, Shinichiro, Kazuto Kawakami, and Satoshi Chiba. "Snails Can Survive Passage Through a Bird's Digestive System." *Journal of Biogeography* 39, no. 1 (2012): 69–73.

Yeung, Norine W., and Kenneth A. Hayes. "Biodiversity and Extinction of Hawaiian Land Snails: How Many Are Left Now and What Must We Do to Conserve Them." *Integrative and Comparative Biology* 58, no. 6 (2018): 1157–69.

CONTRIBUTORS

Anna Boswell is a research associate at the New Zealand Centre for Human-Animal Studies. She is currently completing a law degree at the University of Canterbury to further her interests in environmental history, land management conflicts, and tikanga Māori, and was the recipient of the Anderson Lloyd Prize in Land Law in 2021. She talks and writes about settler colonialism in terms of ecology and pedagogy, and was awarded a Marsden Fund Fast Start grant by the Royal Society of New Zealand for a postdoctoral research project examining zoos and wildlife sanctuaries in the settler south (2016–19). Her most recent work is published in *Humanities*, *Pacific Dynamics*, *Transformations: Journal of Media, Culture and Technology*, and *Animal Studies Journal*.

Nancy Cushing is Associate Professor of History at the University of Newcastle, Australia who lives and works on the unceded land of the Darramurragal and Awabakal peoples. An environmental historian most interested in relations between humans and other animals, she is co-author, with Kevin Markwell, of *Snake-Bitten: Eric Worrell and the Australian Reptile Park* (UNSW Press, 2010), co-editor of *Radical Newcastle* (New South, 2015) and co-editor of *Animals Count: How Population Size Matters in Animal-Human Relations* (Routledge, 2018), and author of *A History of Crime in Australia* (Routledge, 2023). Current projects include an animal-focused history of Australia and a history of the establishment of Australia's coal industry. Cushing is a member of the executives of the Australian Aotearoa New Zealand Environmental History Network and the Australian Historical Association.

Lea Edgar holds master's degrees in library science and archival studies from the University of British Columbia. She has a background in archaeology and over ten years of experience working with heritage organizations. Lea served as the librarian and archivist at the Vancouver Maritime Museum from 2013 to 2021. During her tenure, she wrote a monthly maritime history column for the industry magazine *BC Shipping News*. She had the privilege of examining, preserving, and working with archives from the *St. Roch* crew and the Royal Canadian Mounted Police, which forms the basis of her research.

David Haworth is a senior research officer for the Global Encounters and First Nations Peoples program at Monash Indigenous Studies Centre, in the School of Philosophical, Historical, and International Studies at Monash University. In 2021, David completed his doctoral thesis in English literature at the University of Melbourne, focusing on depictions of nonhuman artfulness and creativity. He conducted part of his doctoral research at the Natural History Museum in London and the Museum of Natural History in Paris. David's master's thesis won the 2013 Percival Serle Prize. His academic publications and presentations explore such topics as the artfulness of scientific illustration, interspecies animal friendships, talking animals in fairy tales, the "feral" or animal-reared child, illusion and mimicry in nature and art, and the cultural histories of the black swan.

Donna Landry is Professor (emeritus) of English and American Literature at the University of Kent and a fellow of the

Royal Asiatic Society. She is the author, co-author, or co-editor of eight books, including *Noble Brutes: How Eastern Horses Transformed English Culture* (2008) and *Cosmopolitan Animals* (2015, co-edited with Kaori Nagai et al). Her current monograph project is a study of Waterloo and its aftermath from the point of view of the horses. Landry is contributing to the Thoroughbred and Arabian strands of Kristen Guest's and Monica Mattfeld's Equine Breeds and Modern Identity project (http://eqbreeds.ca). With Gerald MacLean, she plans to bring the great Ottoman traveler Evliya Çelebi (1611–ca. 1687) to new audiences across the disciplines in a book; they are founding members of the Evliya Çelebi Way project to promote equestrian tourism and knowledge of Ottoman history (https://research.kent.ac.uk/the-evliya-celebi-ride-and-way-project/).

Kaori Nagai is Lecturer in Victorian Literature at the University of Kent. She is the author of *Empire of Analogies: Kipling, India and Ireland* (Cork, 2006), and *Imperial Beast Fables: Animals, Cosmopolitanism and the British Empire* (Palgrave, 2020). She is a founding member of the Kent Animal Humanities Network, and edited a collection of essays titled *Cosmopolitan Animals* (2015, chief editor) with five animal studies colleagues at Kent. She undertook a Caird Short-Term Fellowship at the National Maritime Museum on the topic of seafaring rats in the British Empire, which led to the organization of the "Maritime Animals: Telling Stories of Animals at Sea" conference in April 2019.

Derek Lee Nelson is an environmental scholar interested in coastal and marine environmental histories. He specializes in the role that marine-introduced species have played in the evolution of shipping technology, coastal infrastructure, and even cultural attitudes about the sea. His most recent work, "The Ravages of Teredo," in *Environmental History*, examines the history of marine wood-boring mollusks known colloquially as teredo, or shipworms, which spread around the globe during the age of sail.

Jimmy Packham is Senior Lecturer in North American Literature at the University of Birmingham. His research focuses on maritime writing and Gothic literature, both as distinct and as overlapping areas of study. With Laurence Publicover, he maintains a research interest in literary and cultural representations of the deep sea. He is the author of *Gothic Utterance* (UWP, 2021) and co-editor of *Our Haunted Shores: Tales from the Coasts of the British Isles* (BL, 2022), and has published articles on the poetry of the deep sea, the voice of sea-soaked sailors in *Moby-Dick*, and the role of the coast in contemporary British Gothic fiction. He is also co-organizer of the Haunted Shores research network.

Laurence Publicover is Senior Lecturer in English at the University of Bristol, where he teaches early modern literature and oceanic studies. He is the author of *Dramatic Geography* (Oxford University Press, 2017) and co-editor, with Susann Liebich, of *Shipboard Literary Cultures: Reading, Writing, and Performing at Sea* (Palgrave Macmillan, 2021). His current projects include a study of figures of depth in early modern English tragedy and, alongside Jimmy Packham, a human history of the seabed.

Killian Quigley is a research fellow at the Australian Catholic University's Institute for Humanities and Social Sciences. He is the author of *Reading Underwater Wreckage: An Encrusting Ocean* (Bloomsbury, 2023) and co-editor, with Margaret Cohen, of *The Aesthetics of the Undersea* (Routledge, 2020). Killian is an associate member of the Oceanic Humanities for the Global South research network.

Lynette Russell is the Kathleen Fitzpatrick Laureate Professor at the Monash Indigenous Studies Centre, in the School of Philosophical, Historical, and International Studies at Monash University. A widely published author specializing in Aboriginal history, Lynette has held fellowships at both Oxford and Cambridge Universities and is an elected member of several learned academies.

Adam Sundberg is Associate Professor of Environmental History and Digital Humanities at Creighton University in Omaha, Nebraska. His work focuses on natural disasters in the early modern Netherlands. He has published in *Environmental History*, *Agricultural History*, and *The Low Countries Journal of Social and Economic History*. His book *Natural Disaster at the Closing of the Dutch Golden Age* (Cambridge, 2022) is an environmental history of Dutch disaster and decline during the seventeenth and eighteenth centuries.

Thom van Dooren is deputy director at the Sydney Environment Institute, Associate Professor in the School of Humanities at the University of Sydney, and Professor II in the Oslo School of Environmental Humanities at the University of Oslo. His research and writing focus on some of the many philosophical, ethical, cultural, and political issues that arise in the context of species extinctions and human entanglements with threatened species and places. He is the author of *Flight Ways: Life and Loss at the Edge of Extinction* (Columbia University Press, 2014), *The Wake of Crows: Living and Dying in Shared Worlds* (Columbia University Press, 2019), and *A World in a Shell: Snail Stories for a Time of Extinctions* (MIT, 2022).

INDEX

Note: Italicized page references indicate illustrations. Endnotes are referenced with "n" followed by the endnote number.

www.ingramcontent.com/pod-product-compliance
Ingram Content Group UK Ltd.
Pitfield, Milton Keynes, MK11 3LW, UK
UKHW031910280425
457958UK00002B/47

9 780271 095387